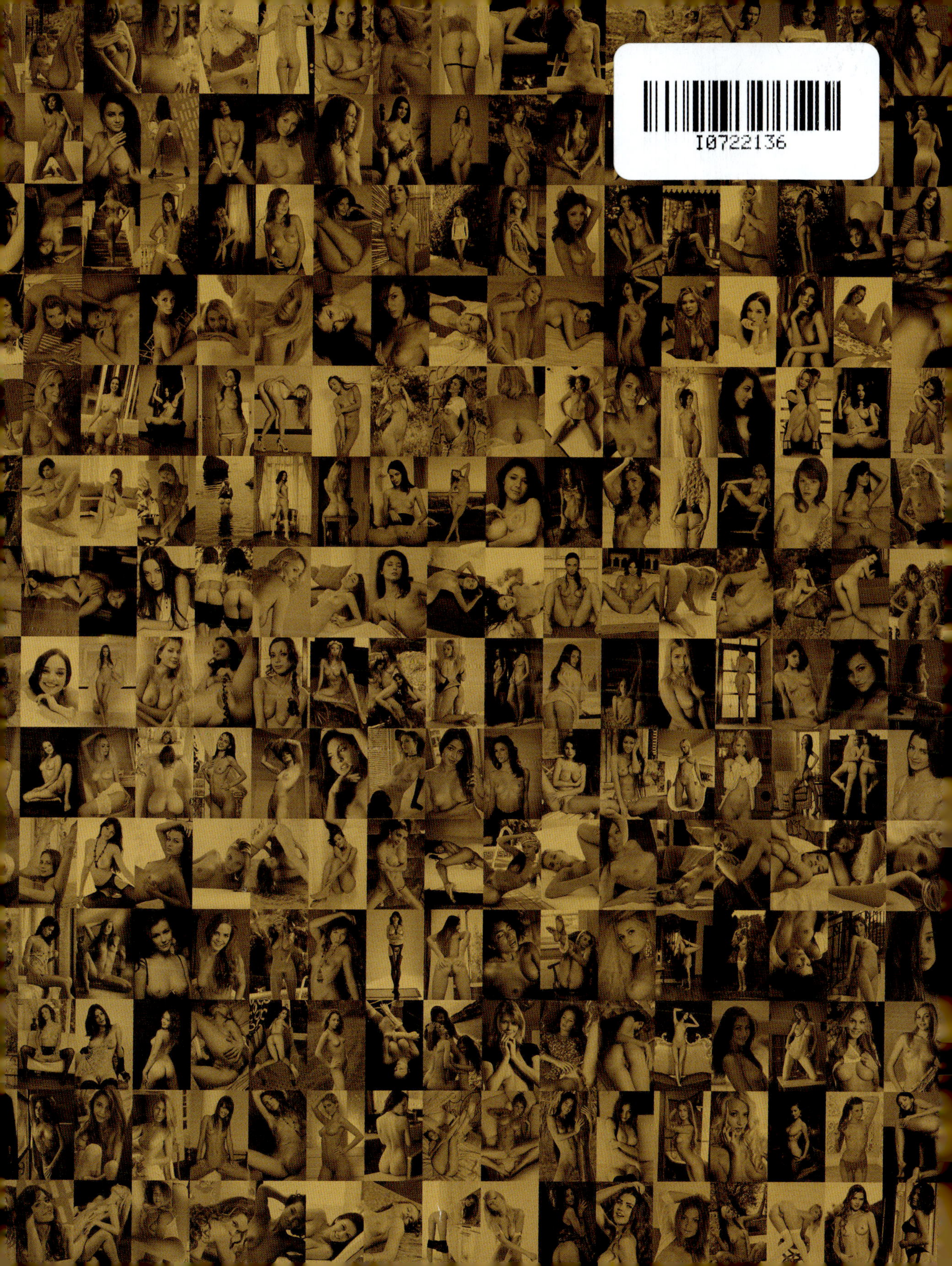
I0722136

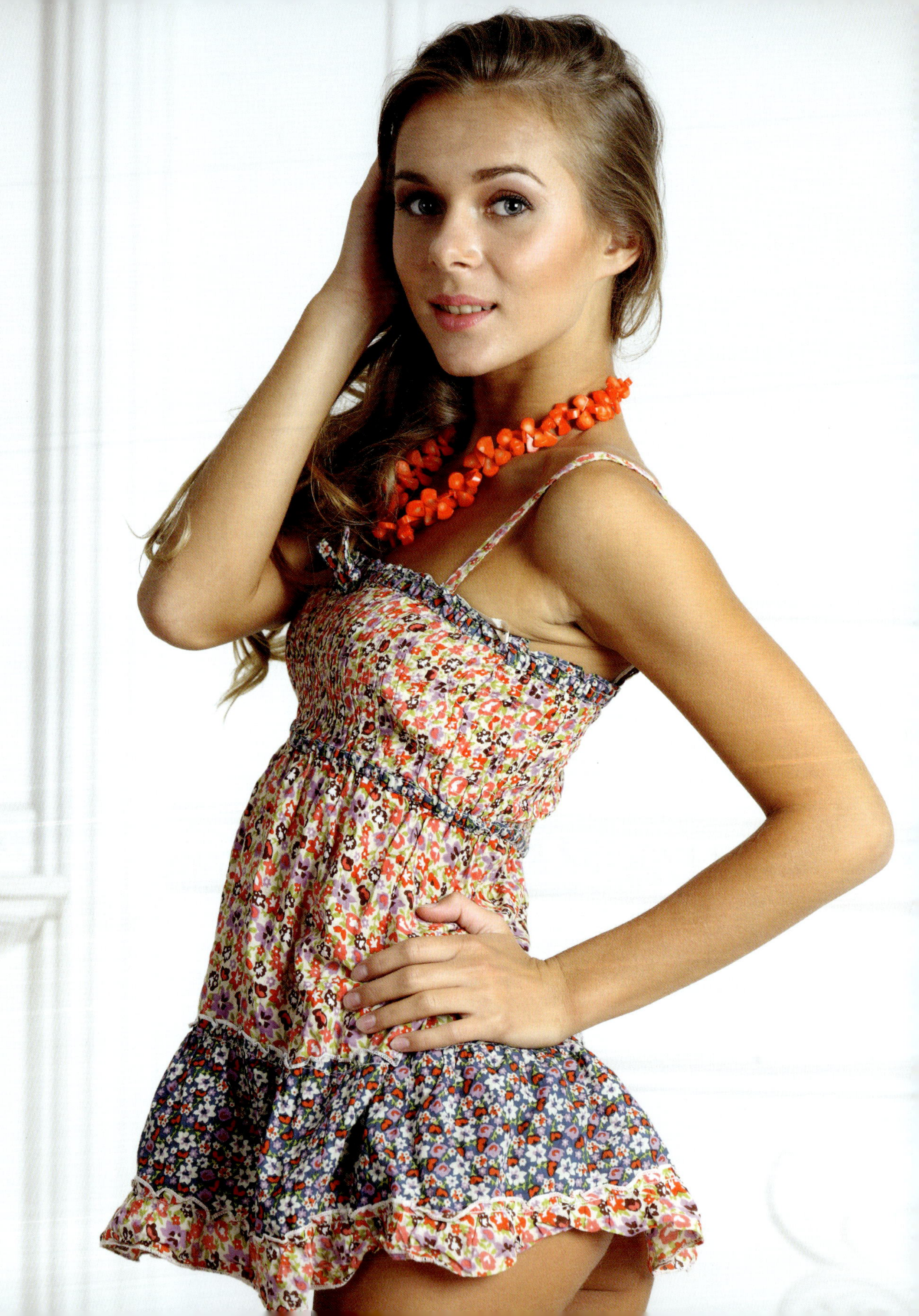

TOP MODELS OF

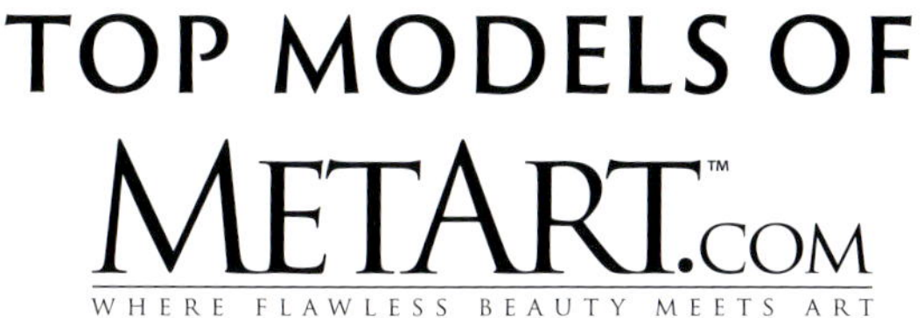

WHERE FLAWLESS BEAUTY MEETS ART

KATIE A

COLLECTED AND EDITED BY ISABELLA CATALINA

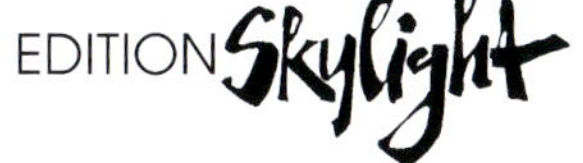

EDITION Skylight

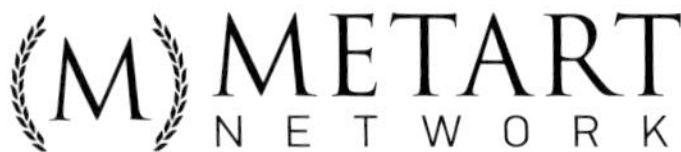

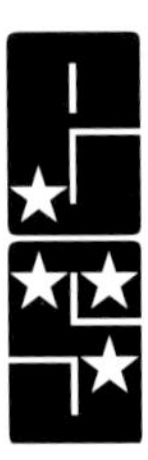

First edition 2025
Copyright © 2025 by Edition Skylight

EDITION SKYLIGHT
Rosengartenstrasse 13B
CH-8608 Bubikon / Zürich
Switzerland
info@edition-skylight.com
www.edition-skylight.com

ISBN 978-3-03766-713-2

Bibliographic information published by Die Deutsche Bibliothek
Die Deutsche Bibliothek lists this publication in the
Deutsche Nationalbibliografie; detailed bibliographic data
are available in the Internet at http://dnb.ddb.de.

Printed in Bosnia and Herzegovina

TWENTY YEARS OLD, SO DAMN GOOD LOOKING, PURE NATURAL AND SEDUCTIVELY SHY!

Cute, perky and with a wonderfully pretty face, **Katie A** is an adorable member of our MetArt 50+ Club, models so popular they have been featured at least 50 times. She's as sweet as she is sexy, with a fresh and almost-innocent allure, and a playful attitude that suggests she's a whole lot of fun.

Ukrainian sweetheart Katie made her debut at the age of 20 on Feb 20, 2013, in a "Presenting" photoset by Alex Iskan. In her bio, the blue-eyed babe says she wants to become a nurse, although we can't help thinking the sight of her would raise blood pressure rather lowering it! Members are devoted to the athletic, angelic cutie with the perfect ass and dazzling smile, describing her as a "stunning beauty" and "absolute goddess".

She is totally mad about theatre and cinema and now Katie is studying her third year at an acting school in Los Angeles. She wants to be a star of a soap opera, playing the sexy girl next door, the role of a dangerous heartbreaker, the seducer of men who wrecks every relationship around her. But for now she enjoys to show her beauty just for us, totally naked.

ZWANZIG JAHRE ALT, VERDAMMT GUT AUSSEHEND UND SO NATÜRLICH UND VERFÜHRERISCH SCHÜCHTERN!

So süß, vorwitzig und mit einem wunderbar hübschen Gesicht: **Katie A** ist ein besonders bezauberndes Mitglied unseres MetArt 50+ Clubs. Diese Models sind so beliebt, dass sie mindestens 50-mal vorgestellt wurden. Sie ist ebenso zuckersüß wie sexy, mit einer frischen und fast unschuldigen Ausstrahlung und einer verspielten Art, die darauf hindeutet, dass sie eine Menge Spaß macht.

Die ukrainische Schönheit Katie debütierte am 20. Februar 2013 im Alter von 20 Jahren in einem „Presenting"-Fotoset von Alex Iskan. In ihrer ersten Biografie sagt die blauäugige Schönheit, sie wolle Krankenschwester werden, obwohl wir uns nicht helfen können zu glauben, dass ihr Anblick den Blutdruck eher erhöhen als senken würde! Die Metart-Mitglieder sind der athletischen, engelsgleichen Schönheit mit dem perfekten Hintern und dem strahlenden Lächeln ergeben und beschreiben sie als „atemberaubende Schönheit" und „absolute Göttin".

Sie ist total verrückt nach Theater und Kino und studiert inzwischen im dritten Jahr an einer Schauspielschule in Los Angeles. Sie möchte Star einer Seifenoper werden, das sexy Mädchen von nebenan spielen, die gefährliche Herzensbrecherin, die Männer verführt und jede Beziehung um sie herum zerstört. Doch noch zeigt sie ihre Schönheit nur für uns, völlig nackt.

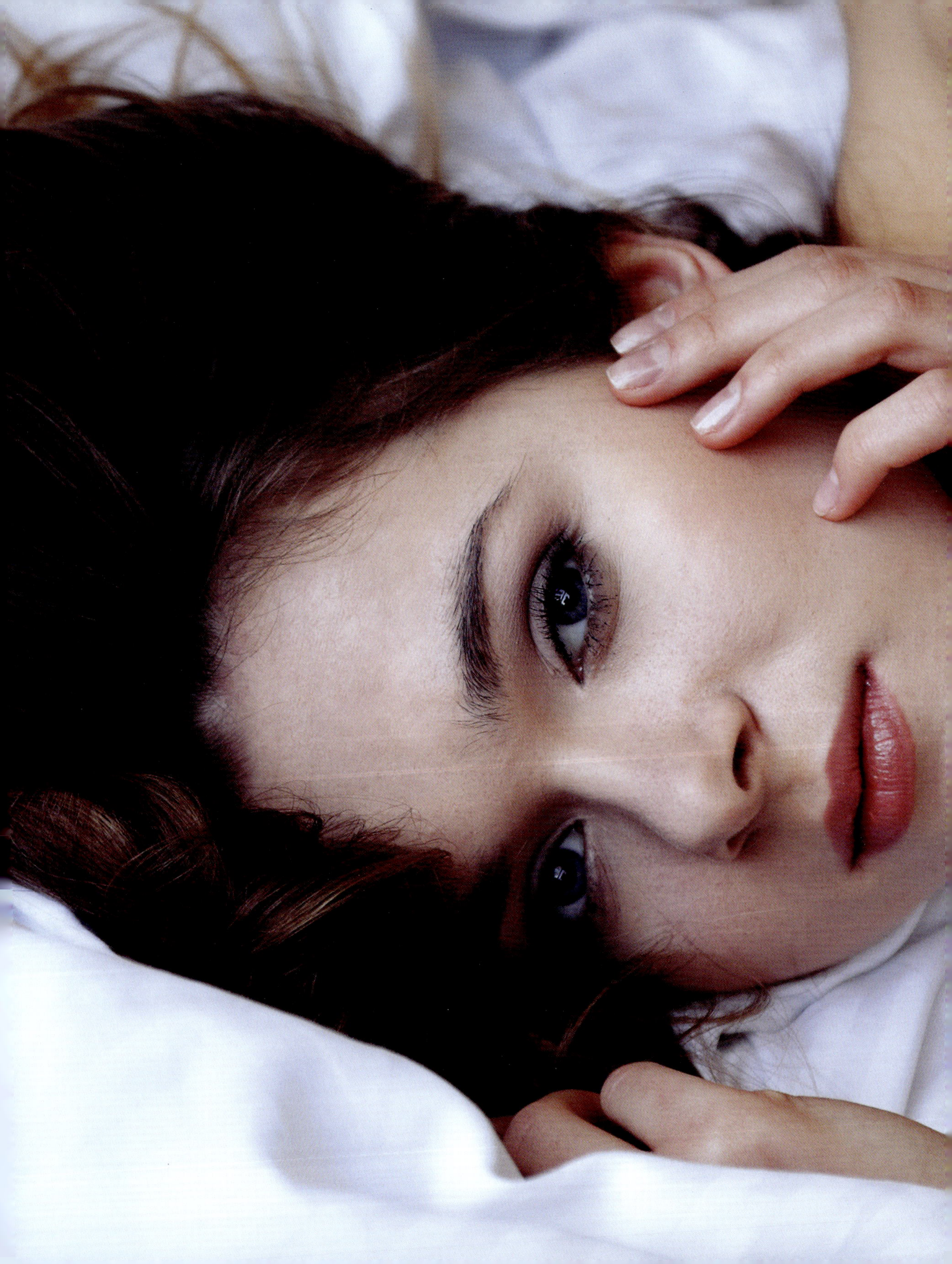

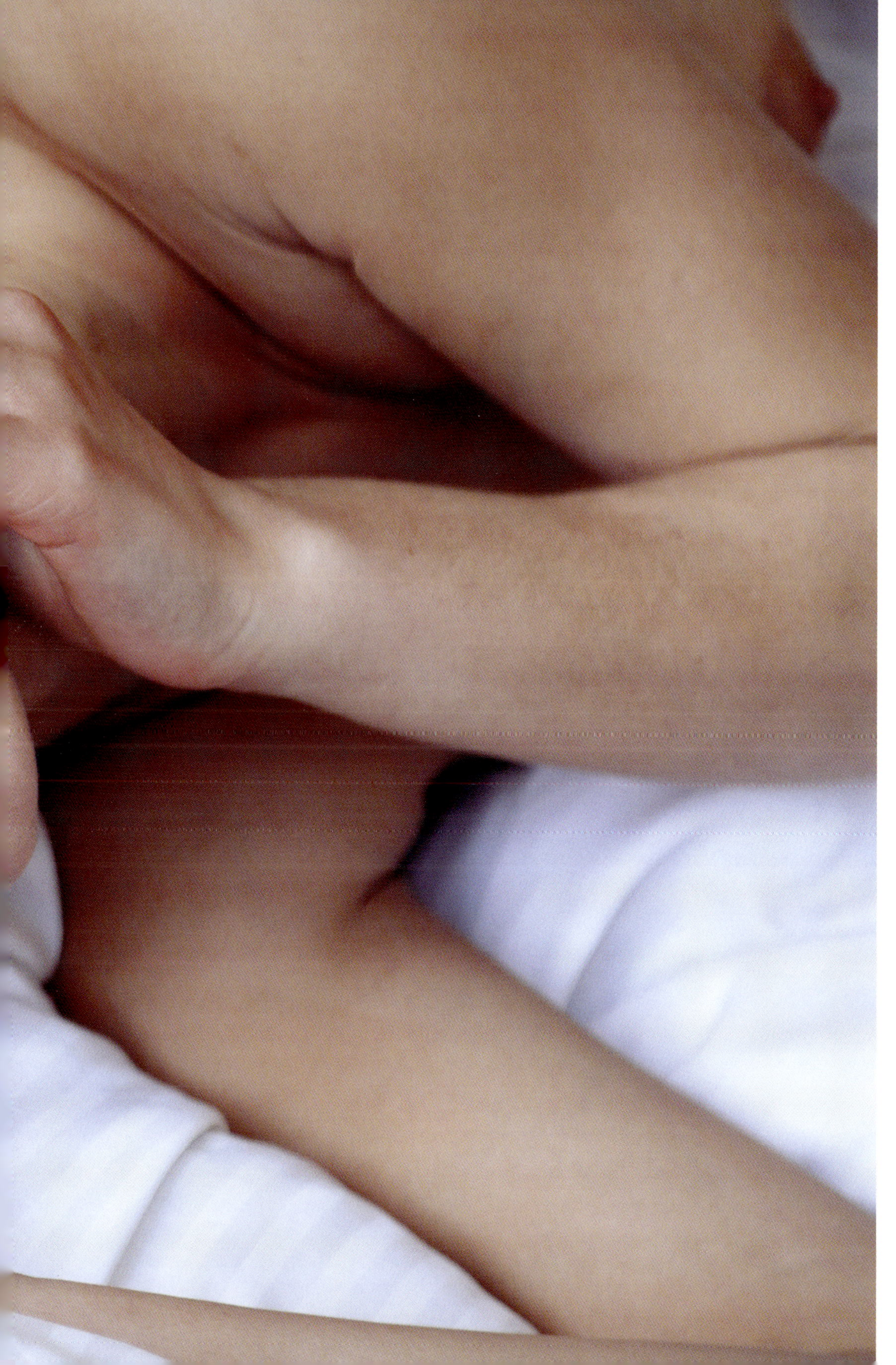

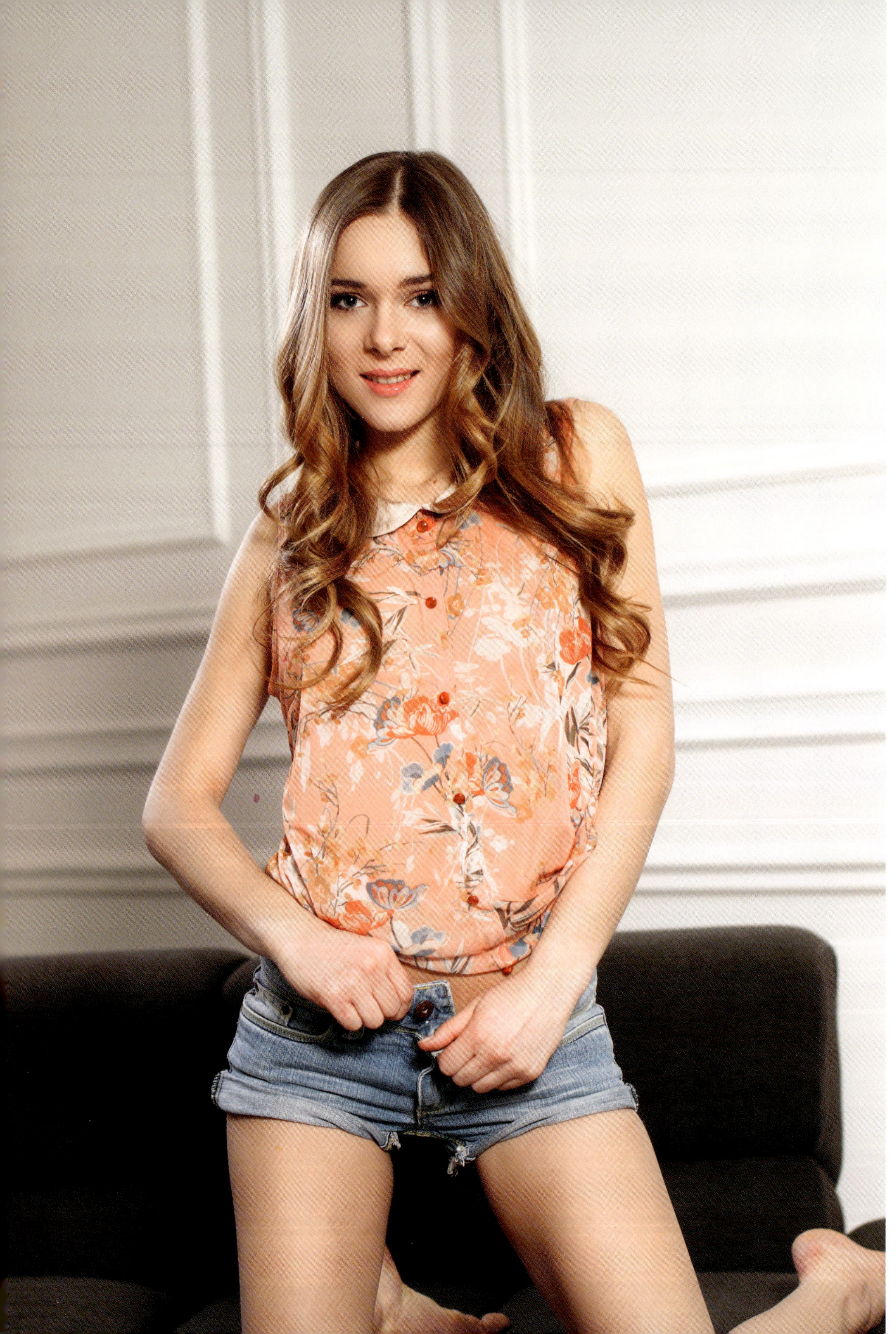

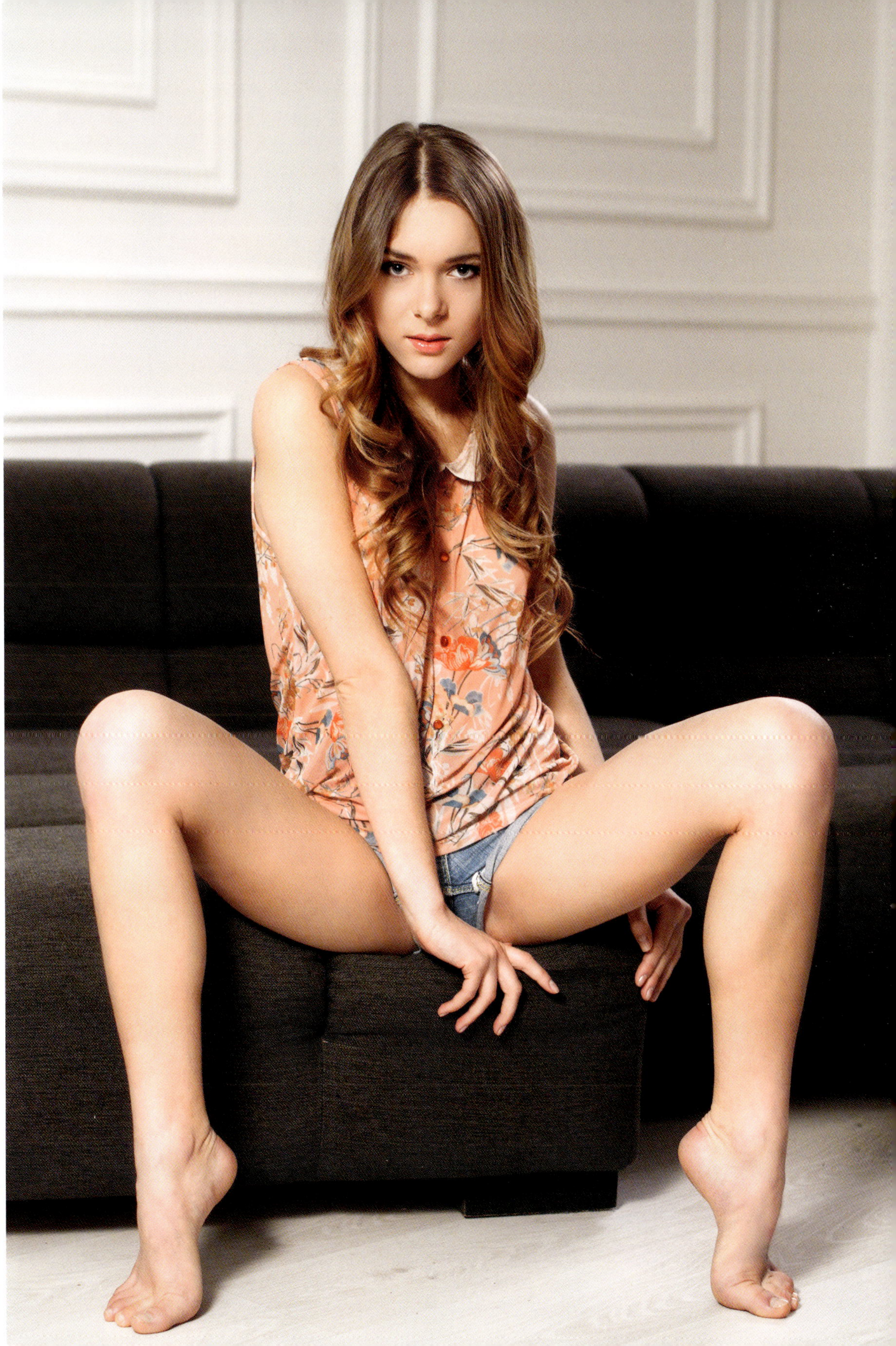

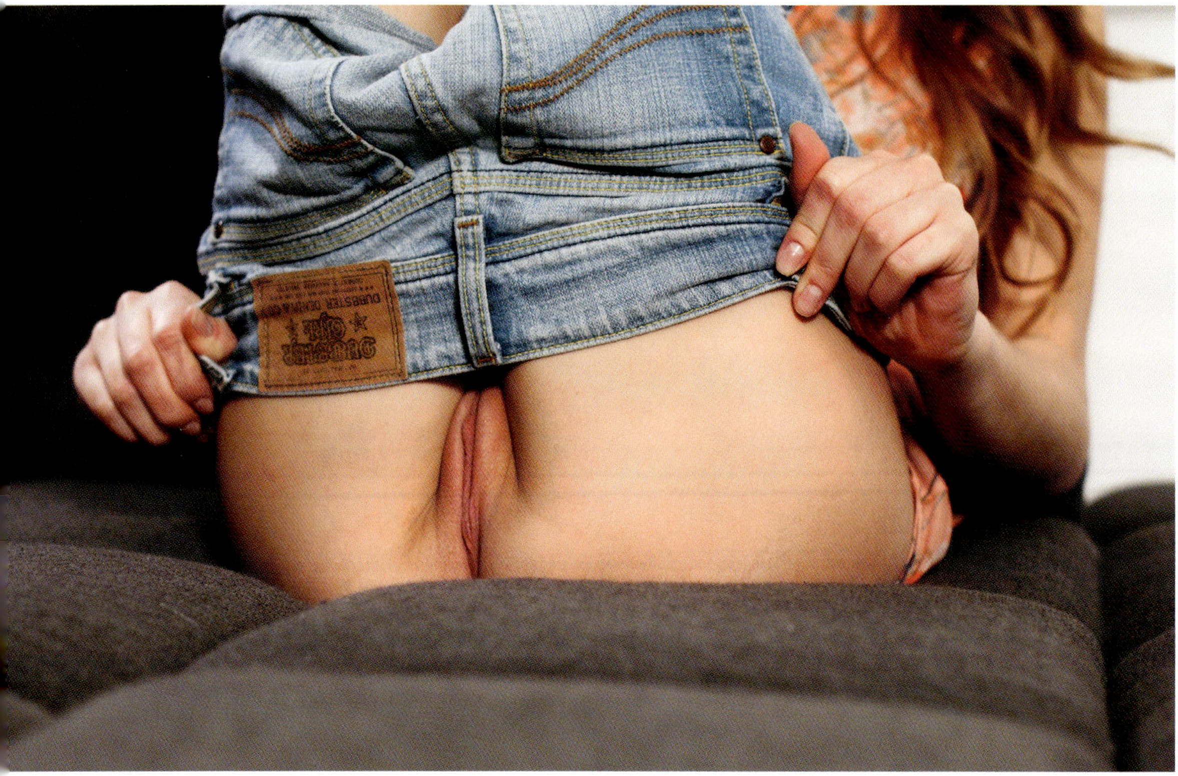

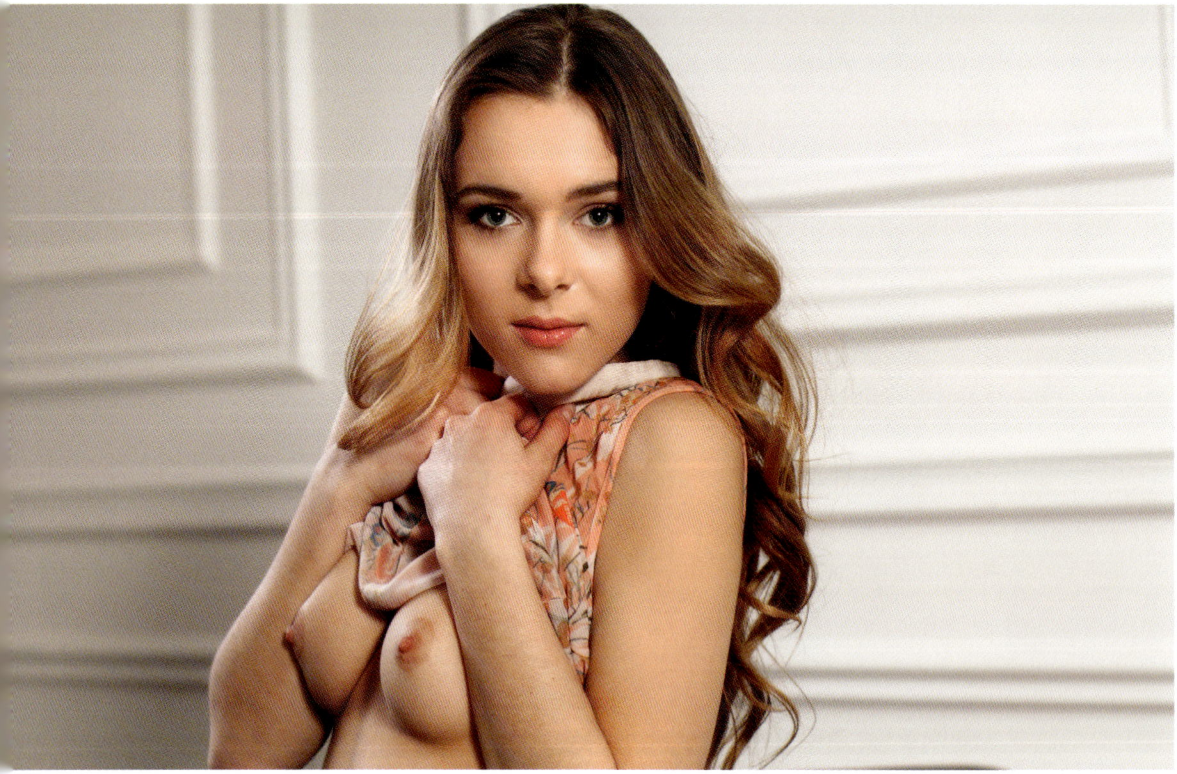

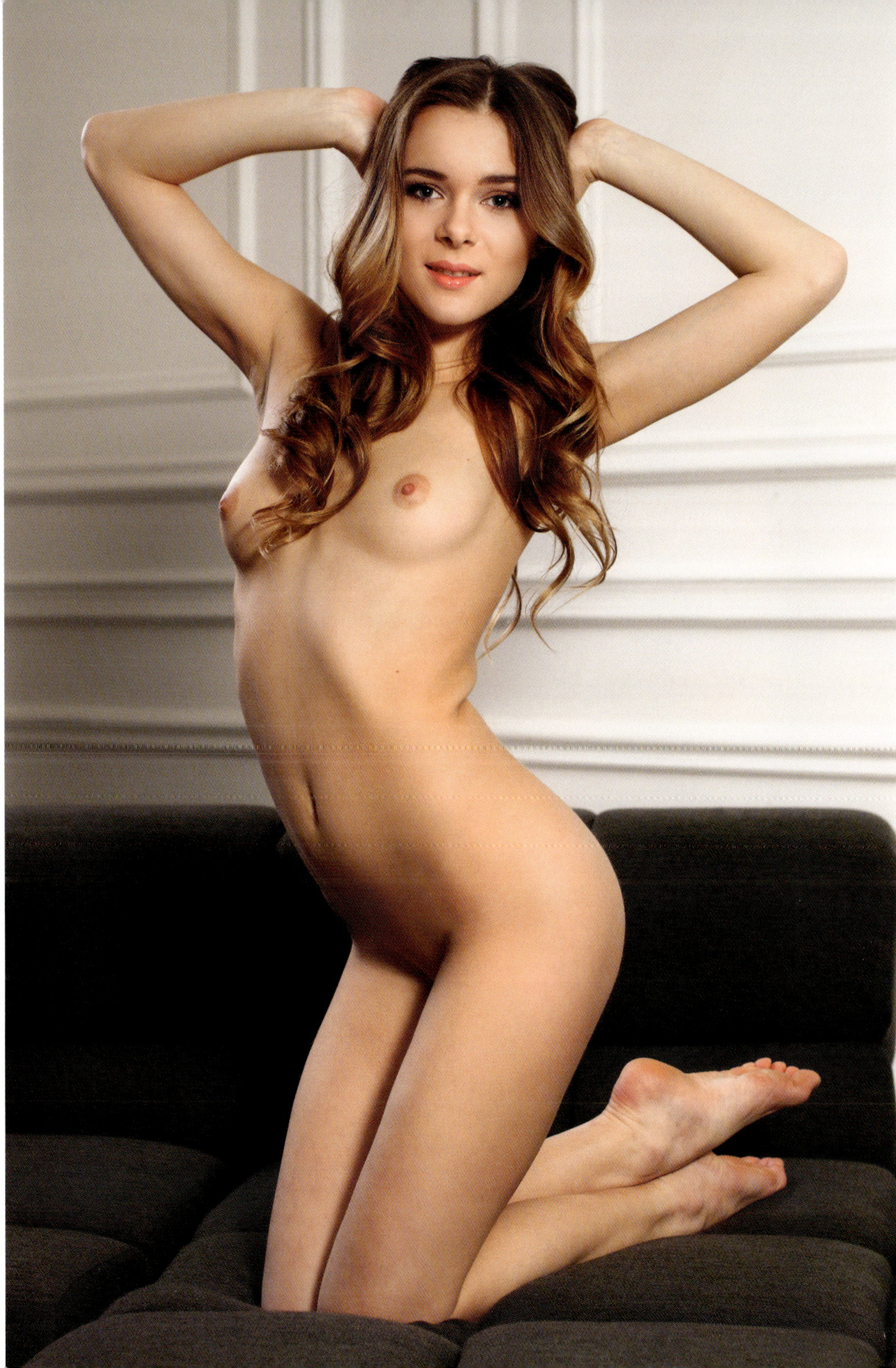

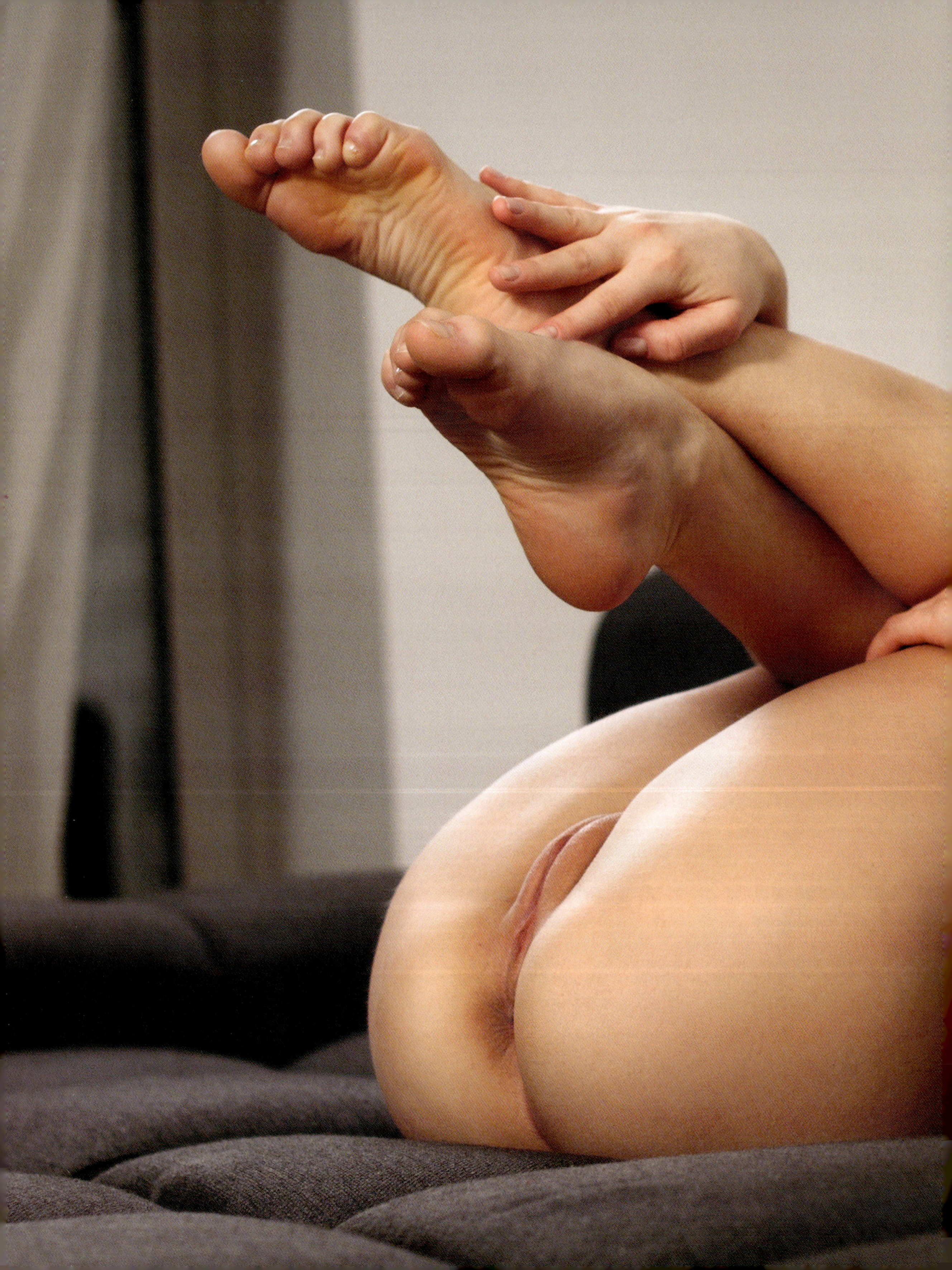

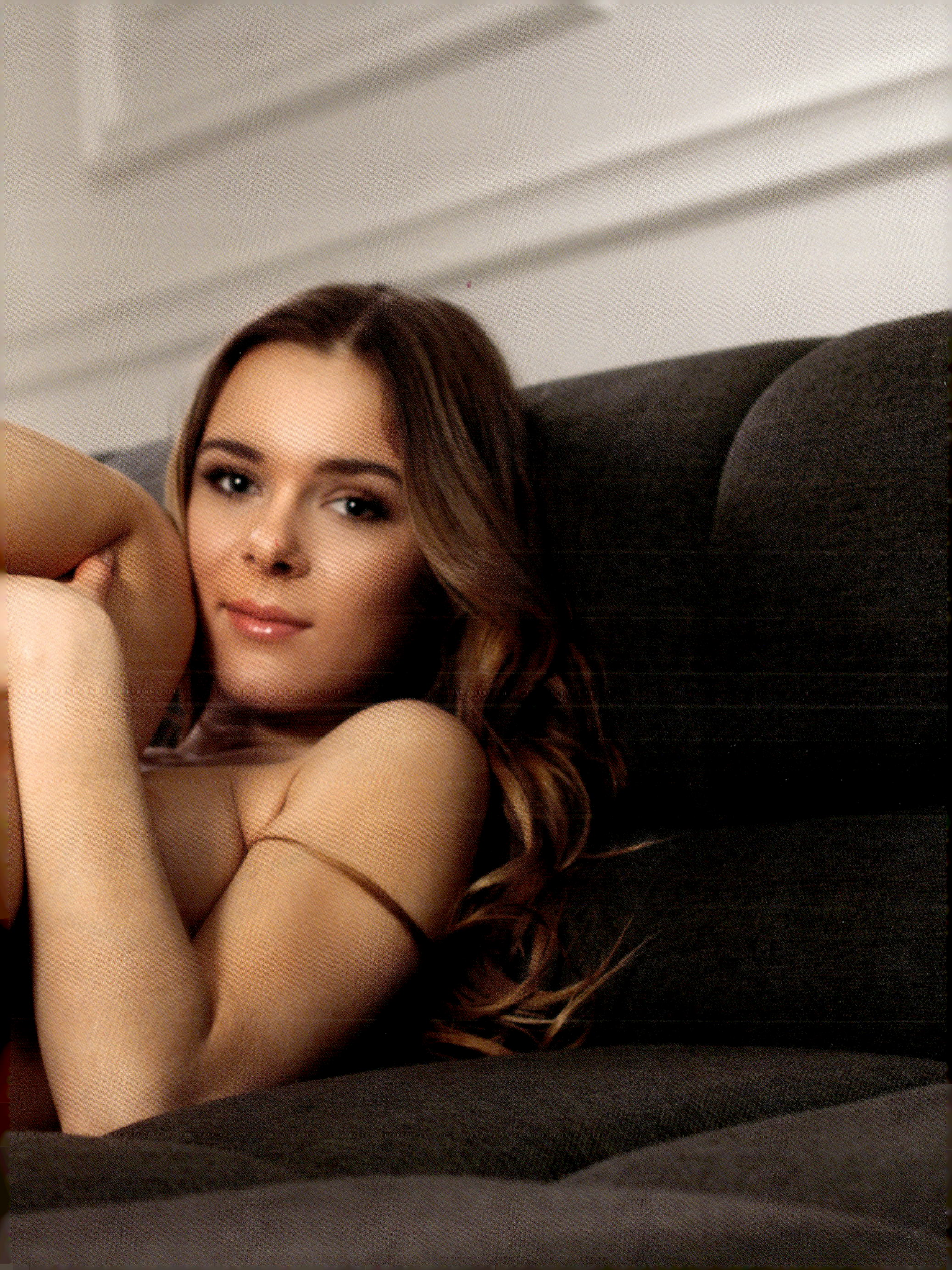

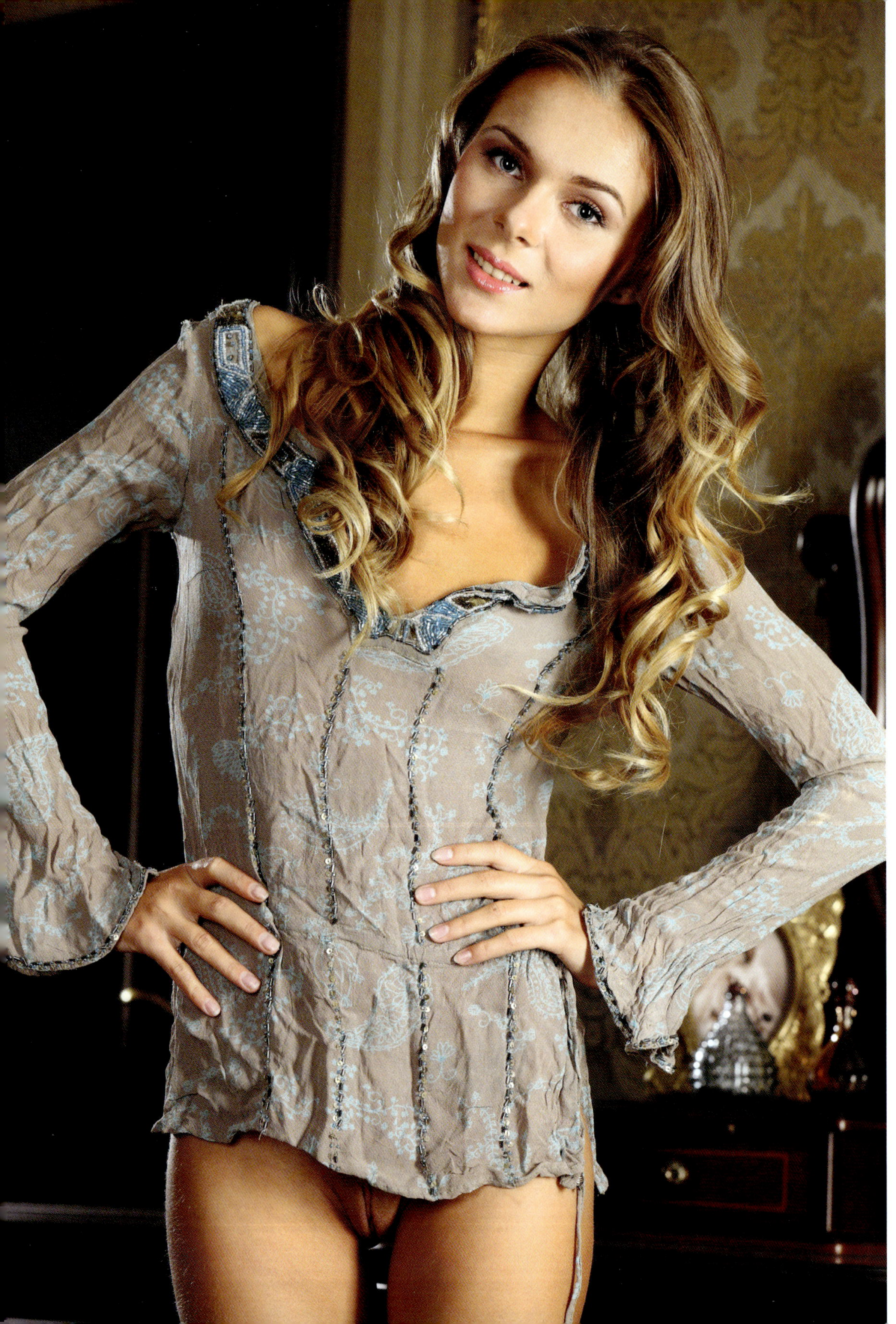

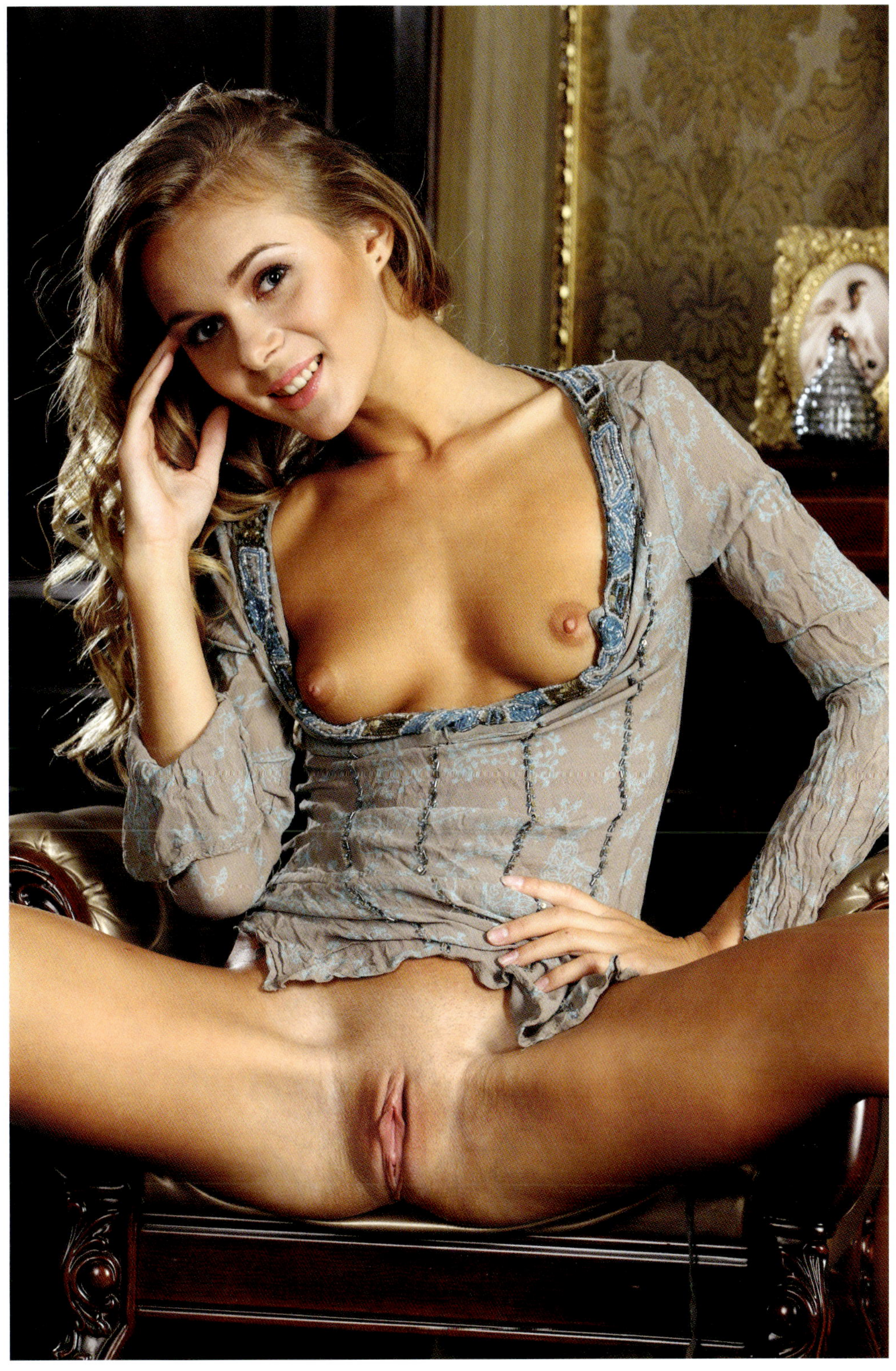

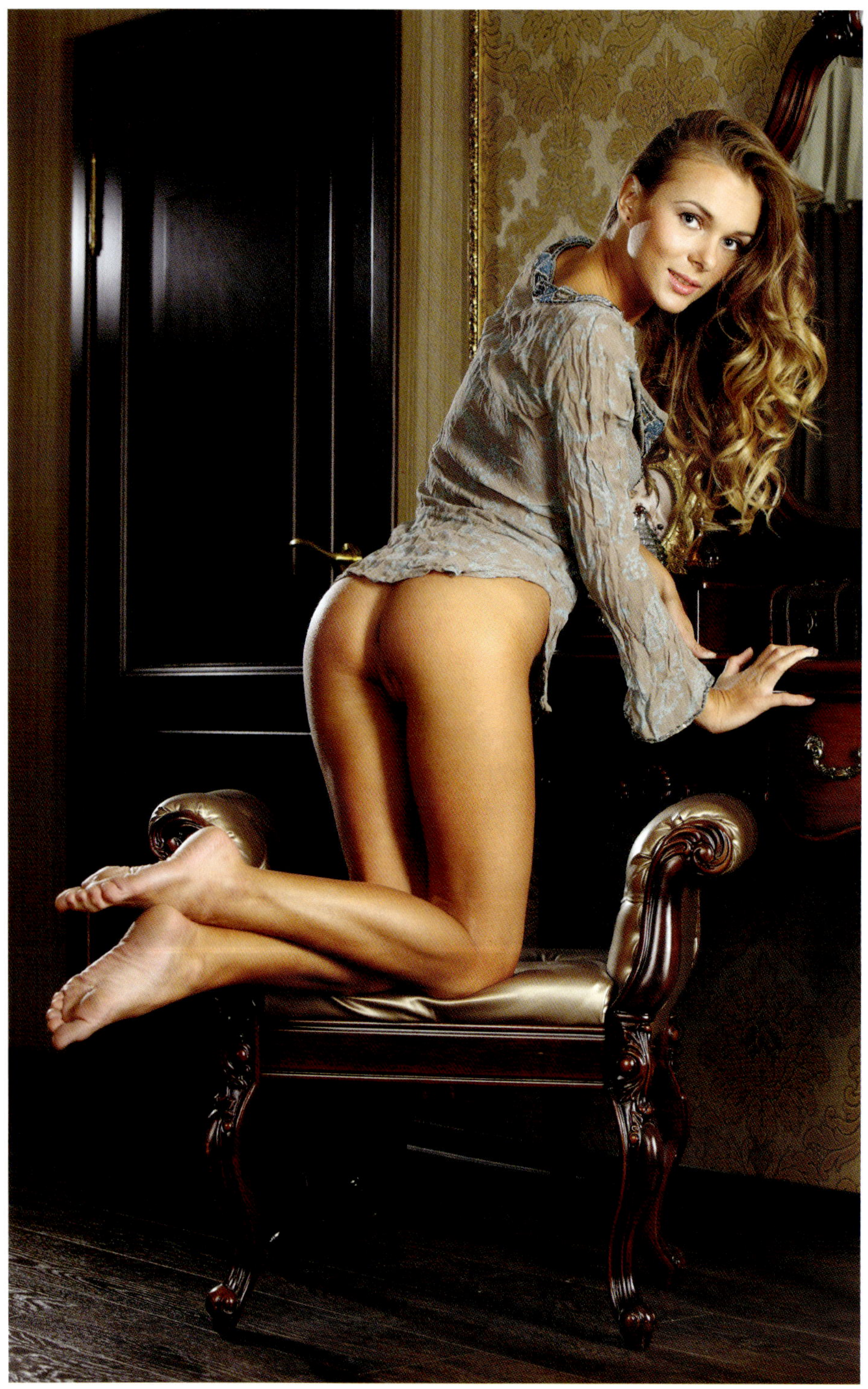

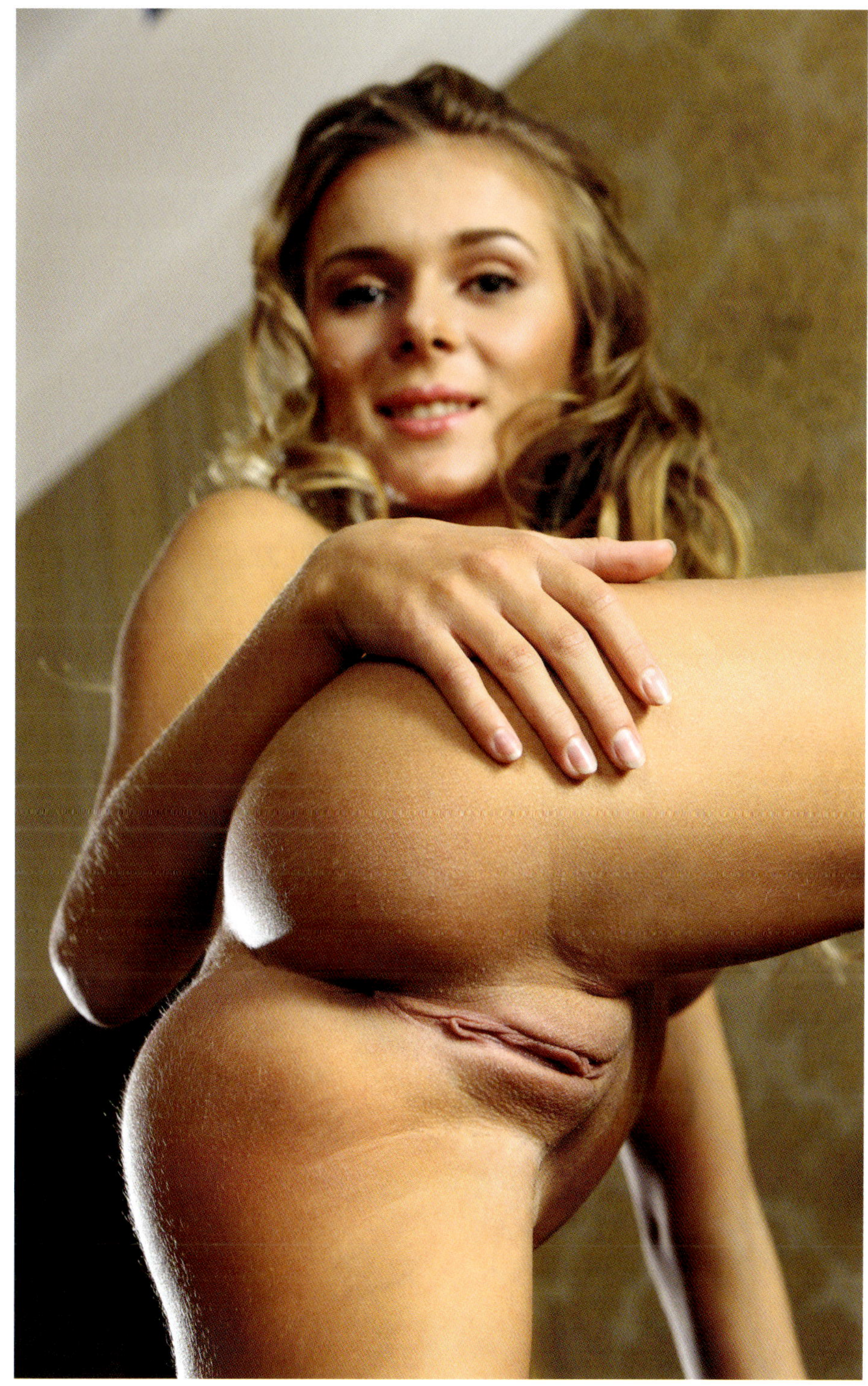

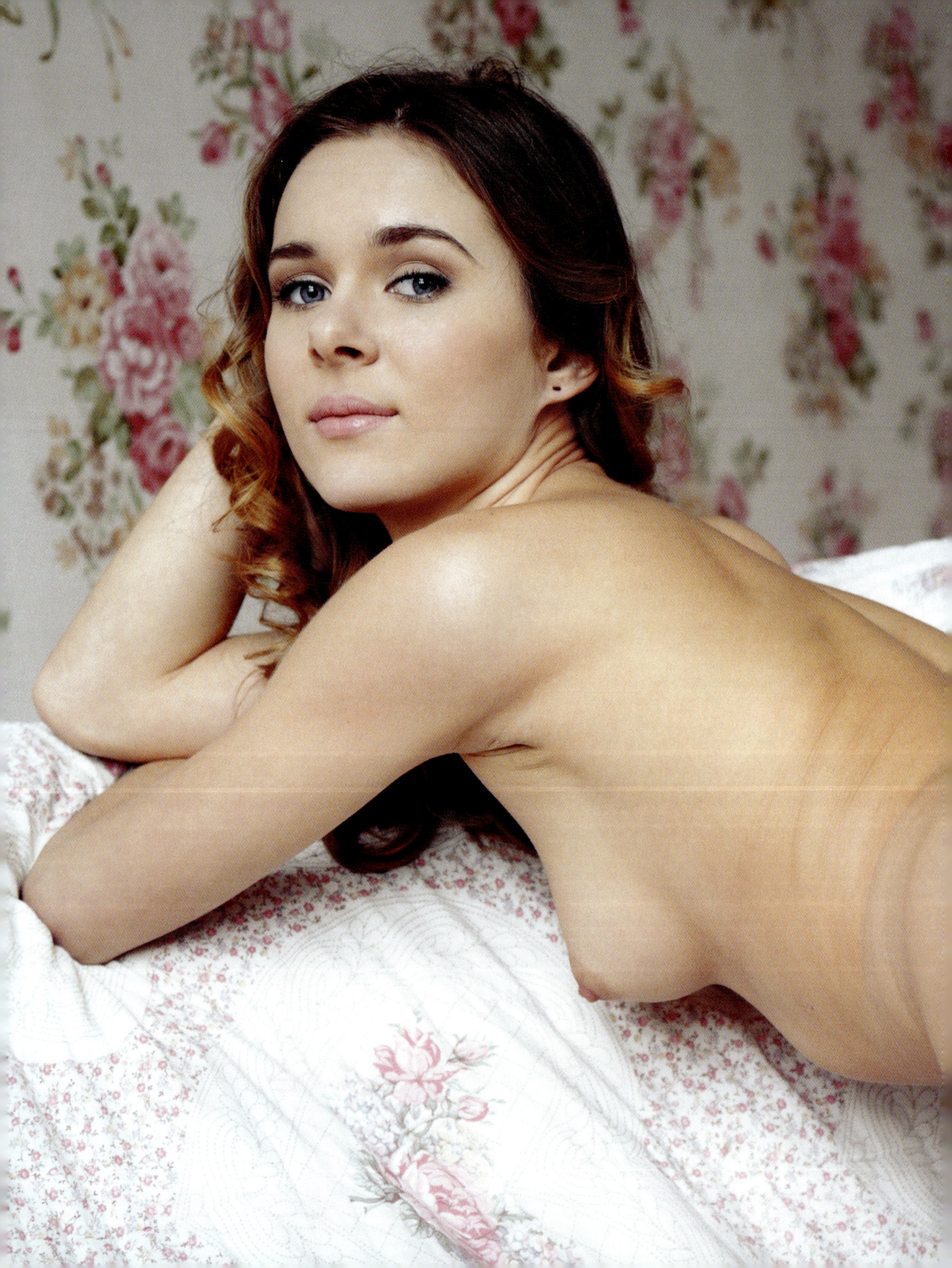

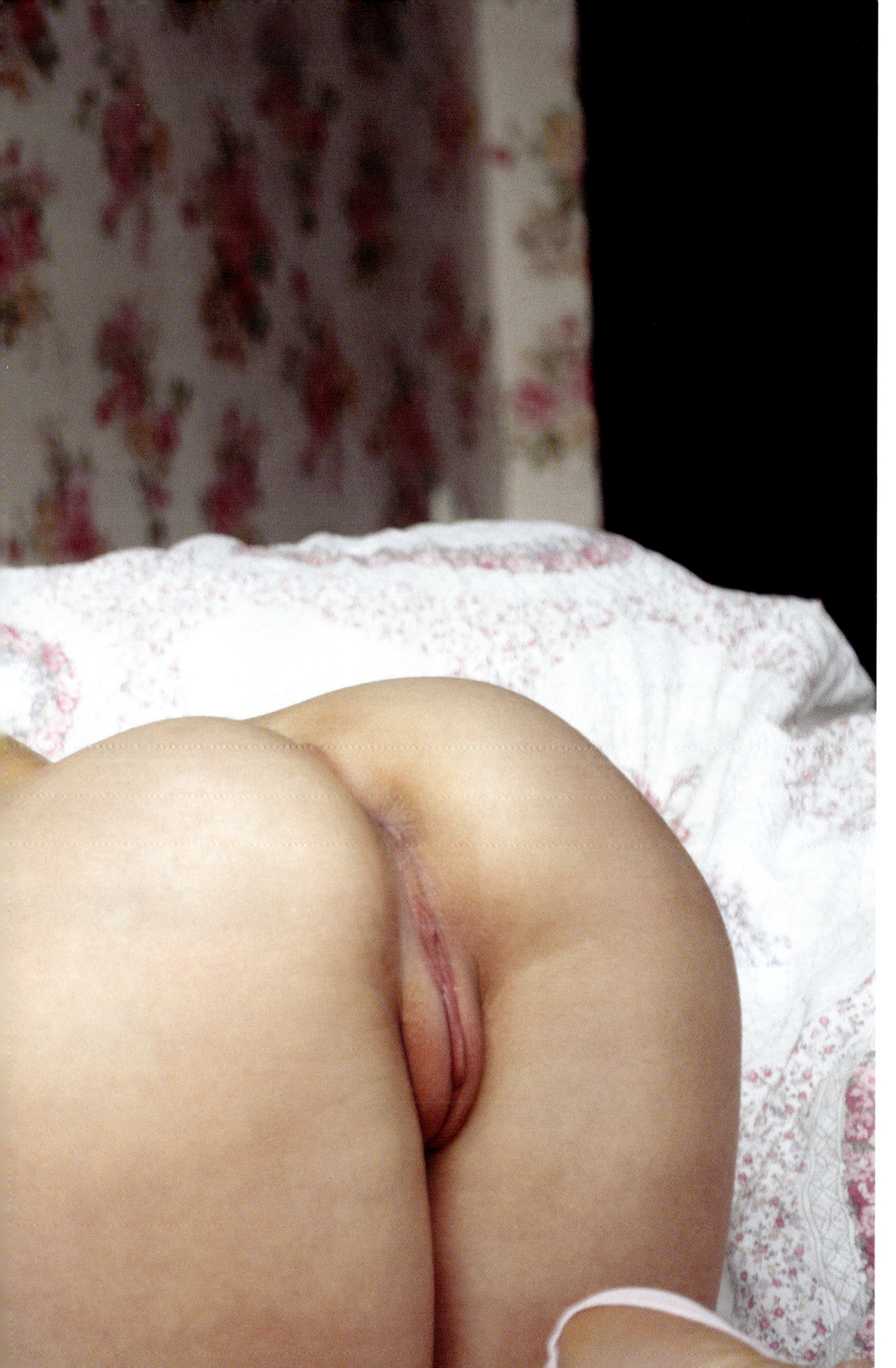

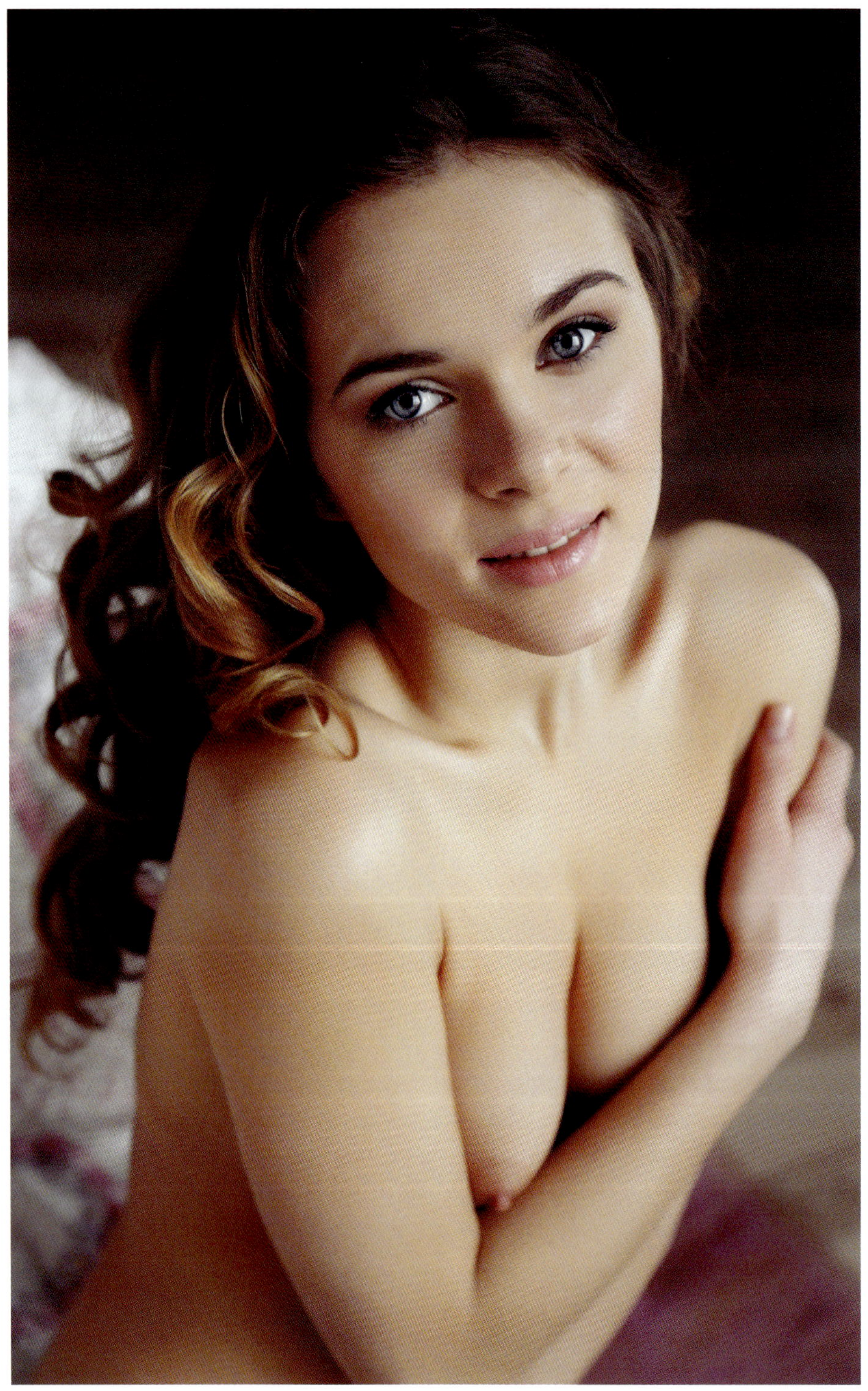

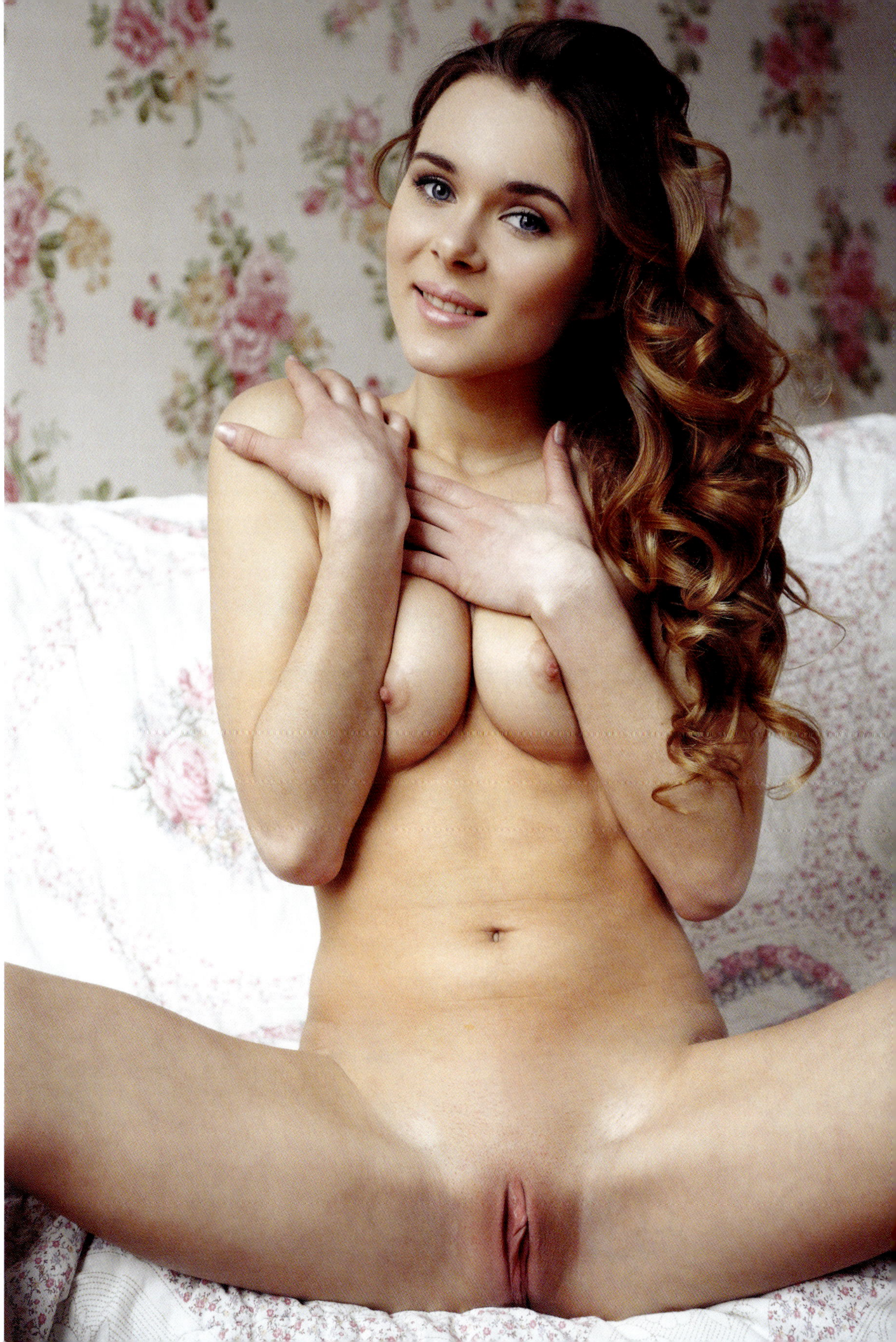

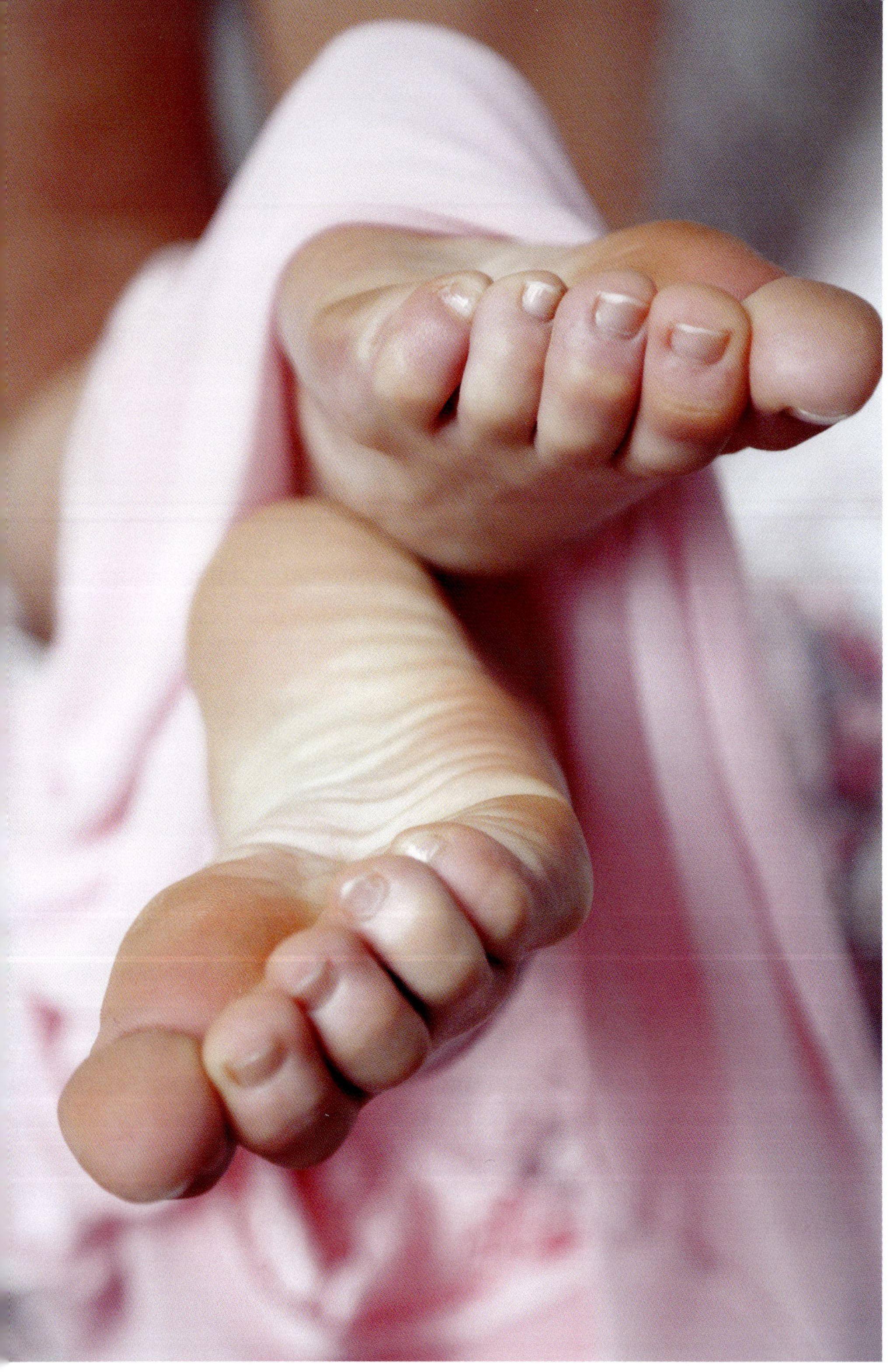

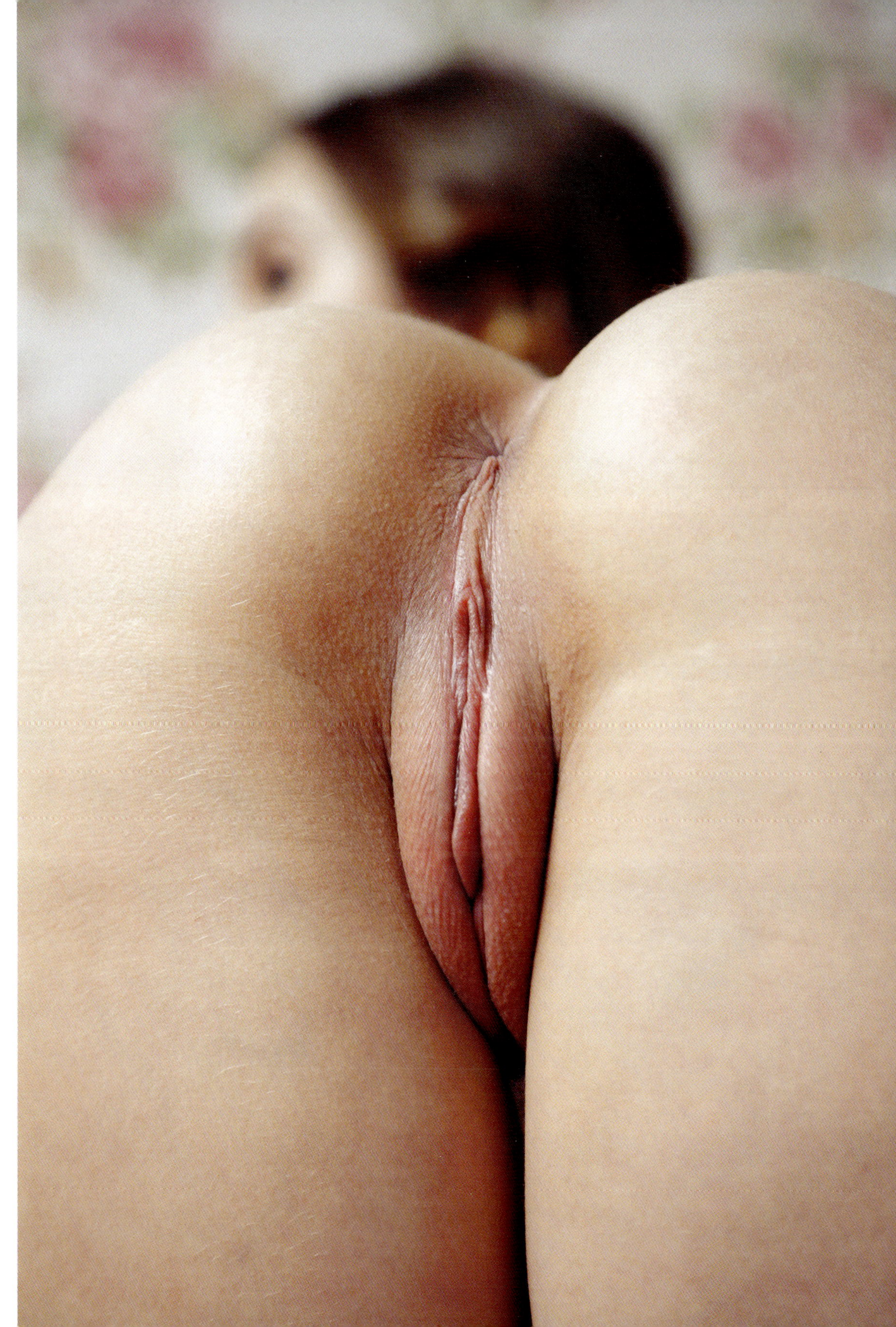

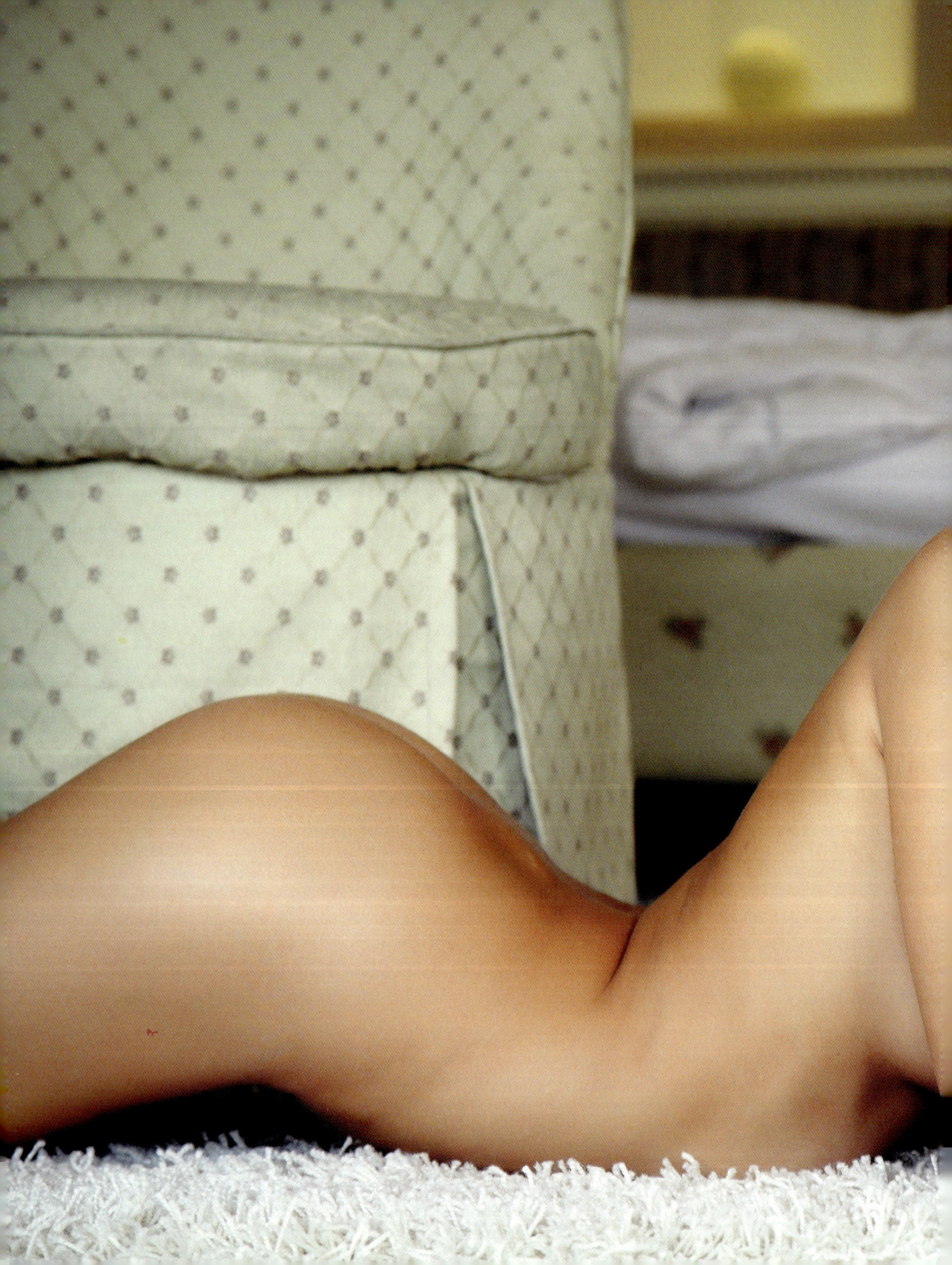

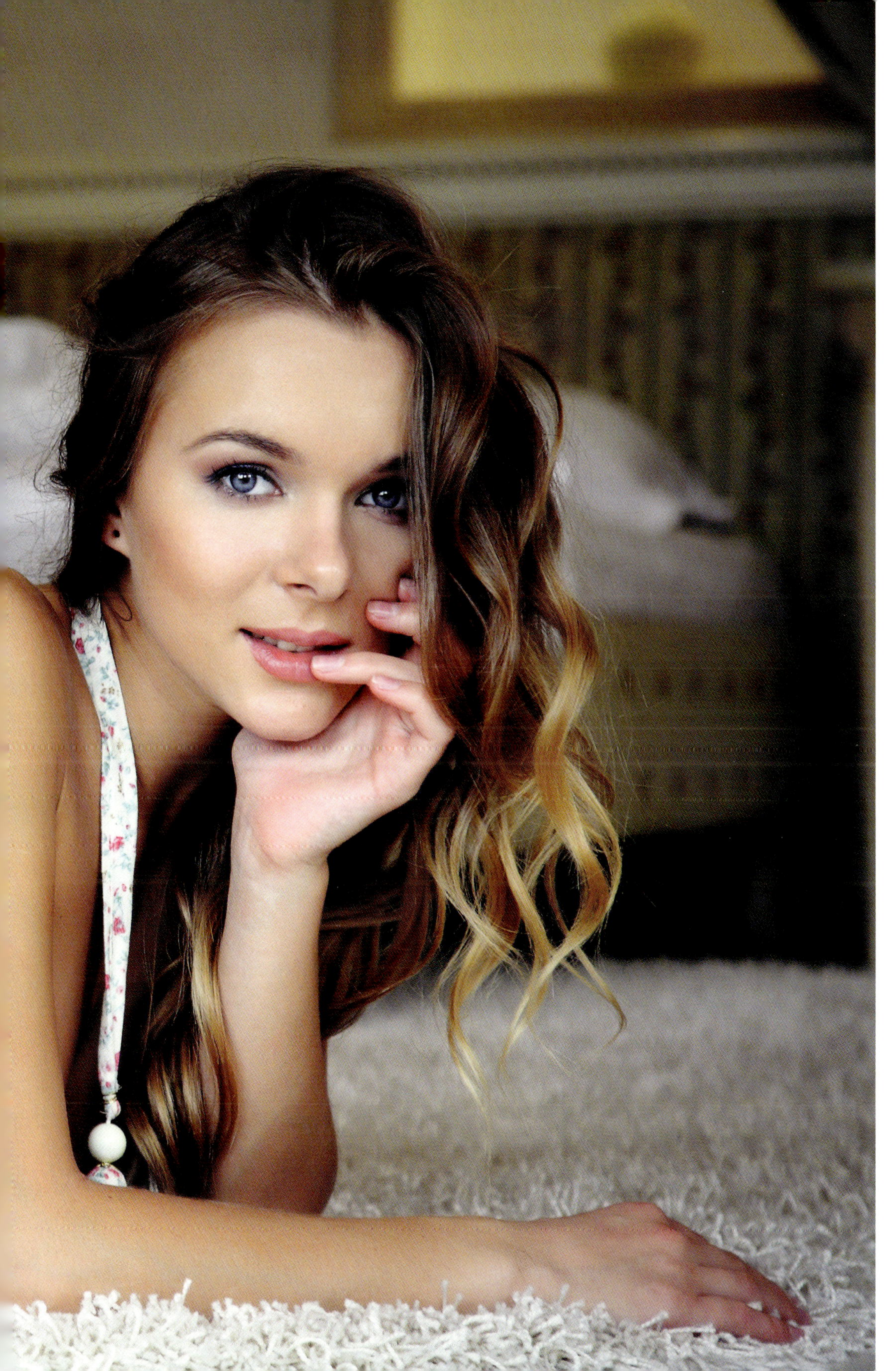

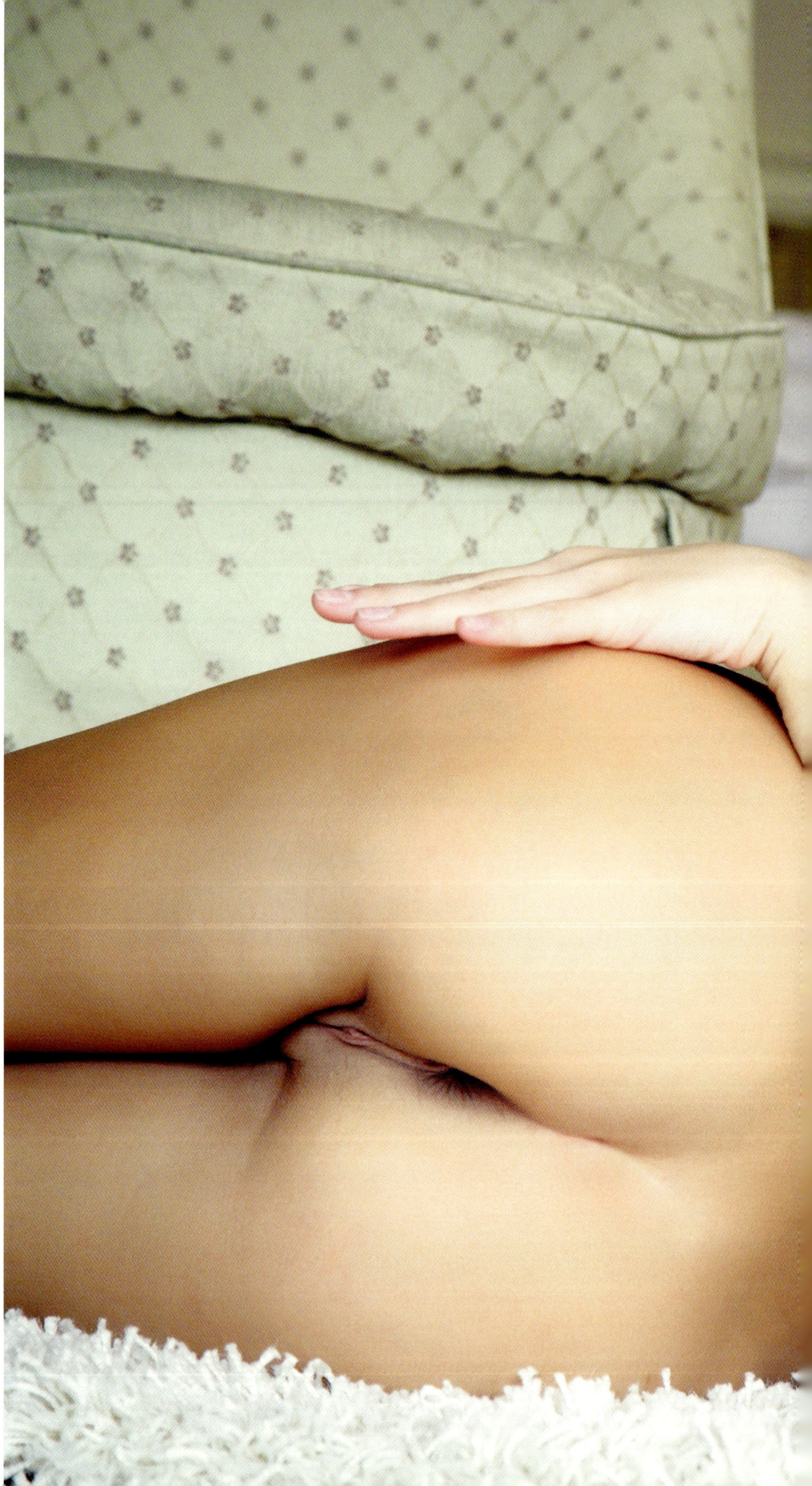

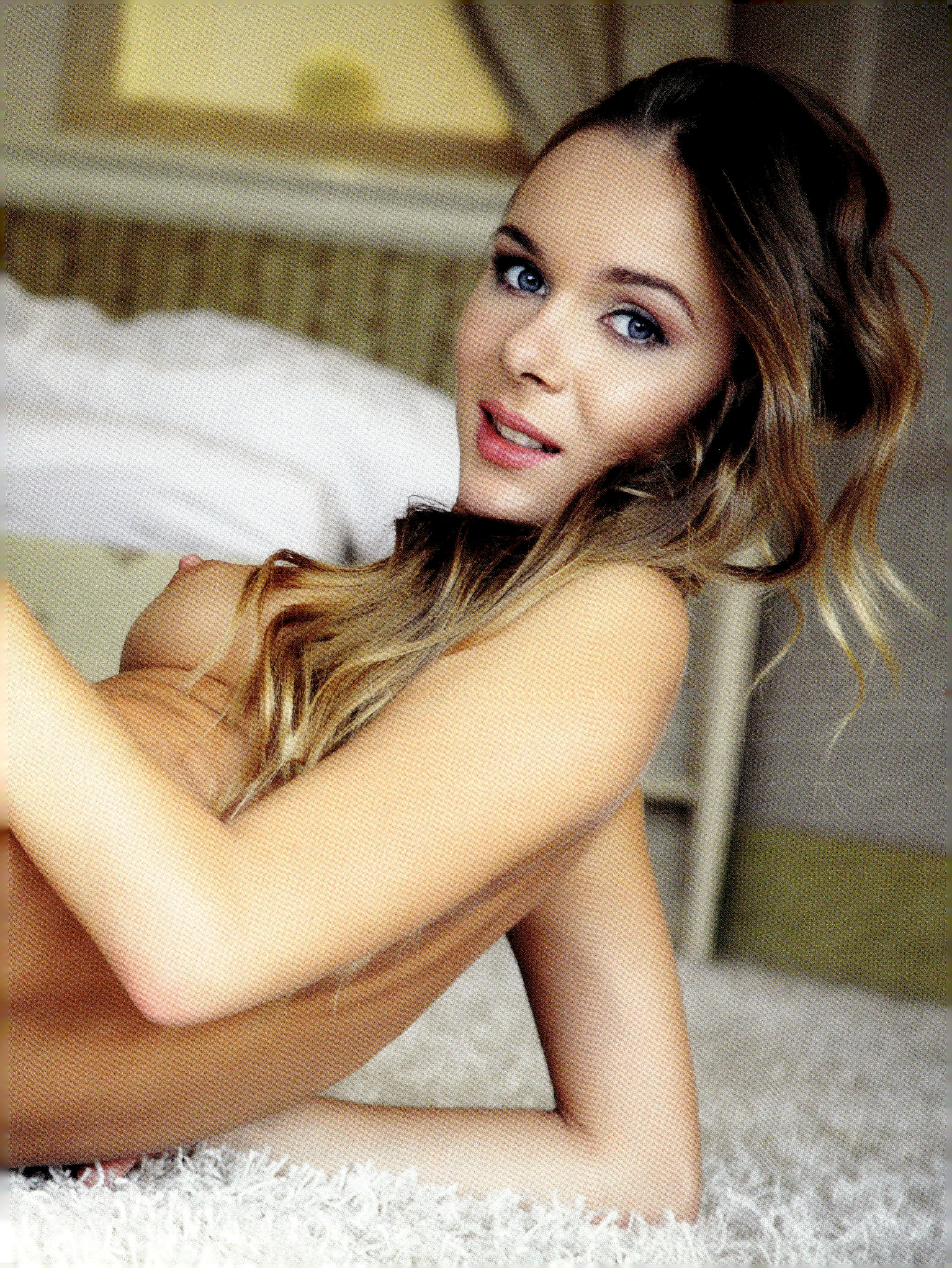

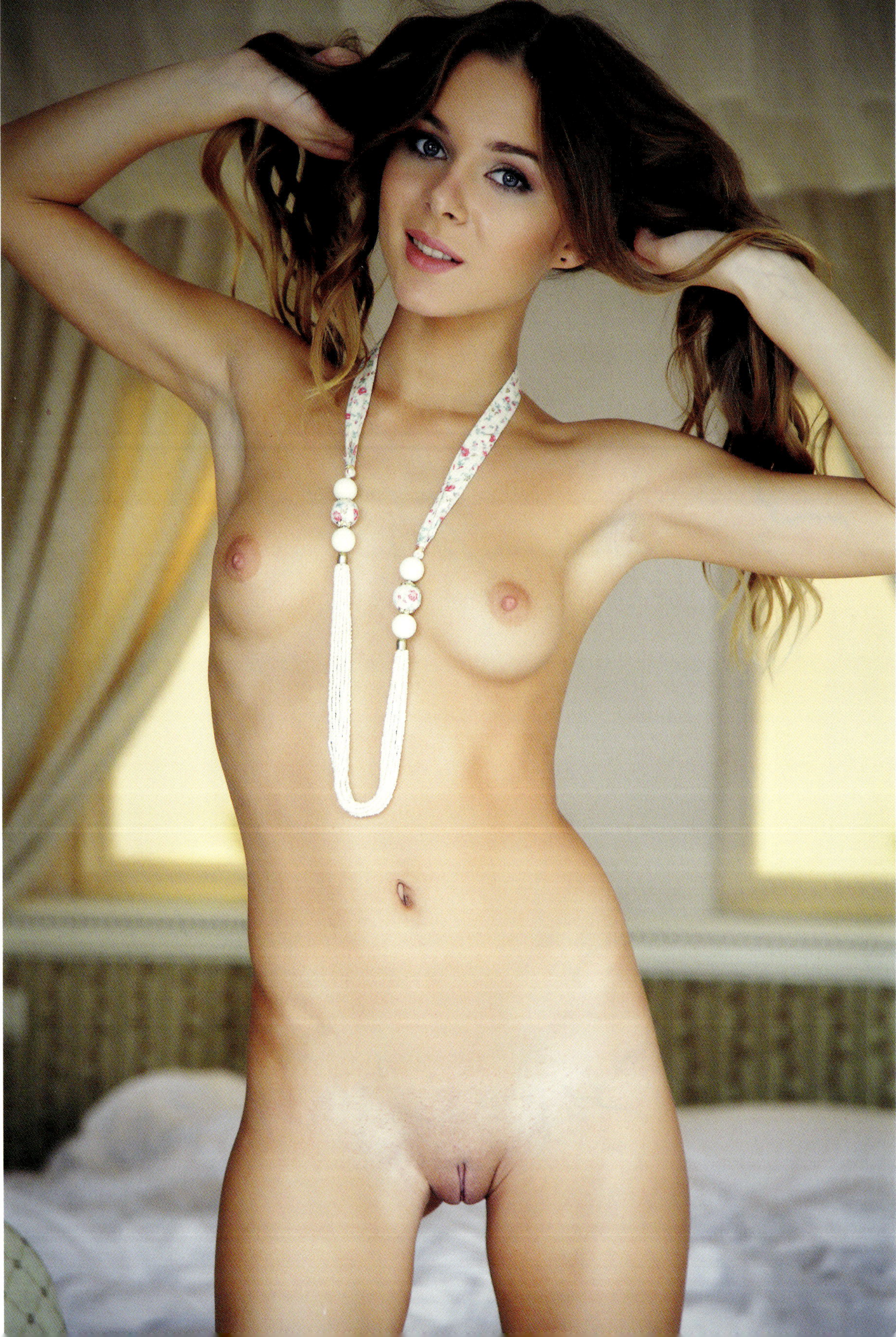

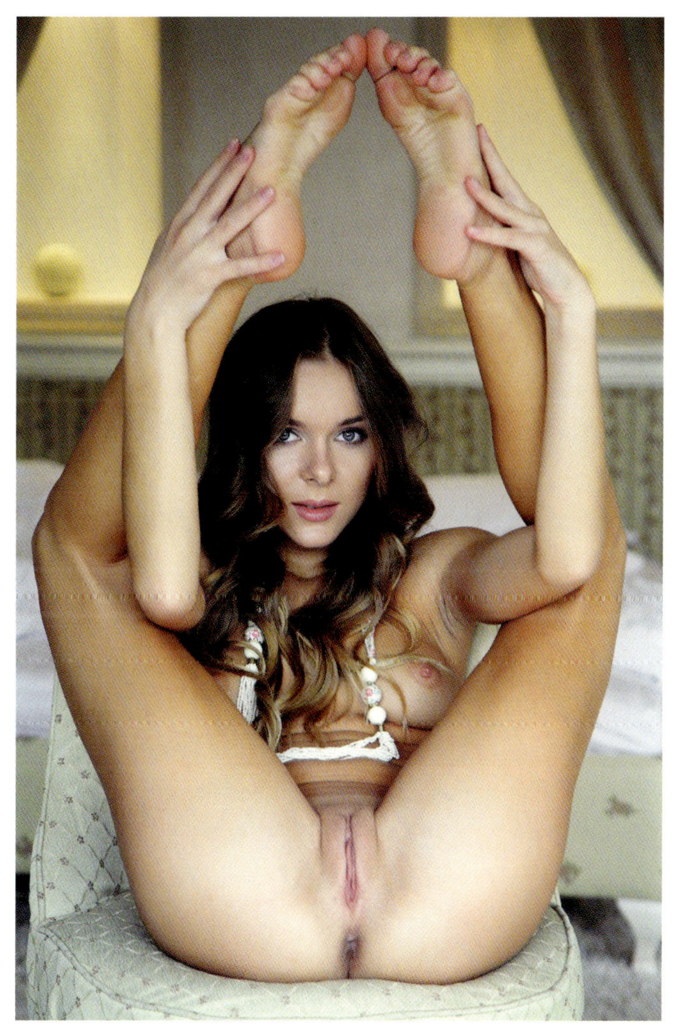

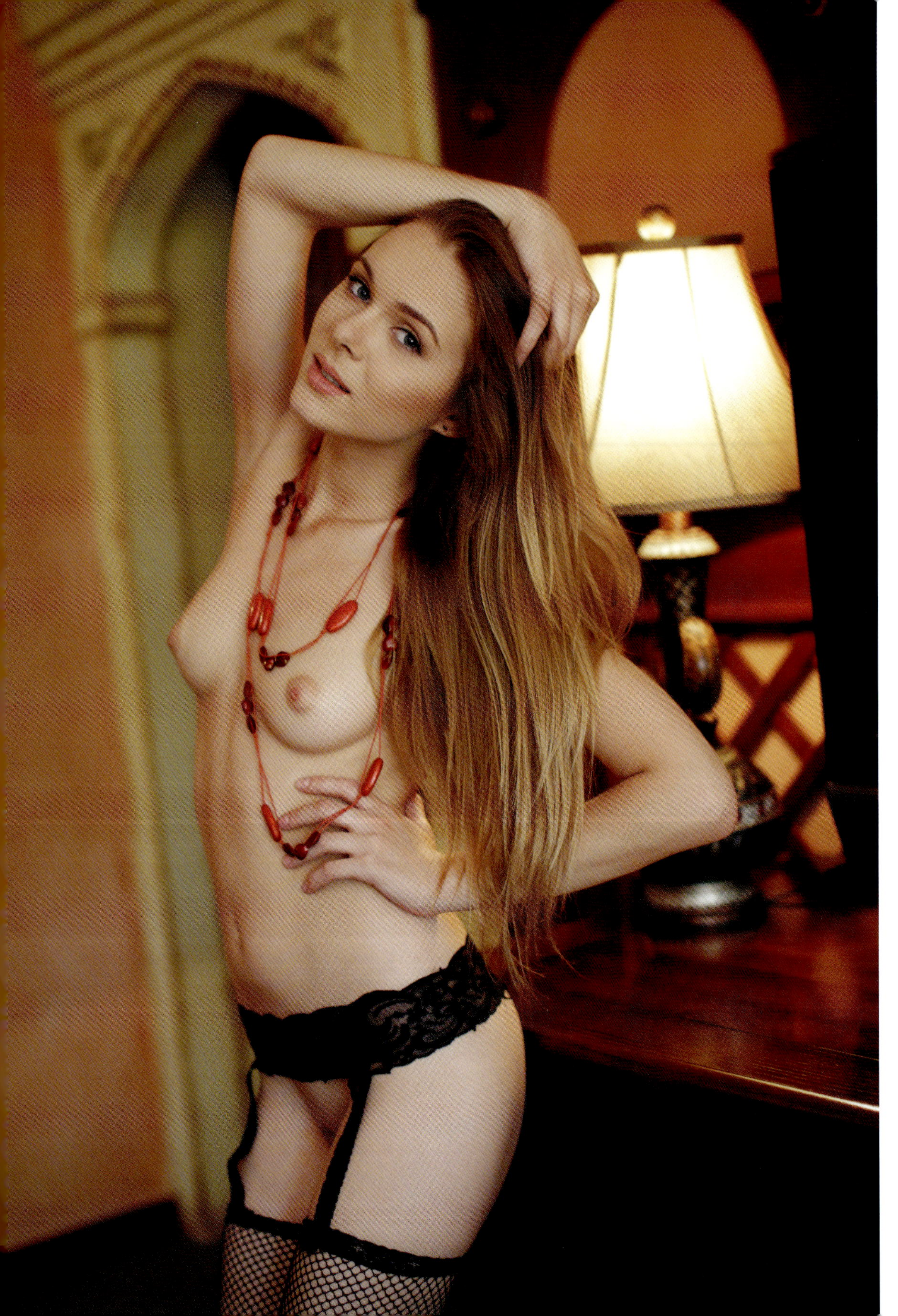

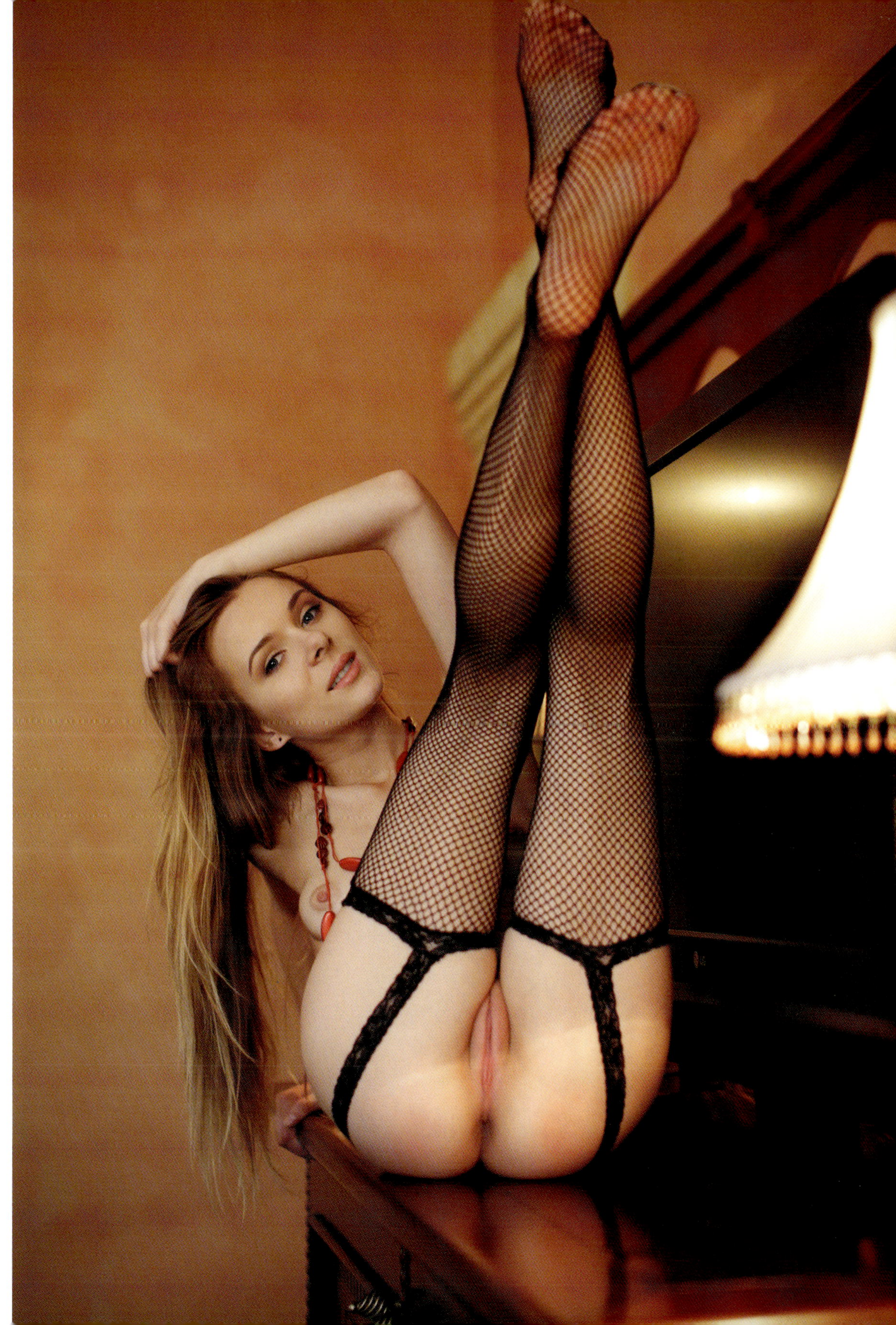

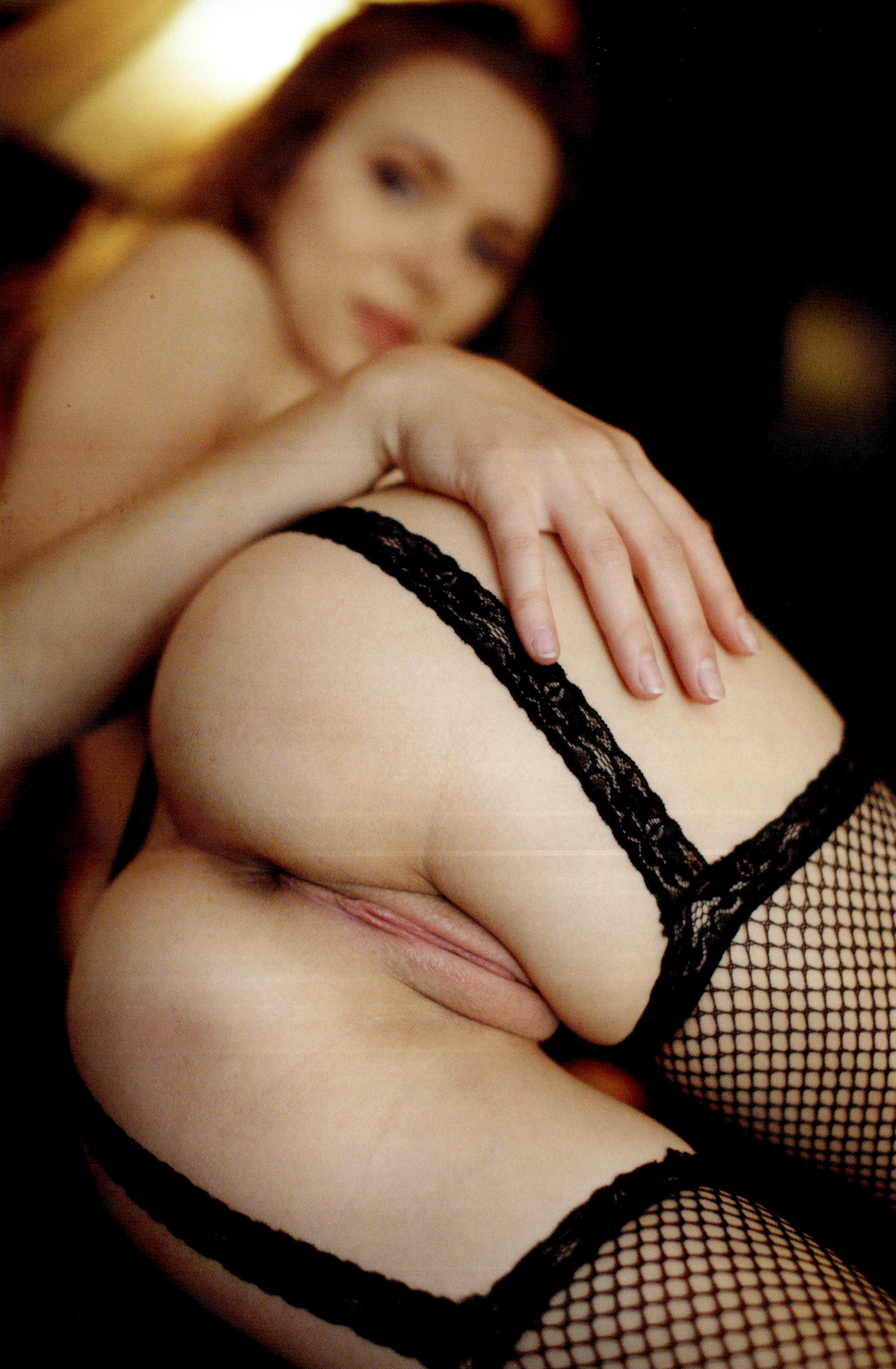

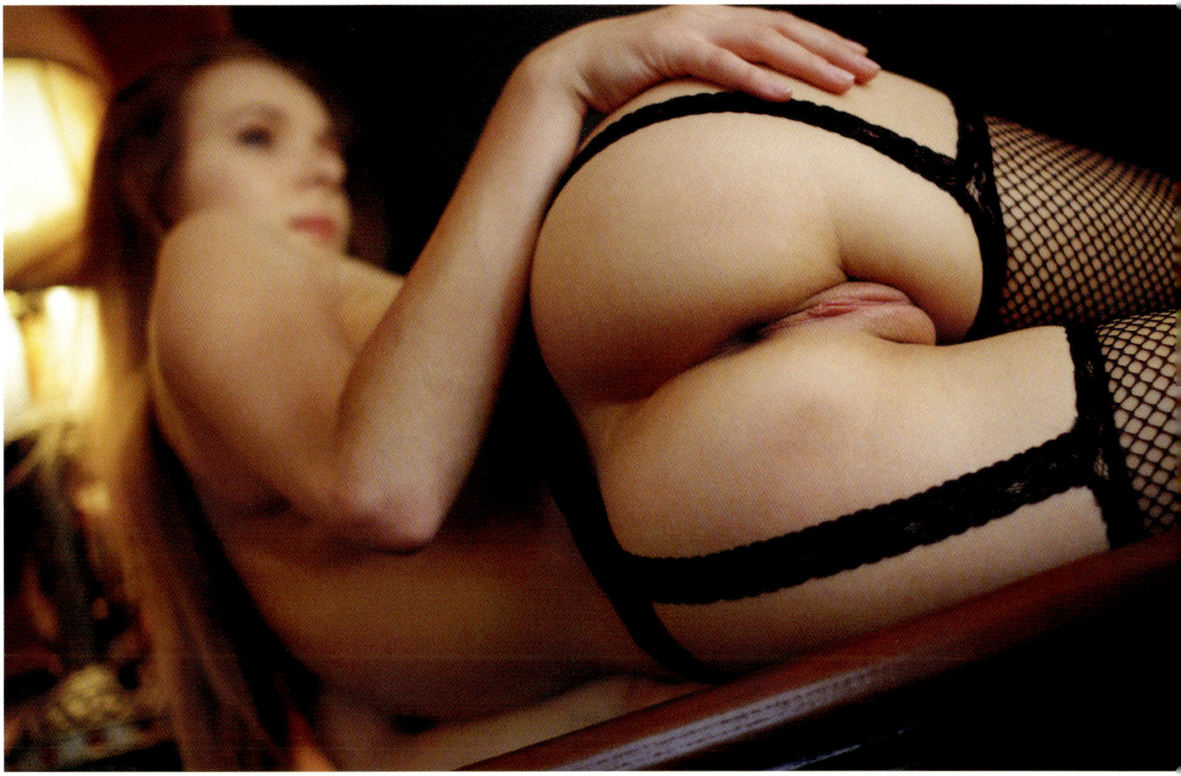

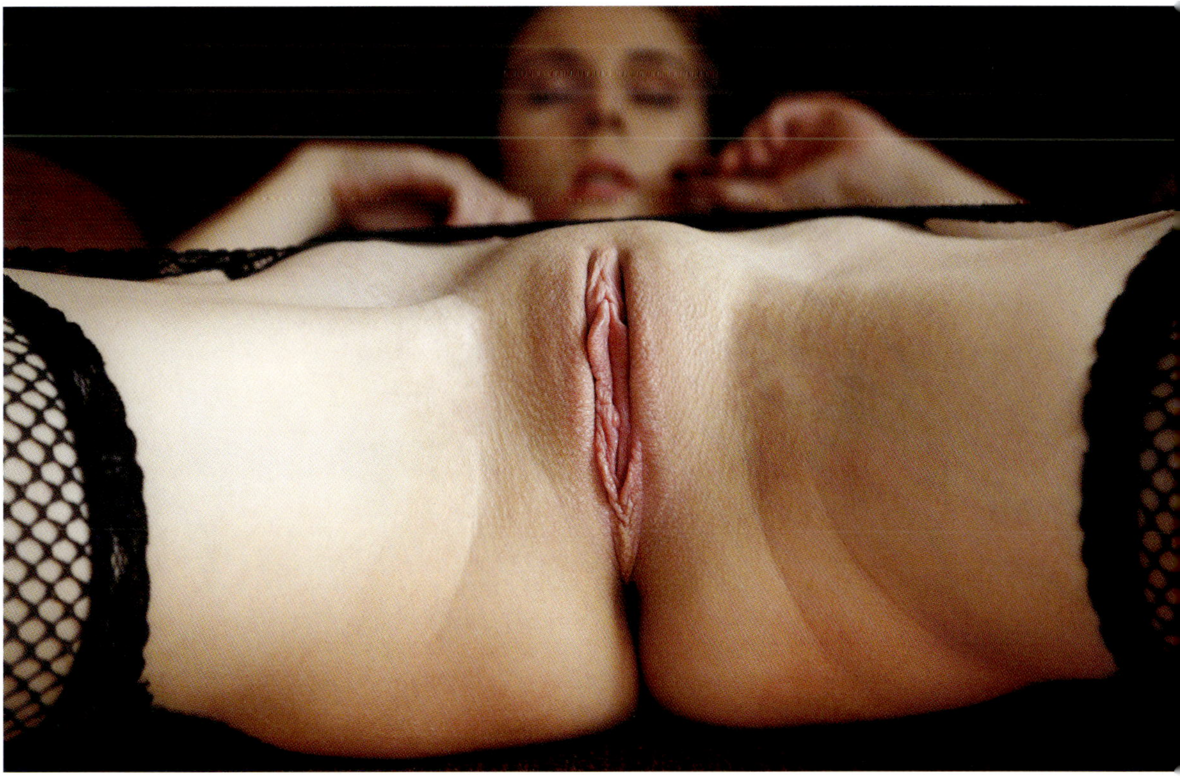

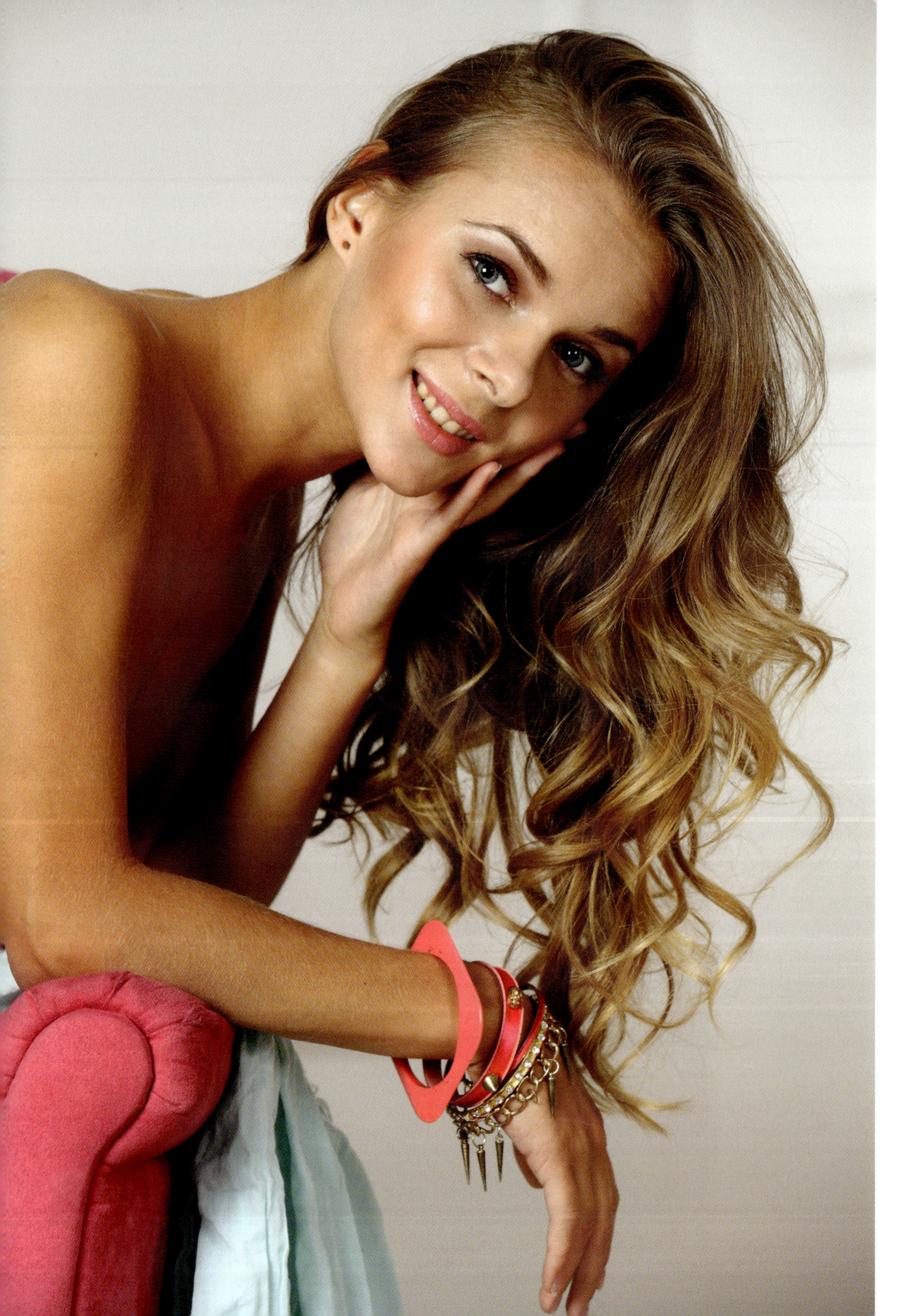

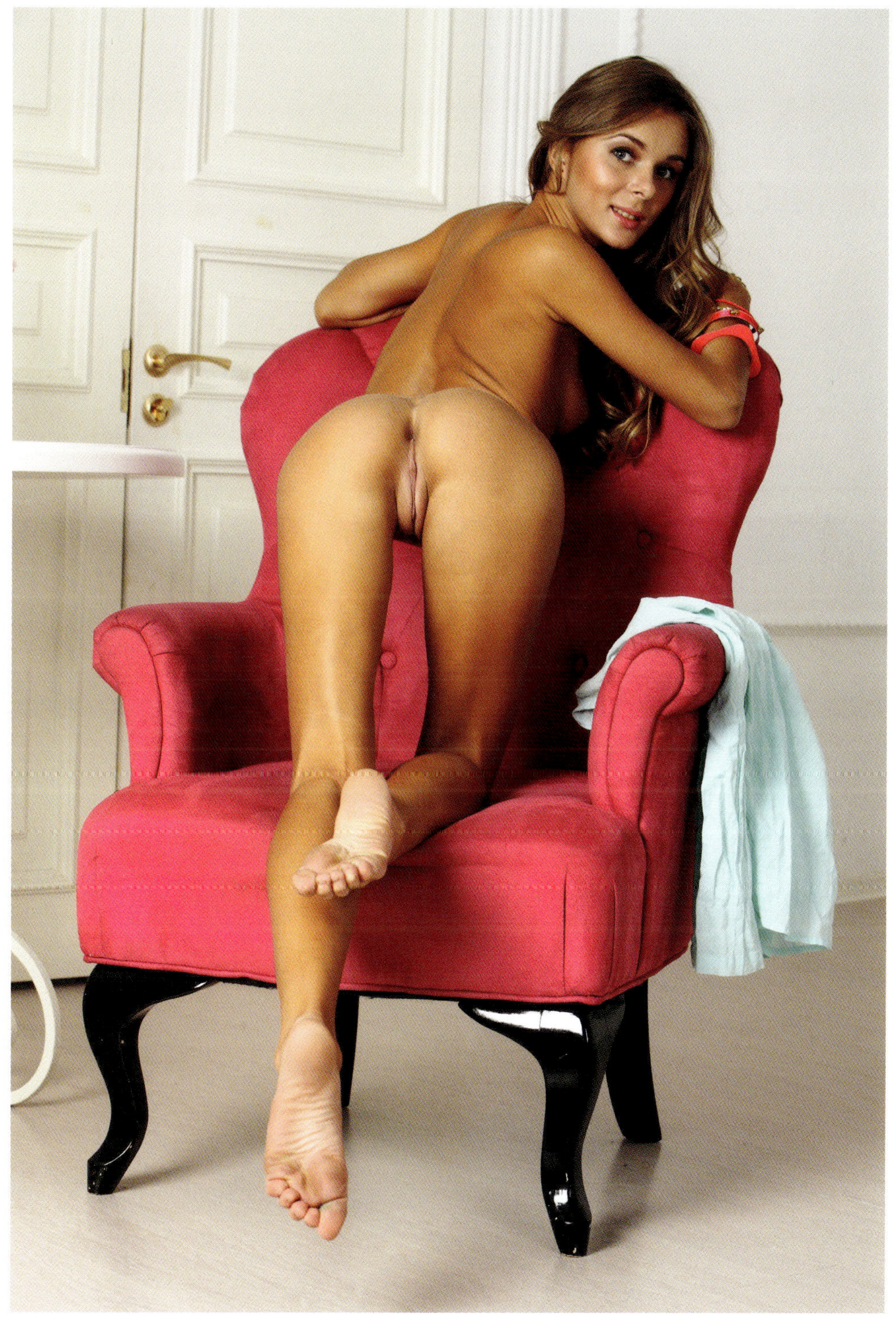

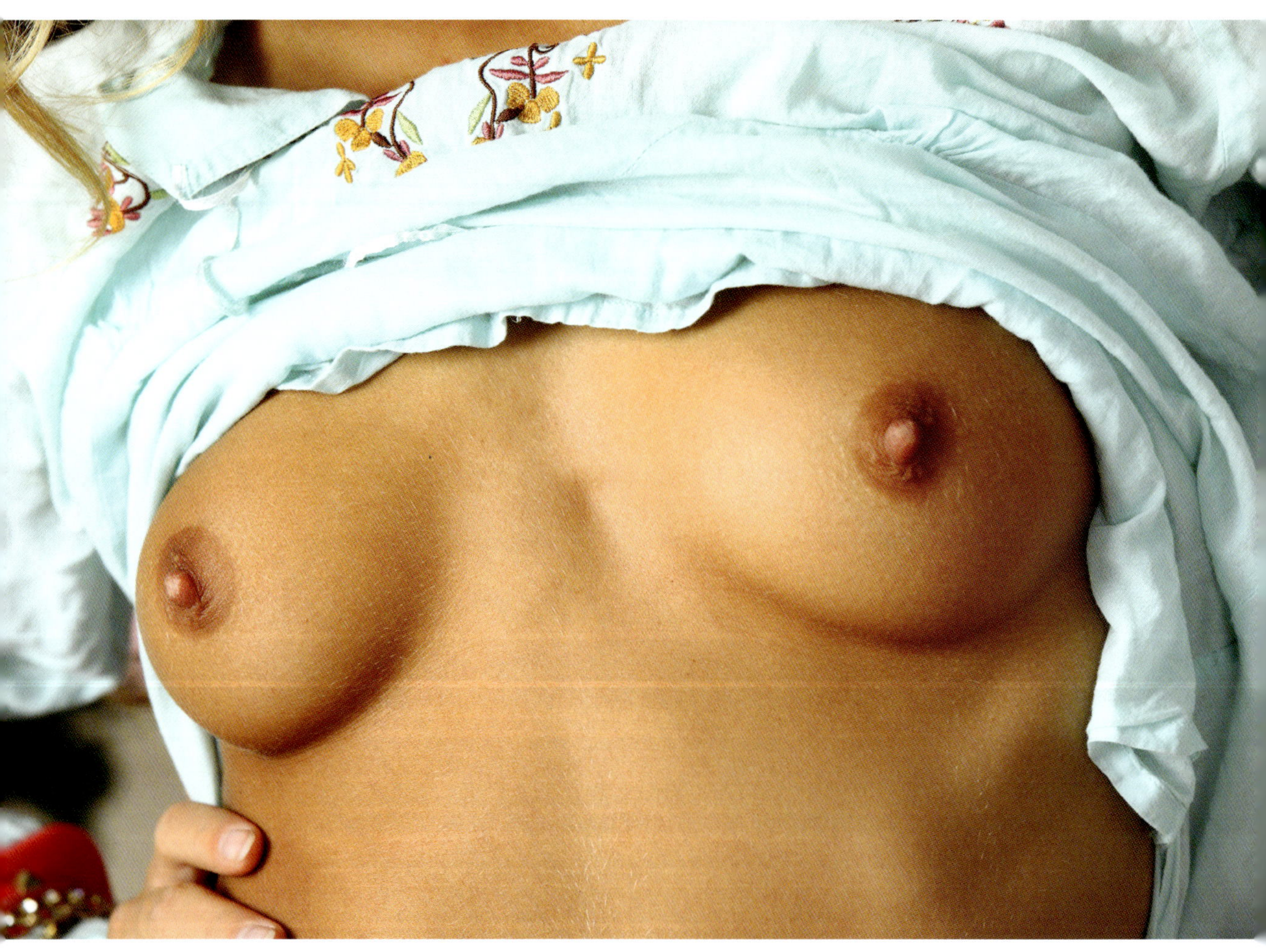

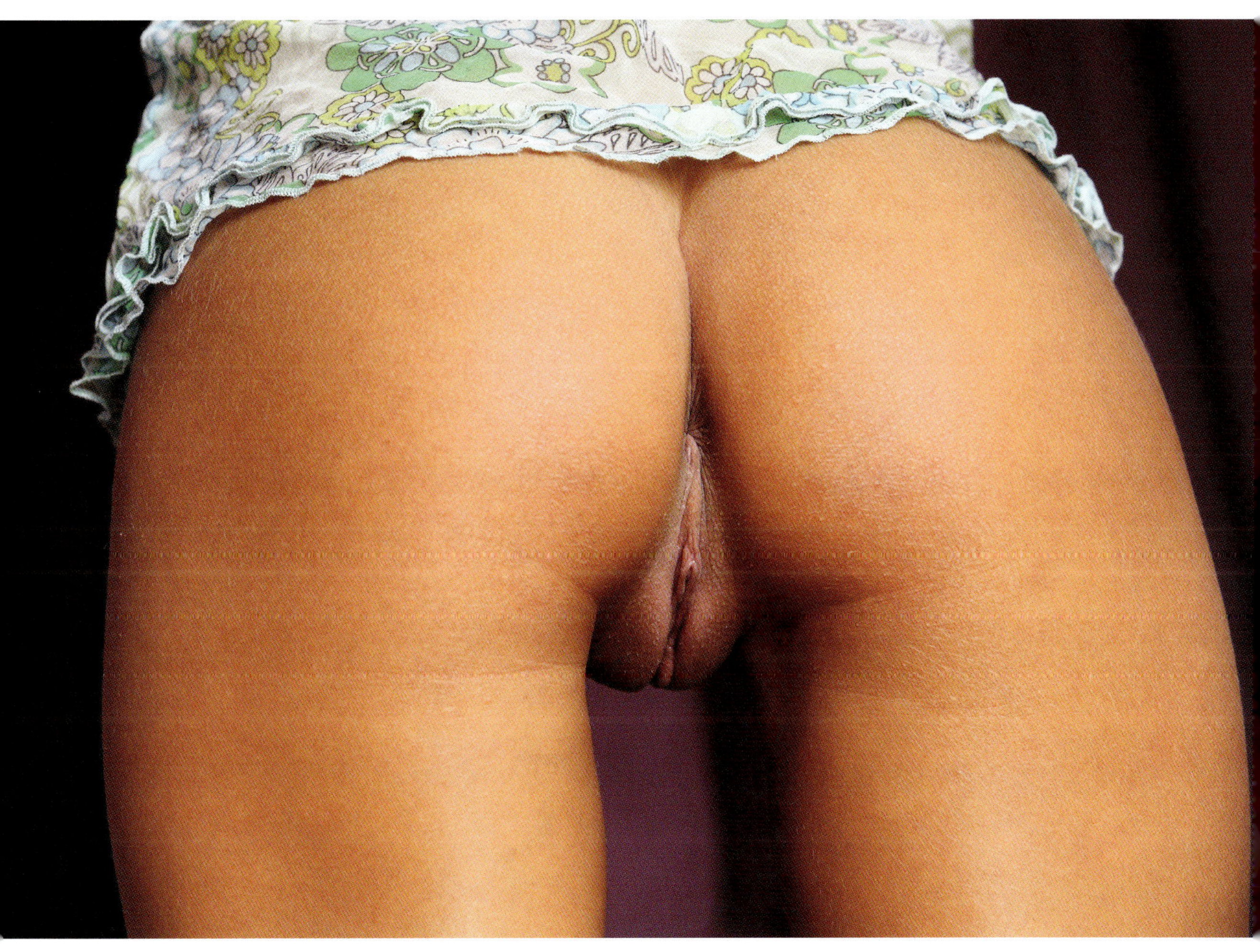

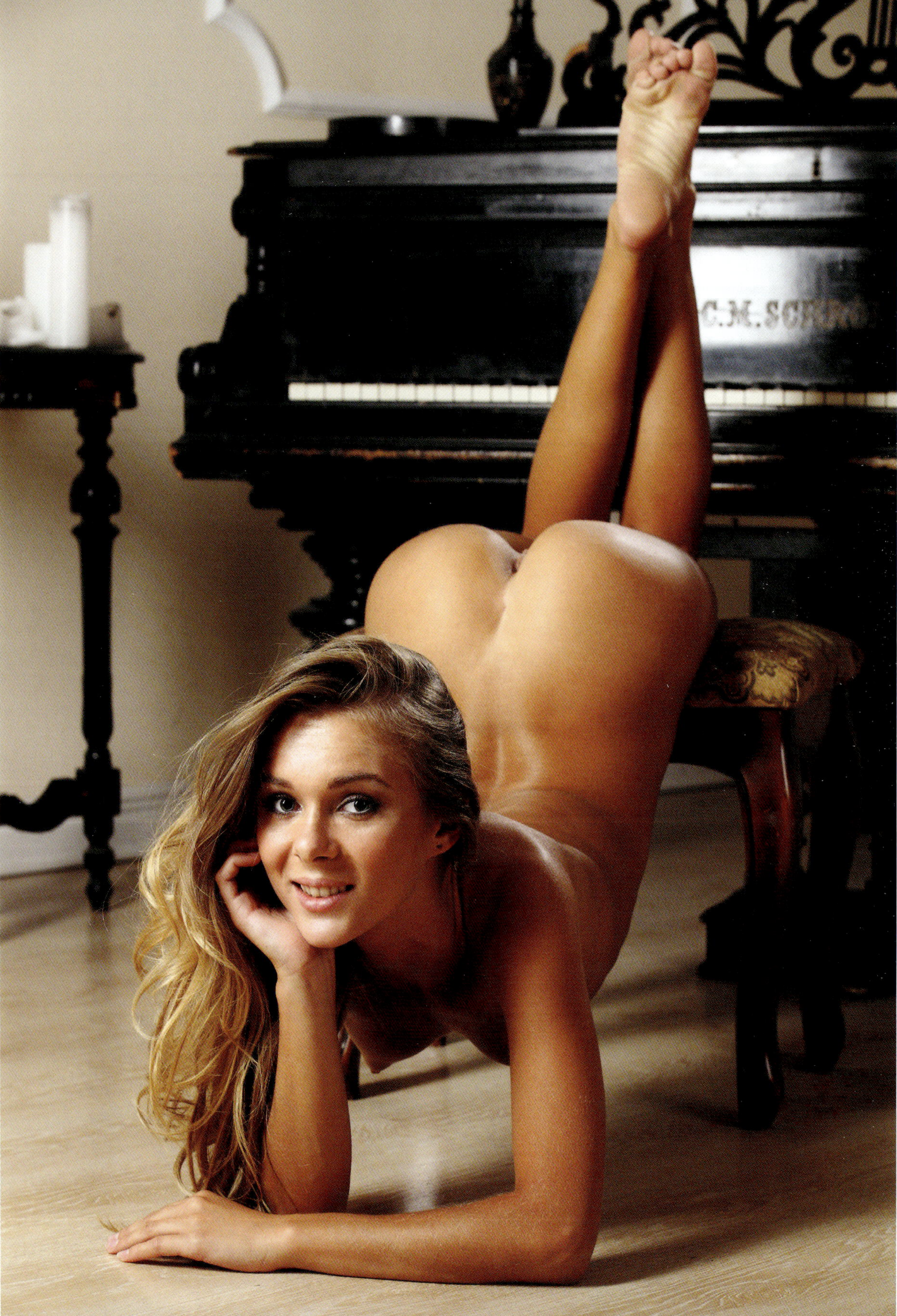

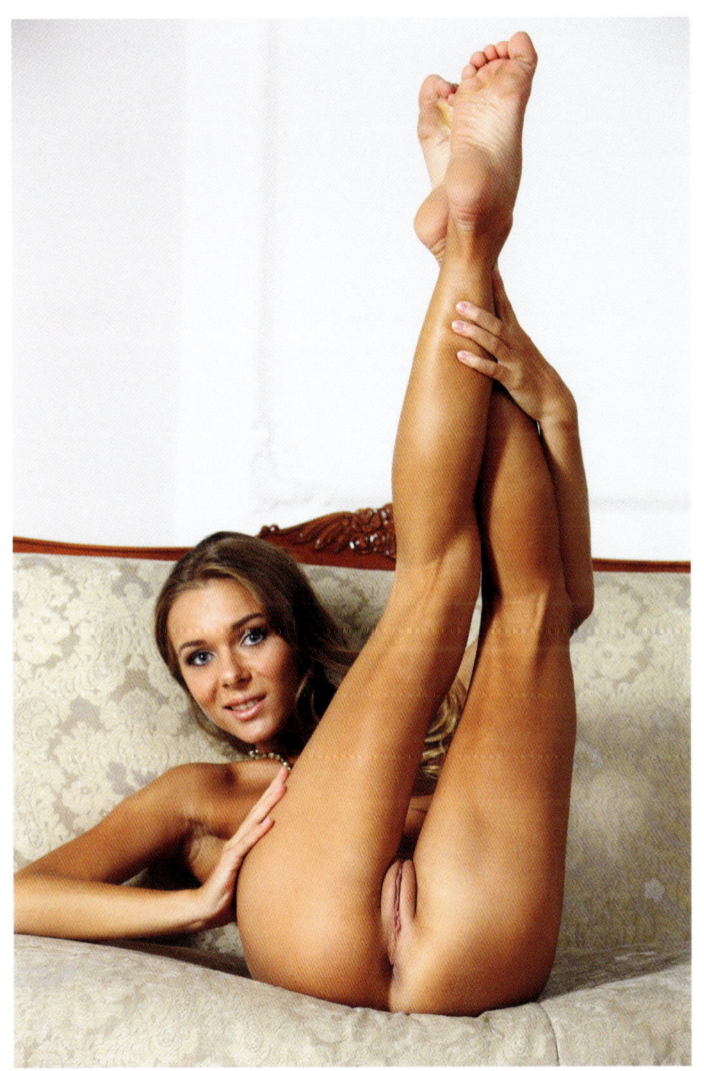

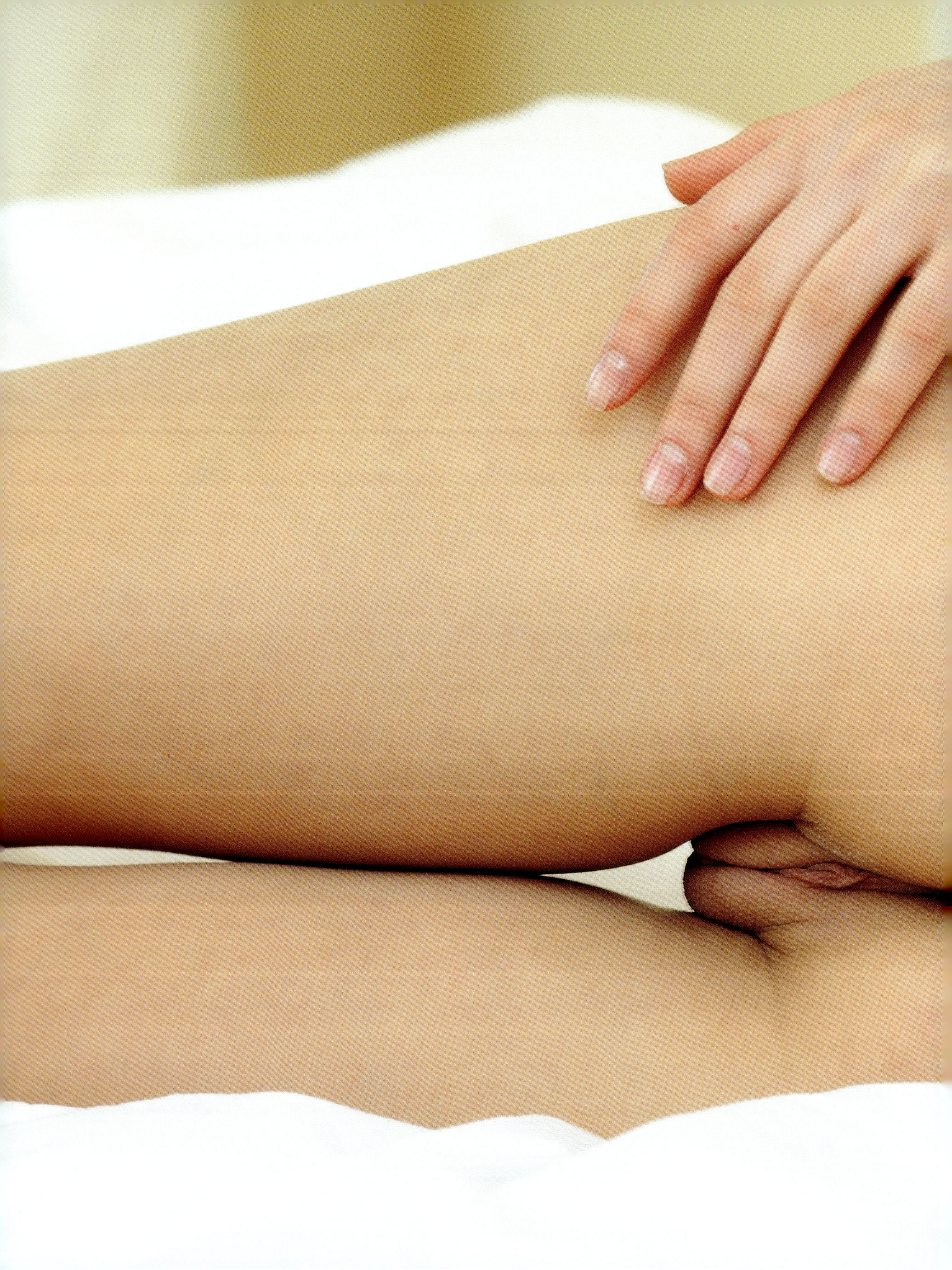

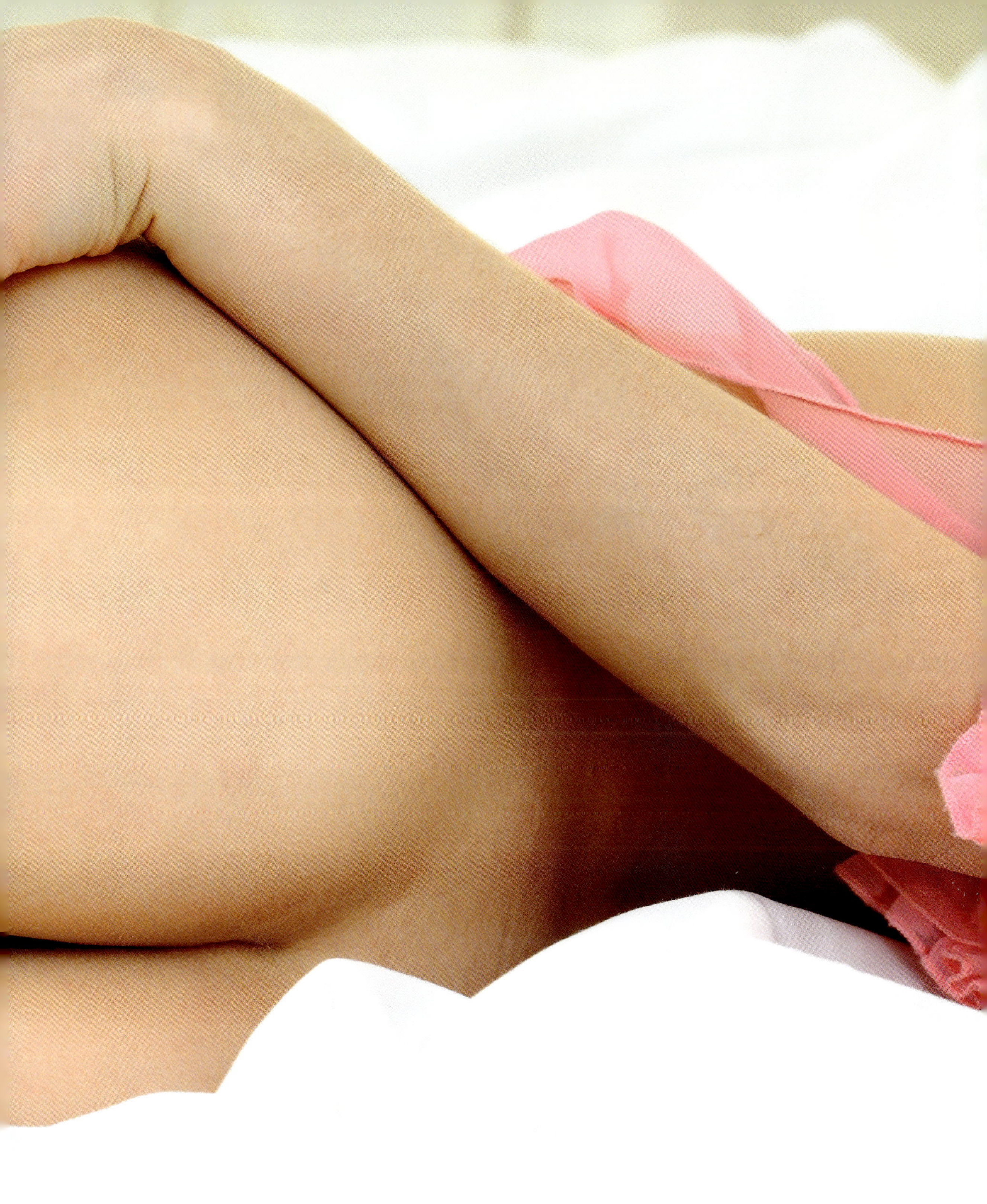

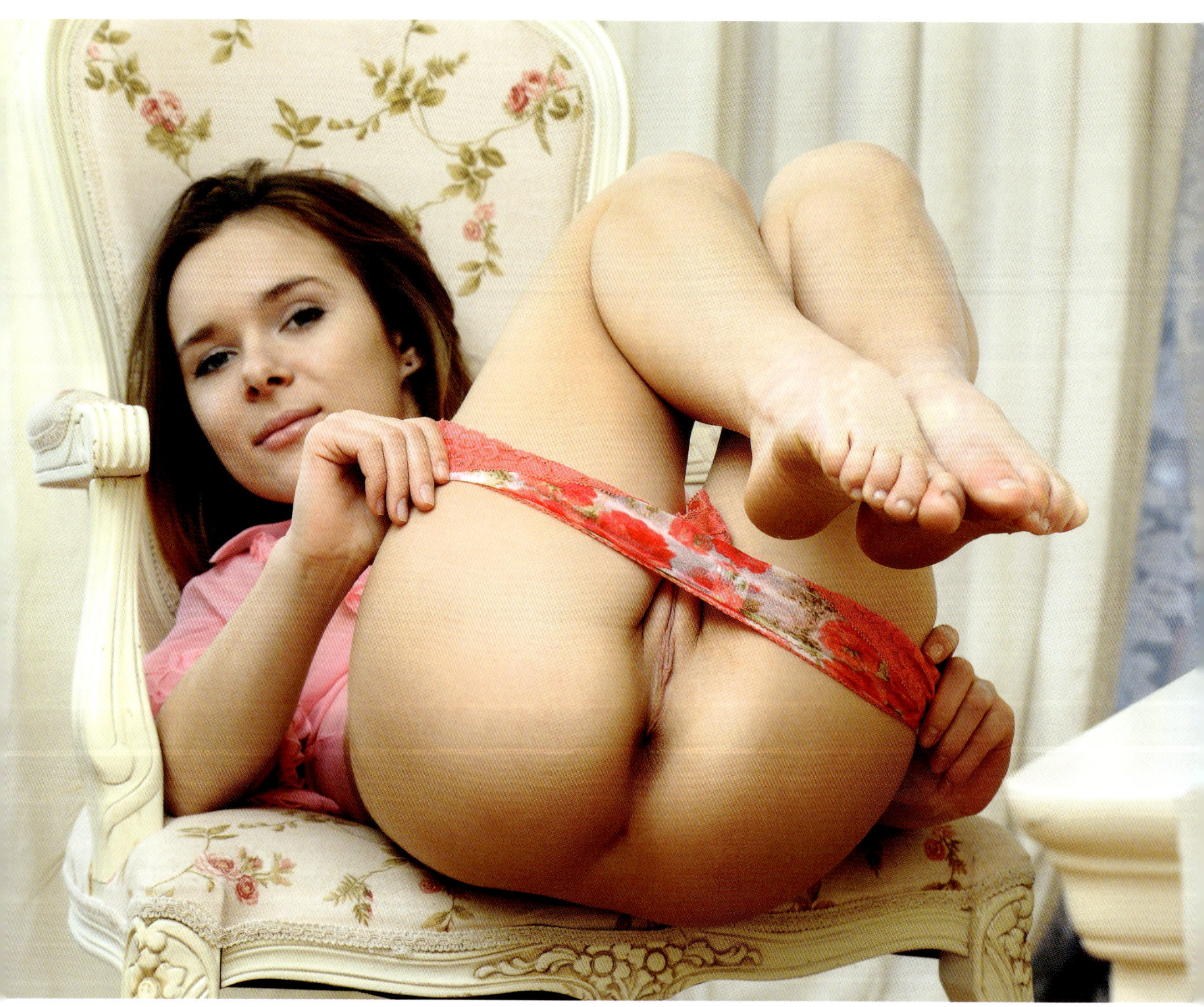

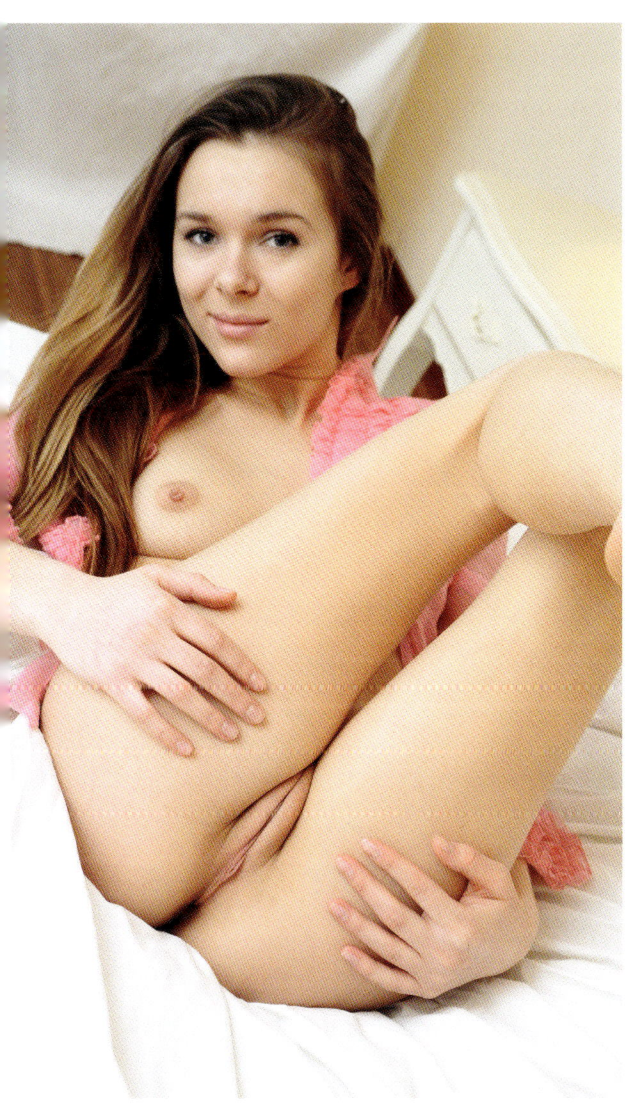
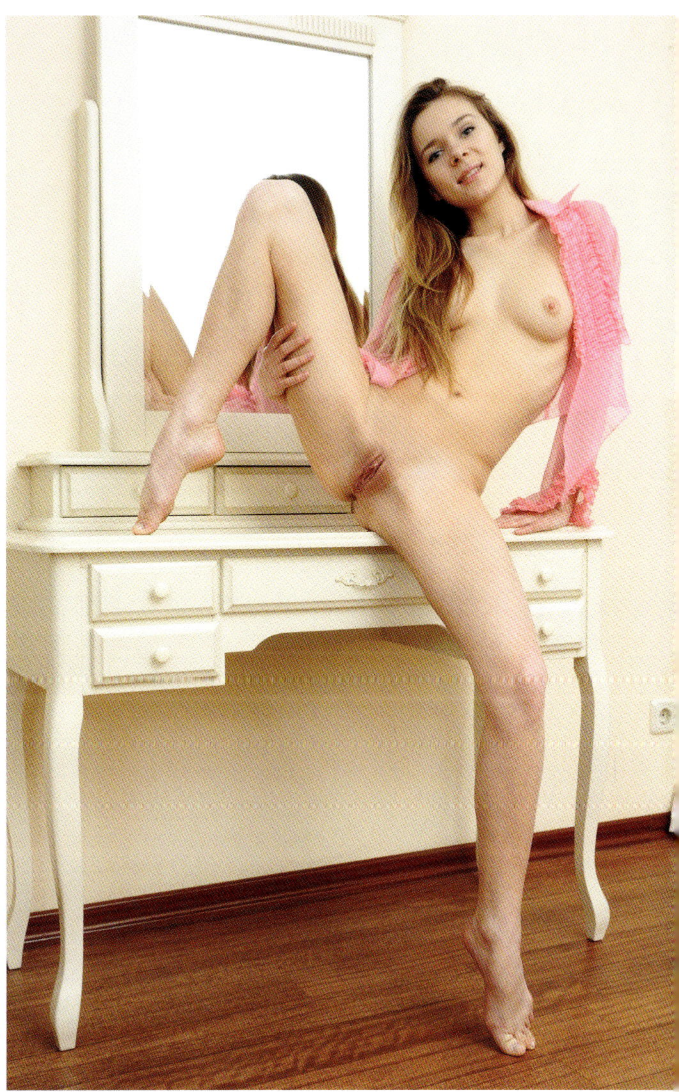

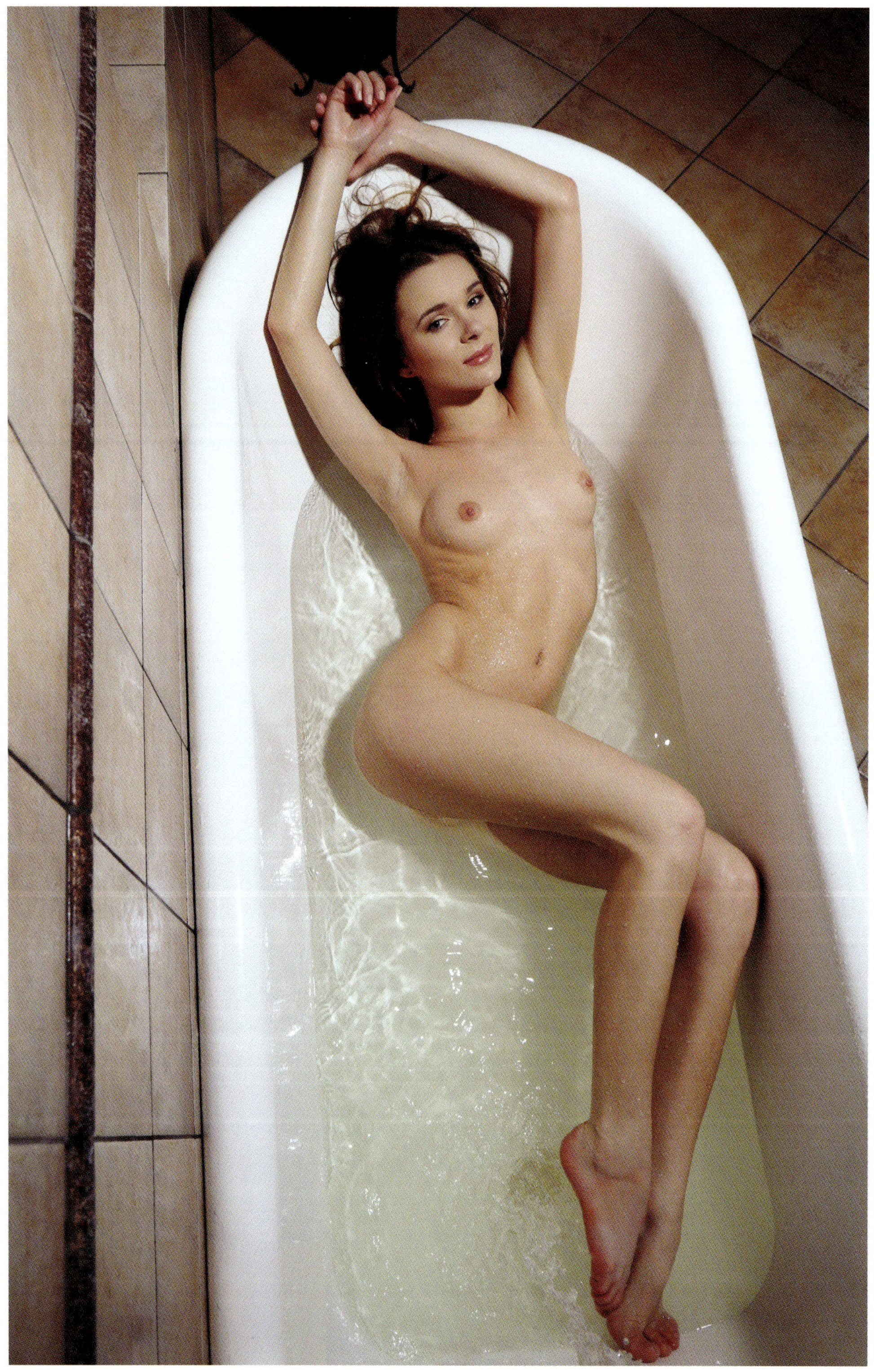

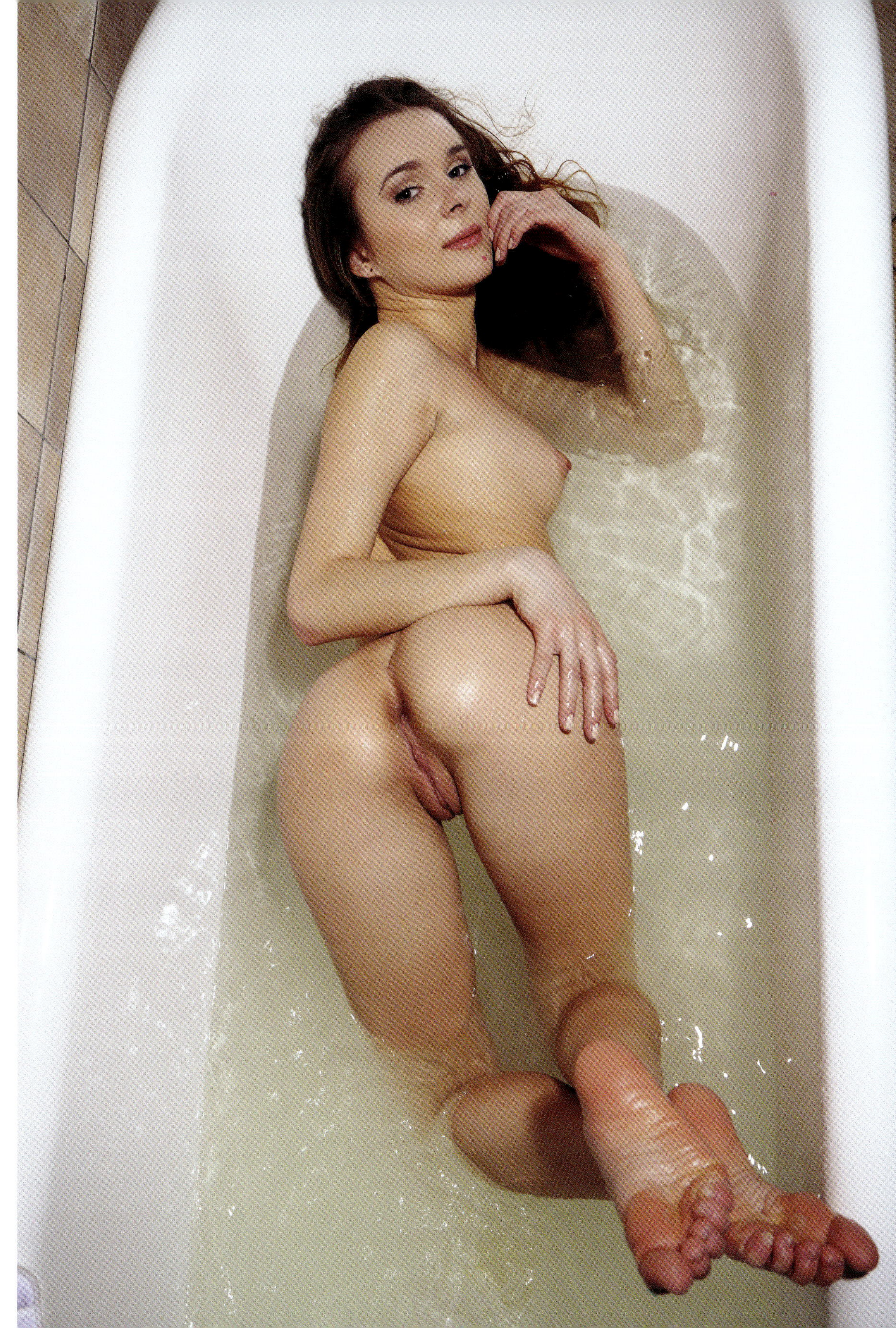

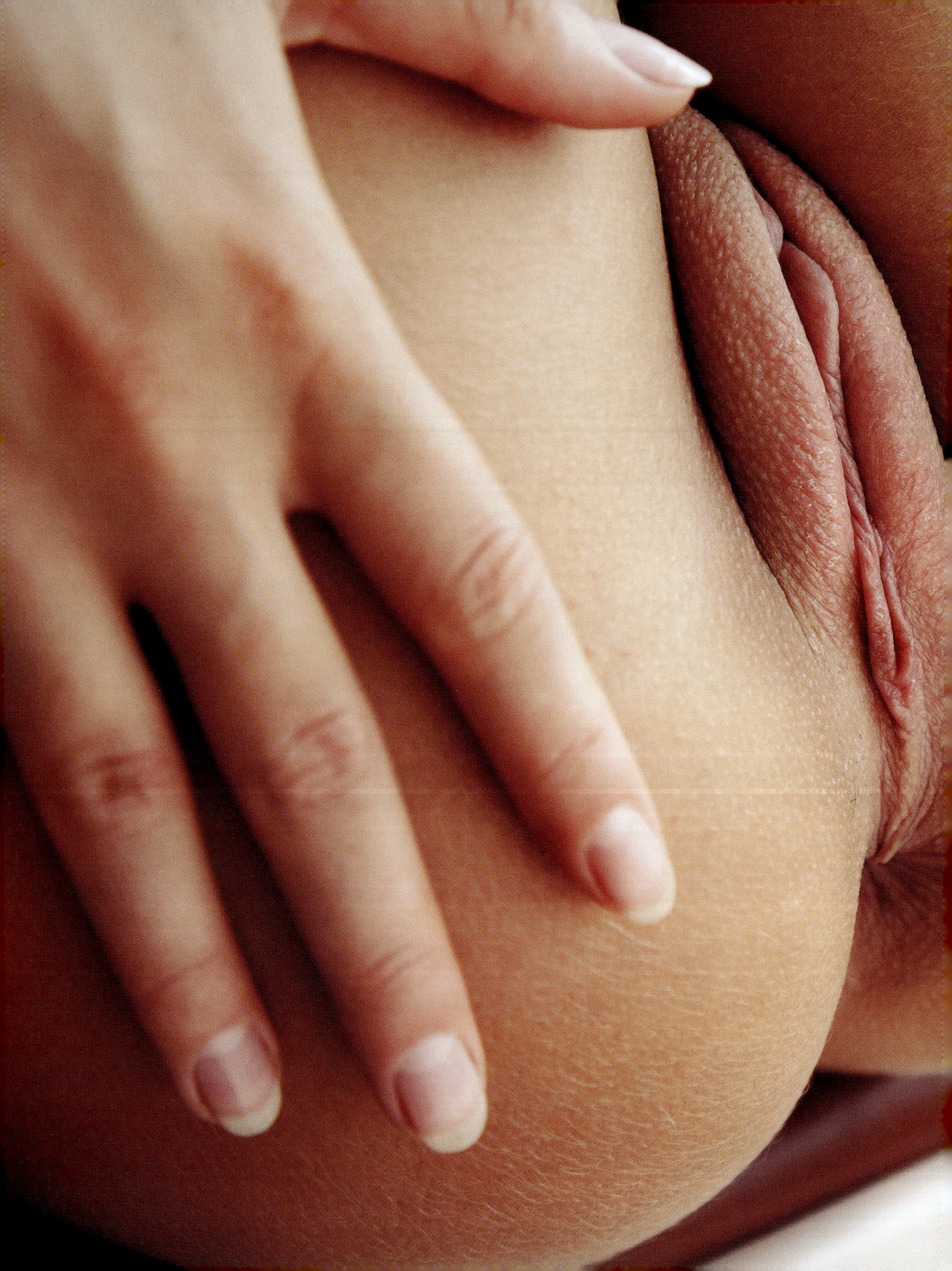

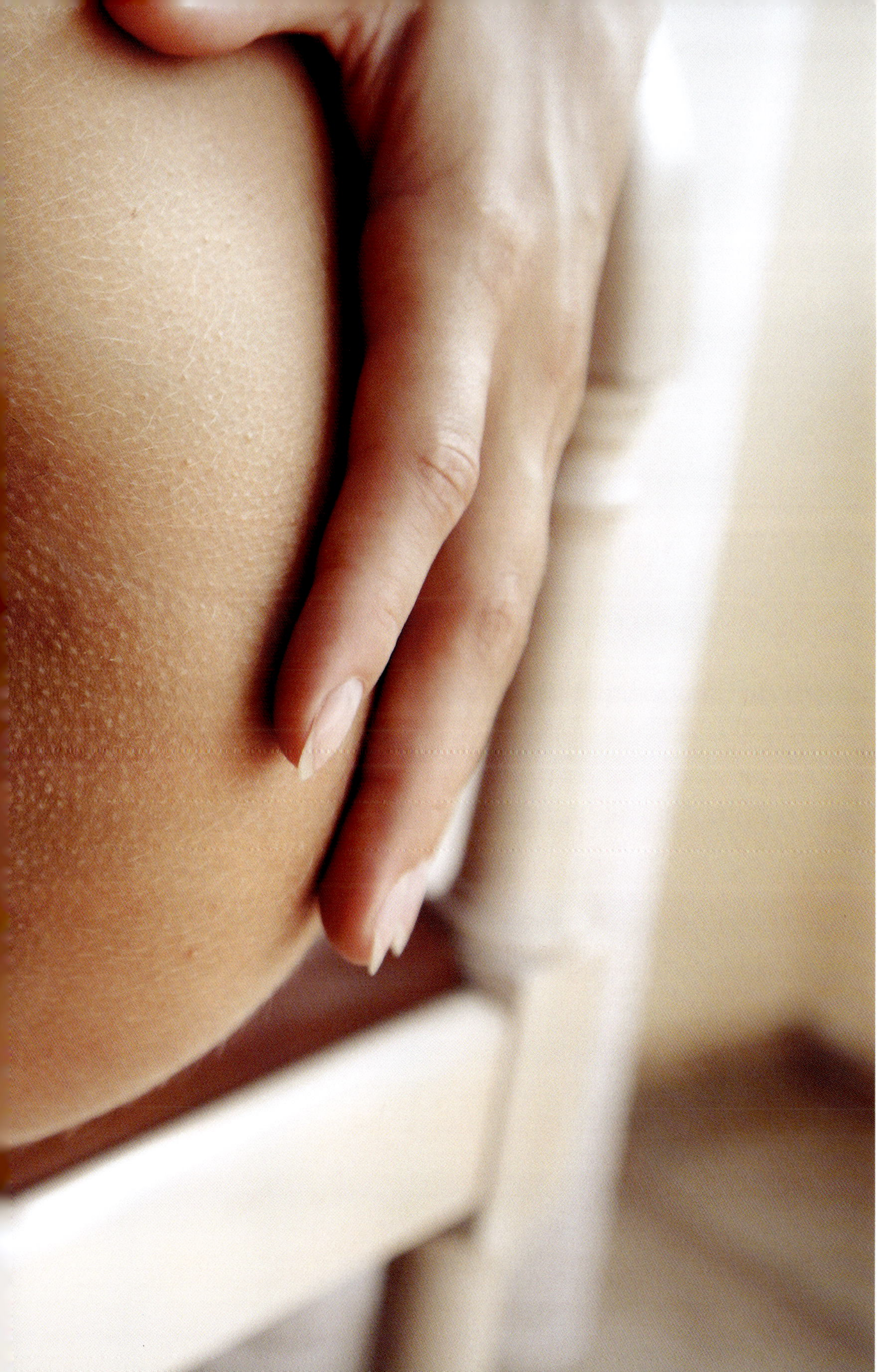

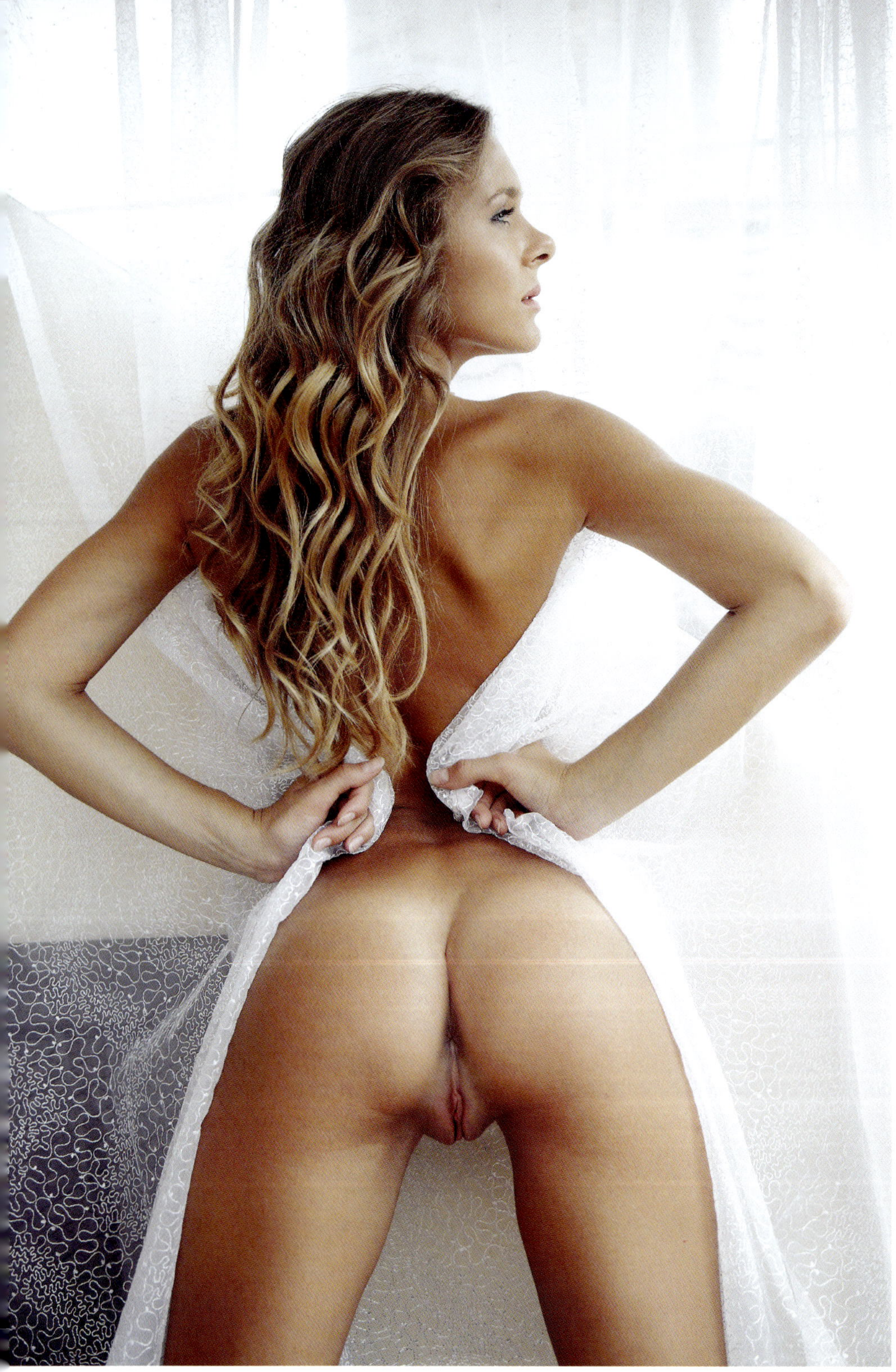

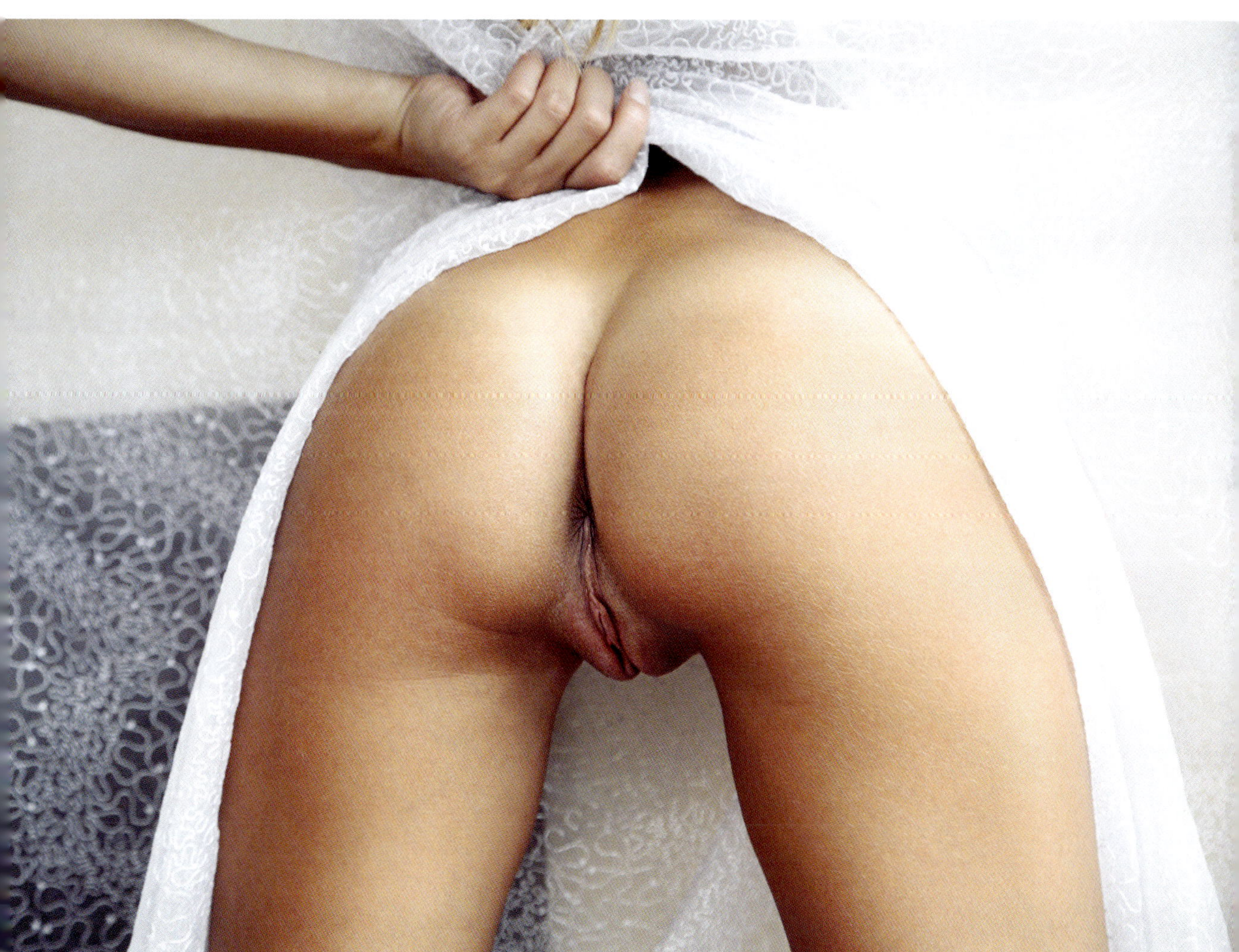

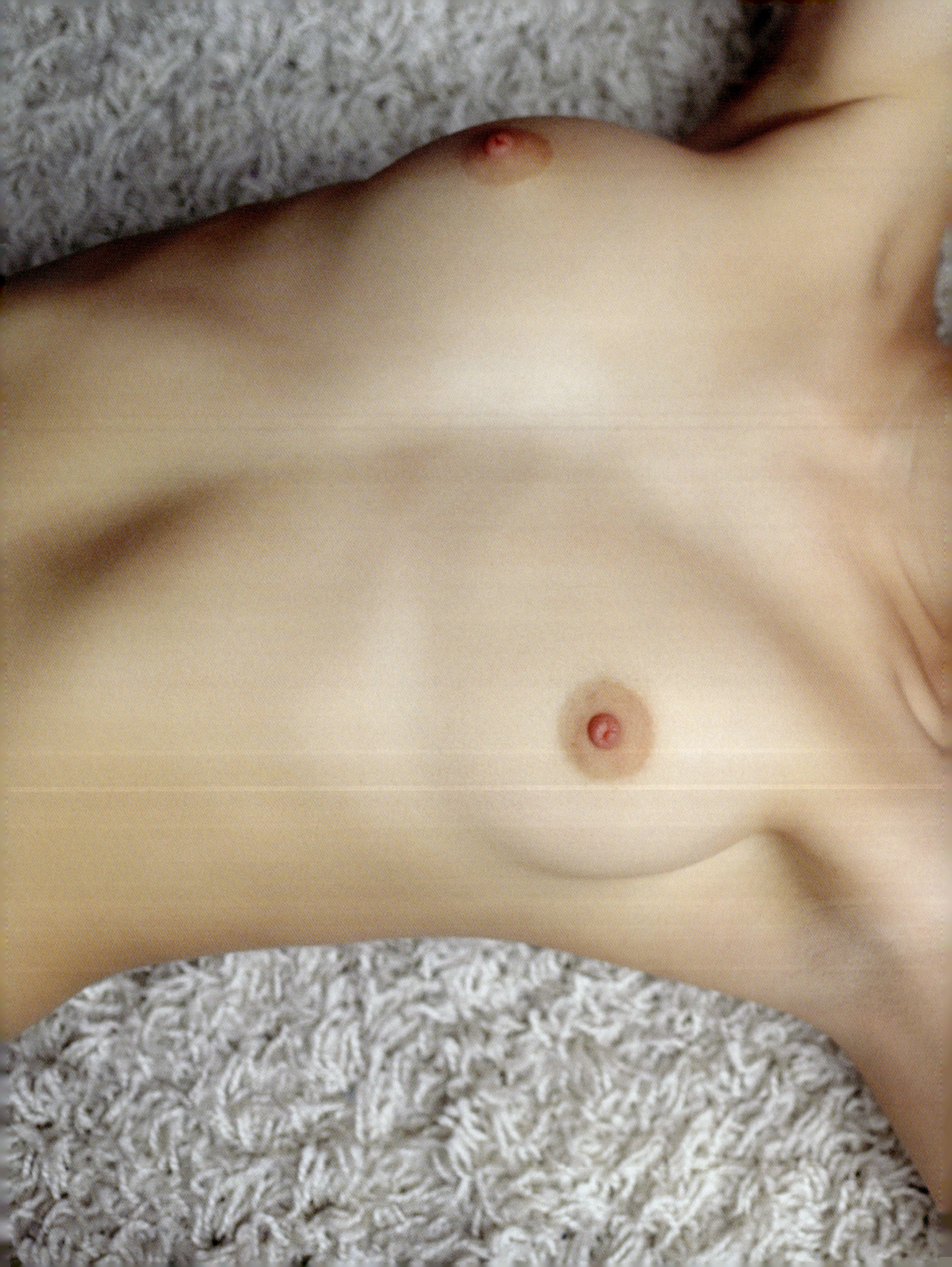

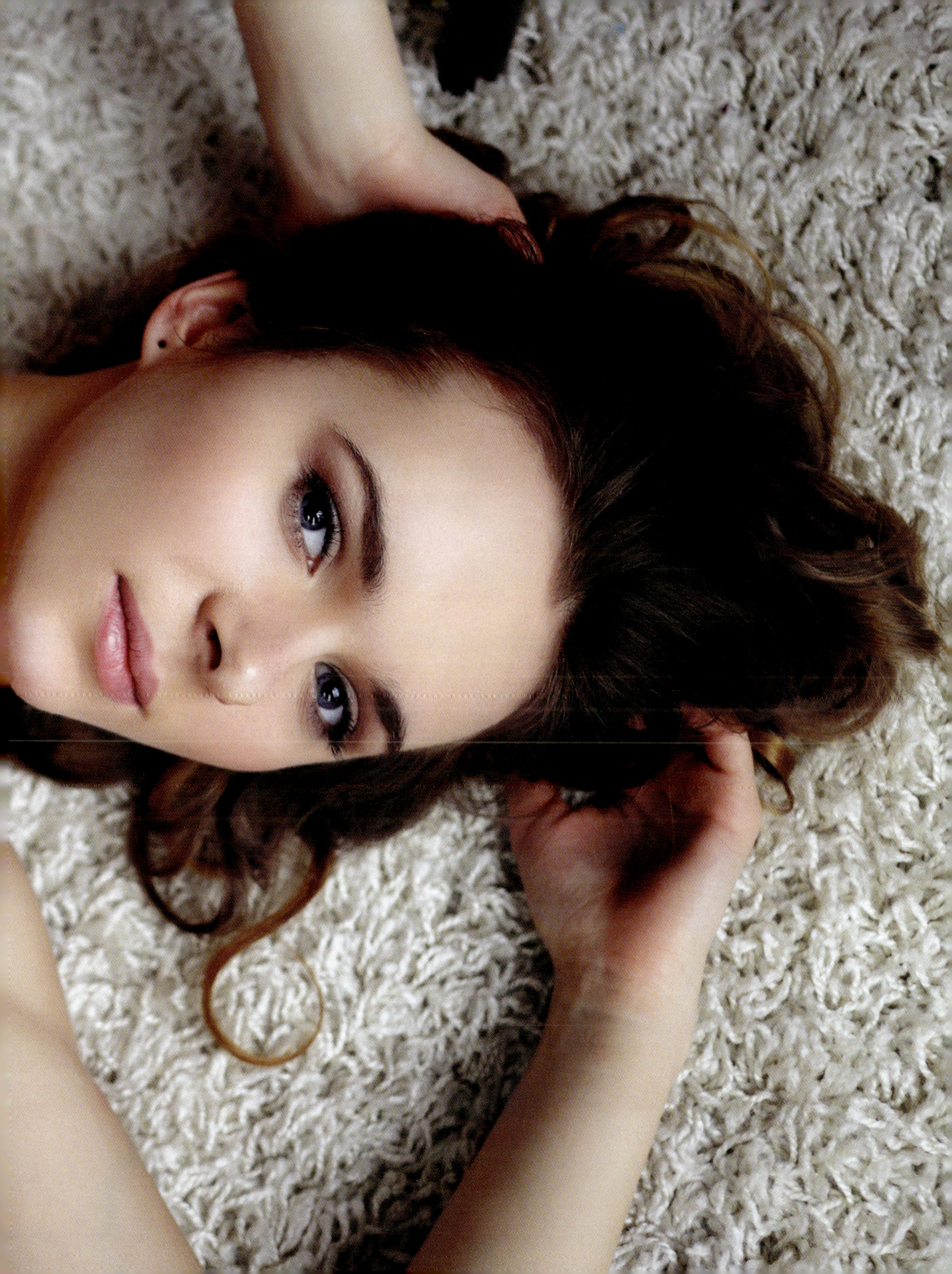

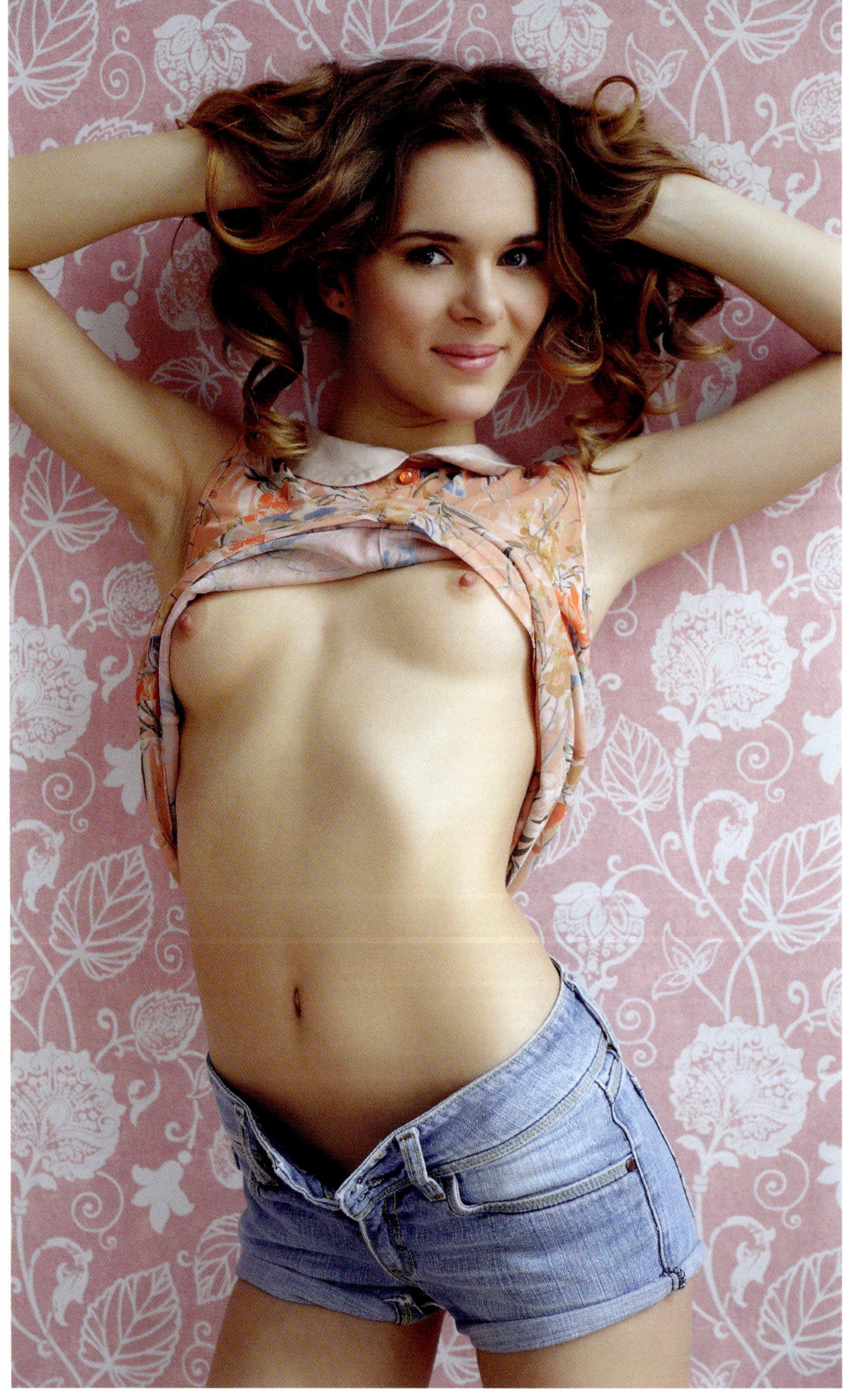

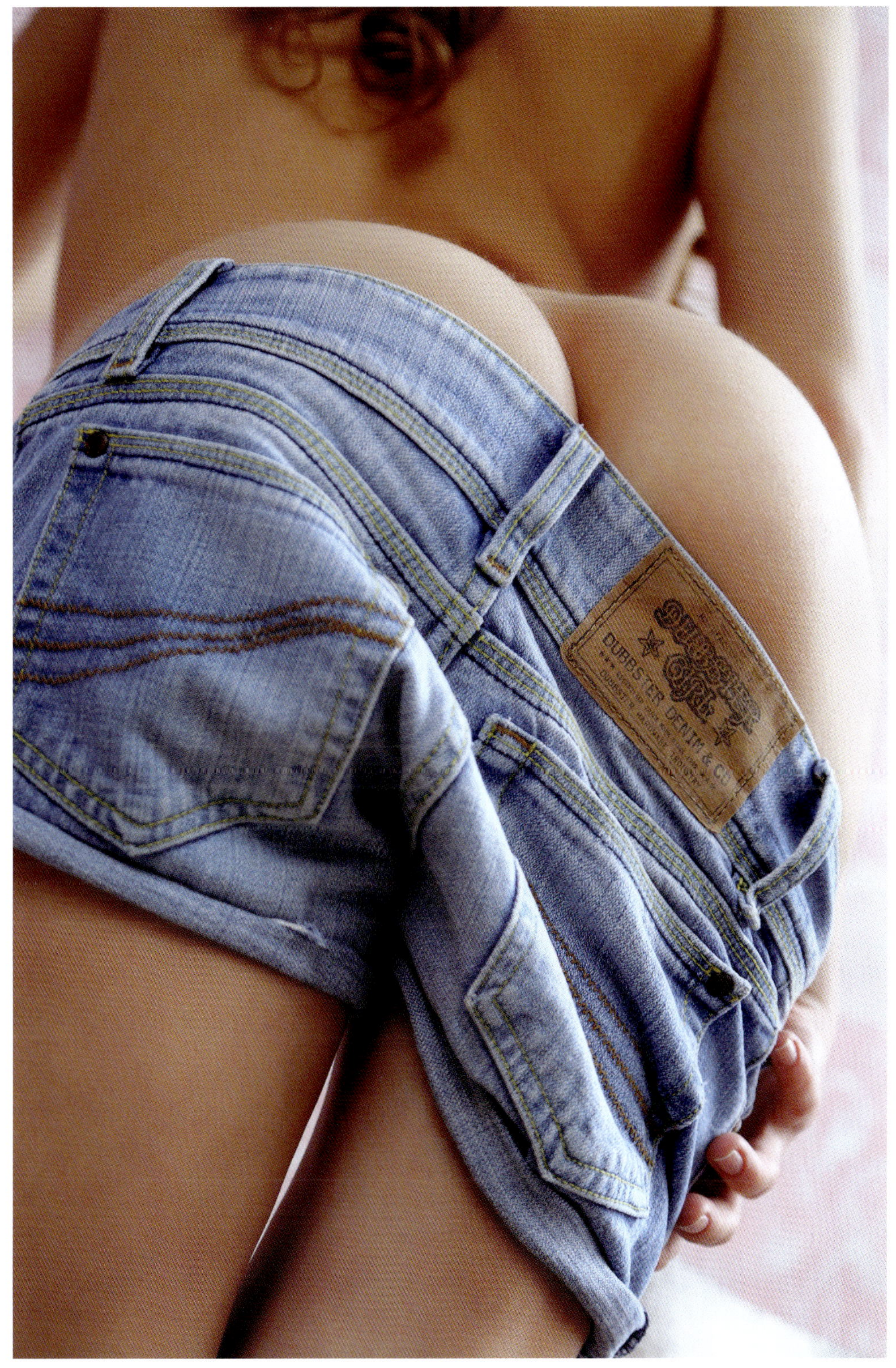
DUBSTER DENIM & CO

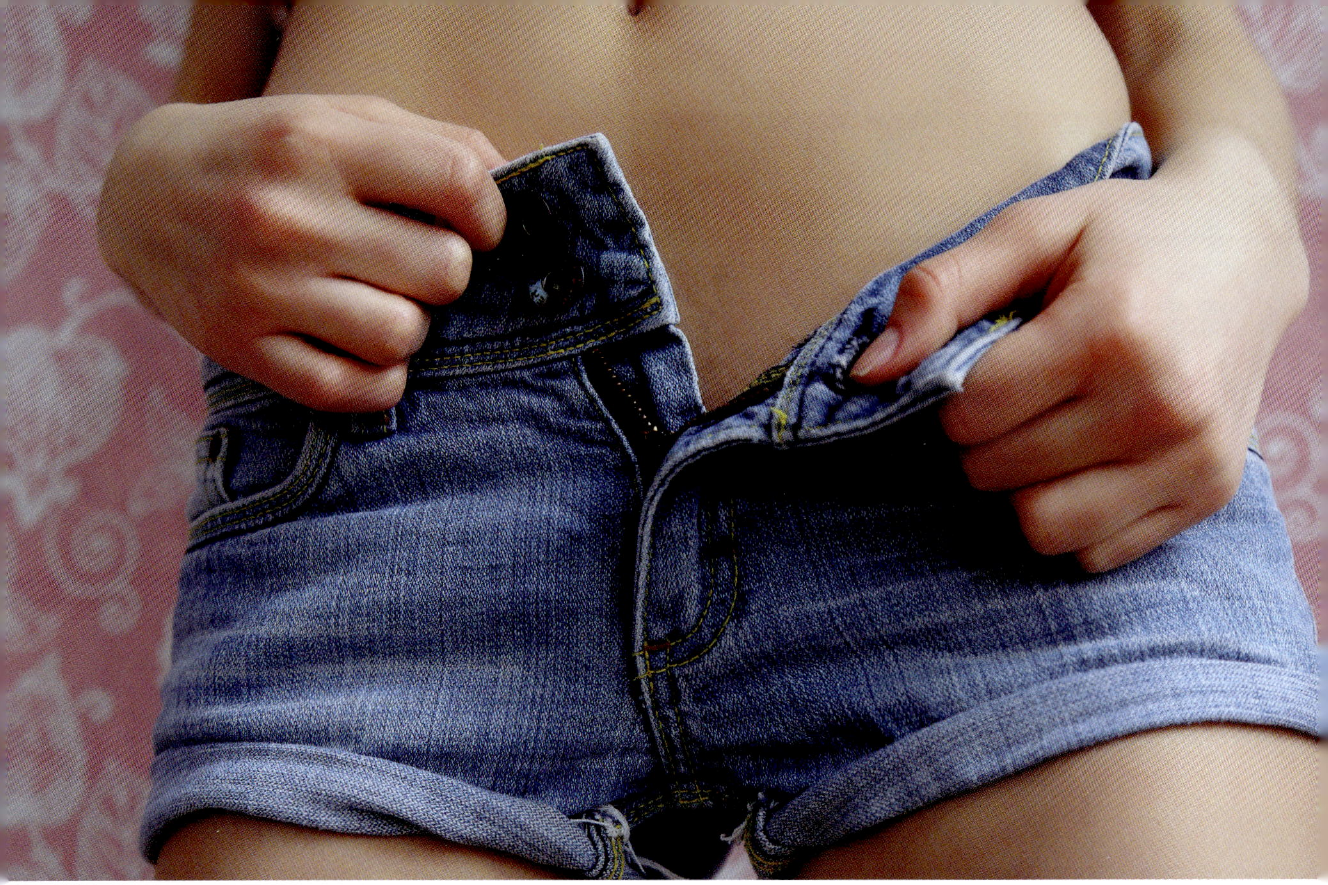

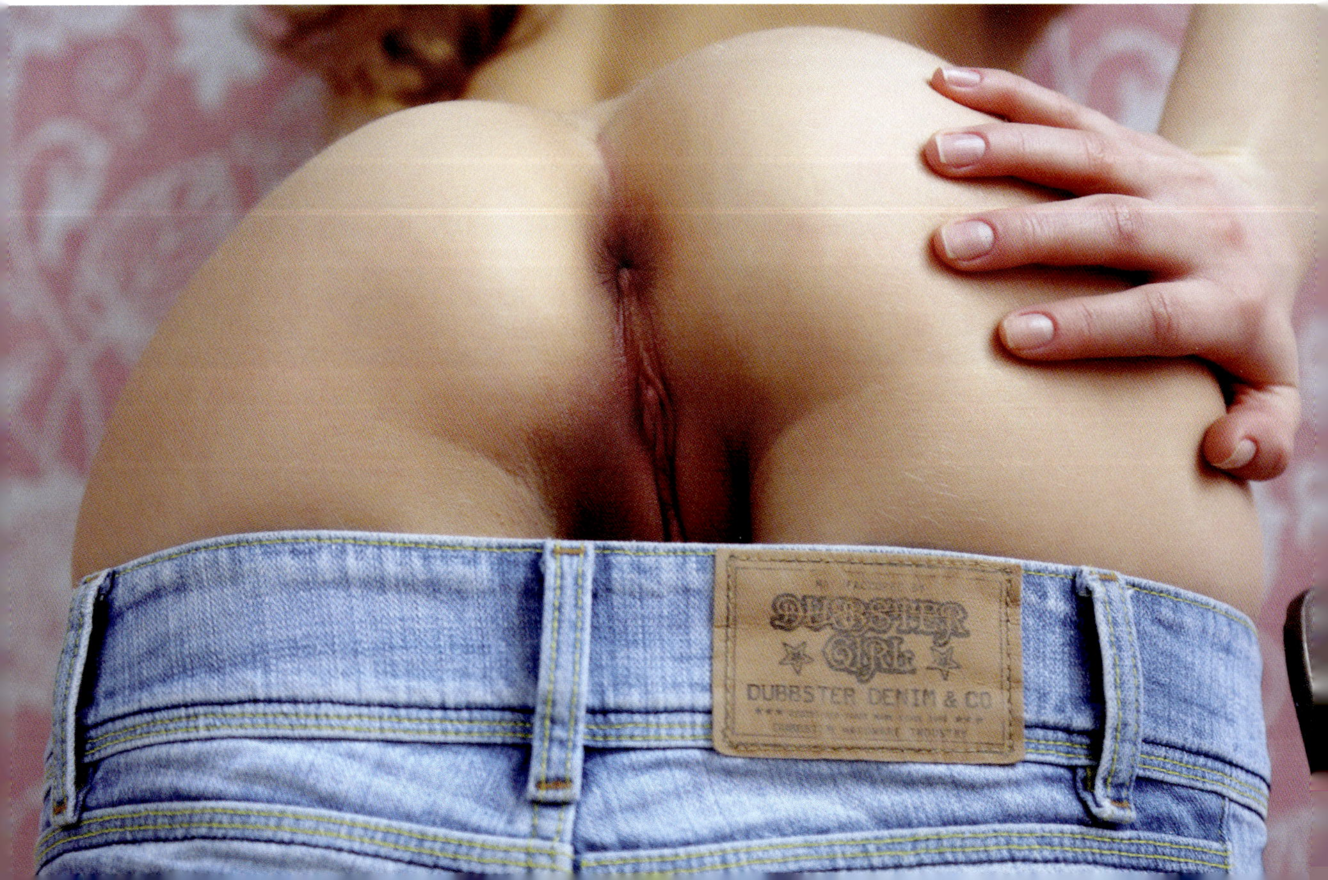

DUBBSTER GIRL
DUBBSTER DENIM & CO.

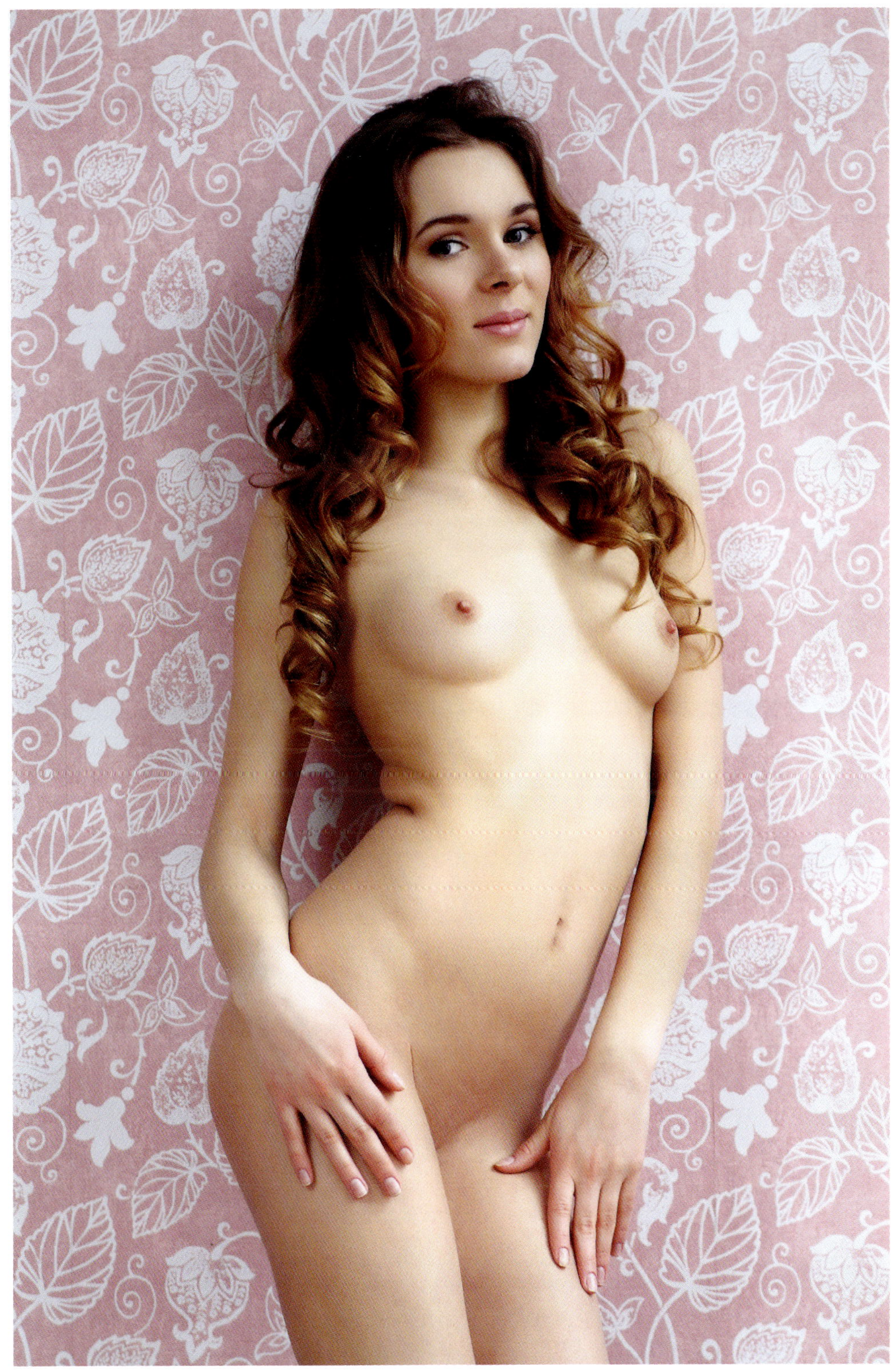

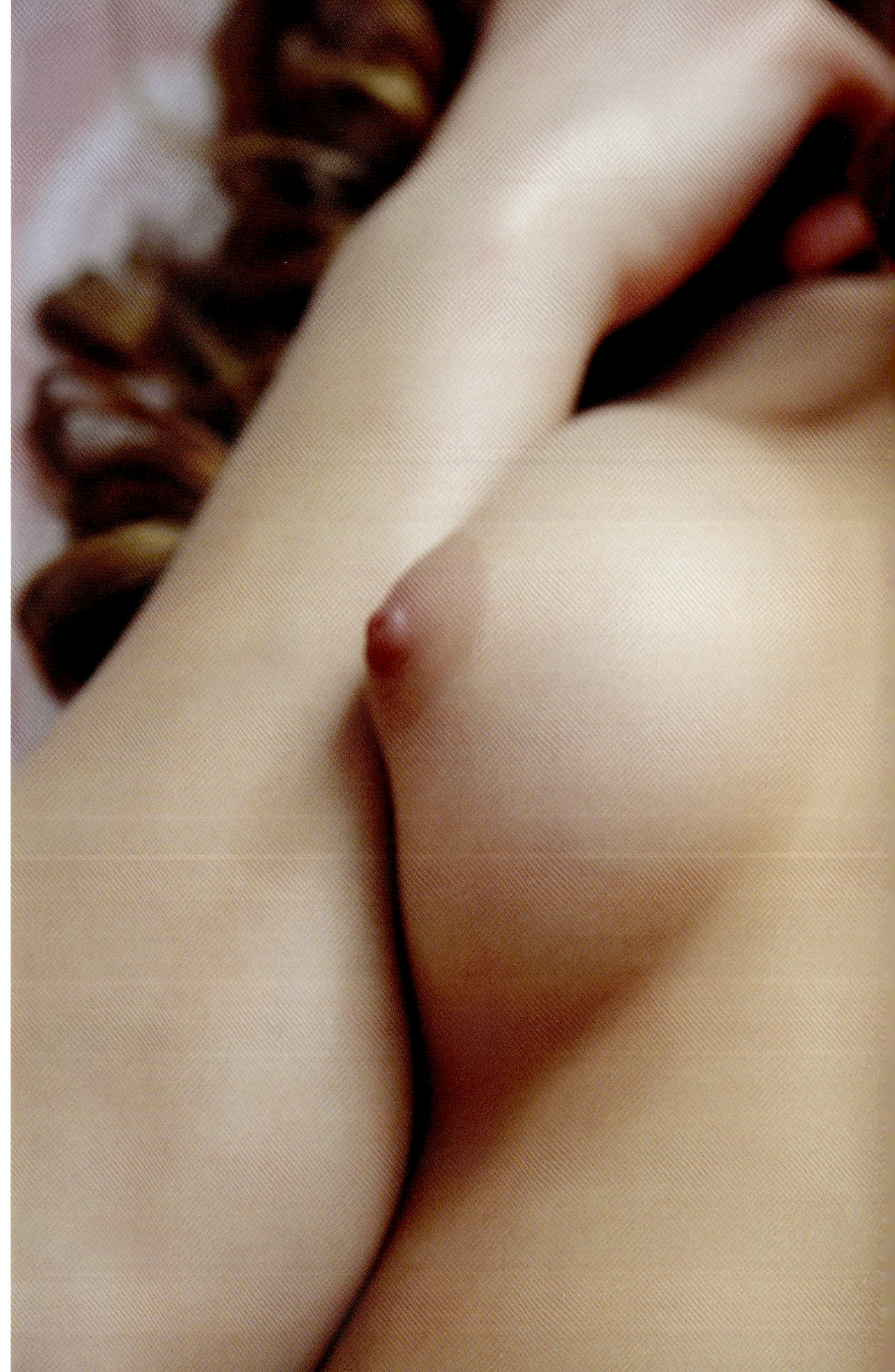

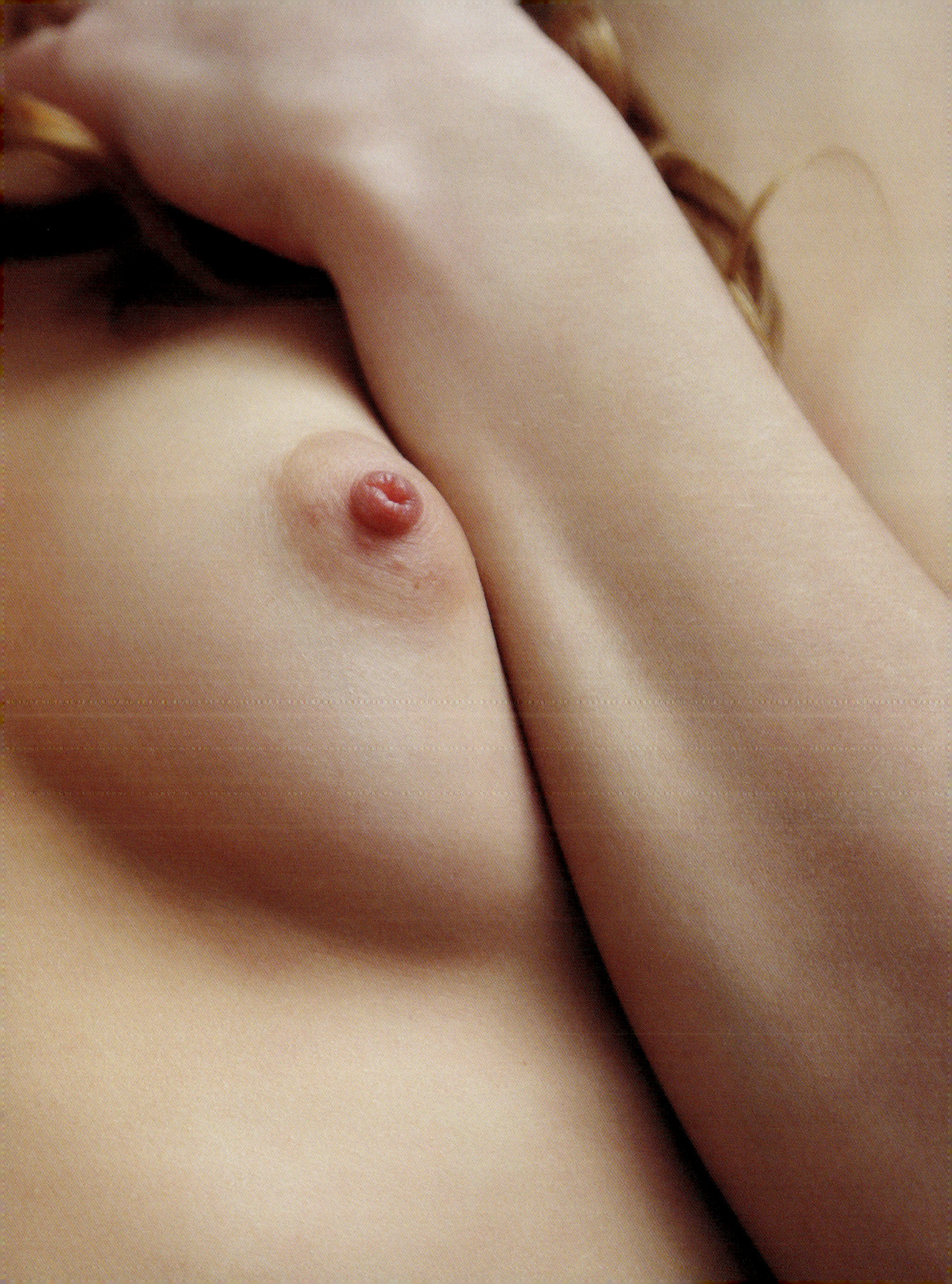

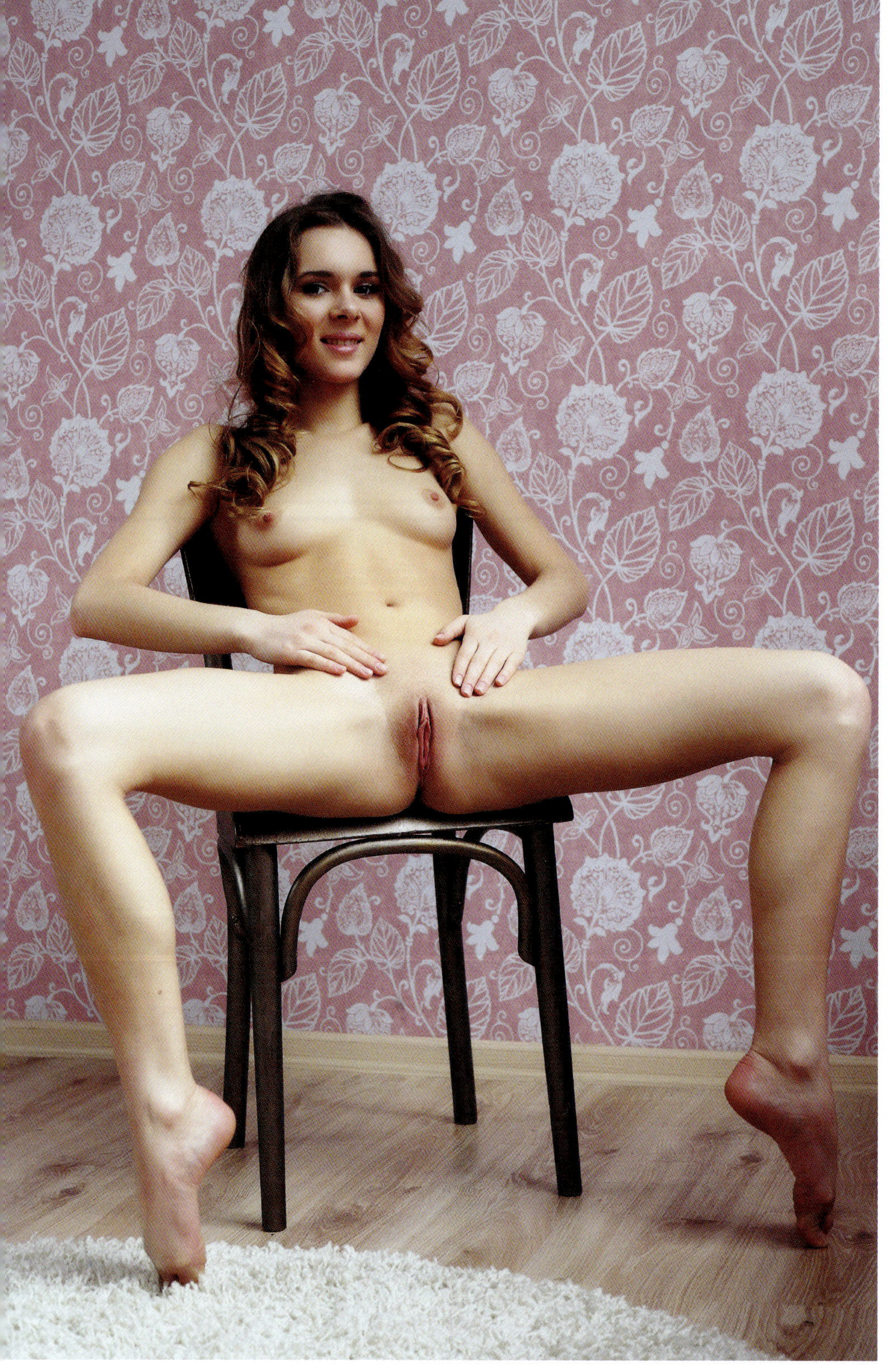

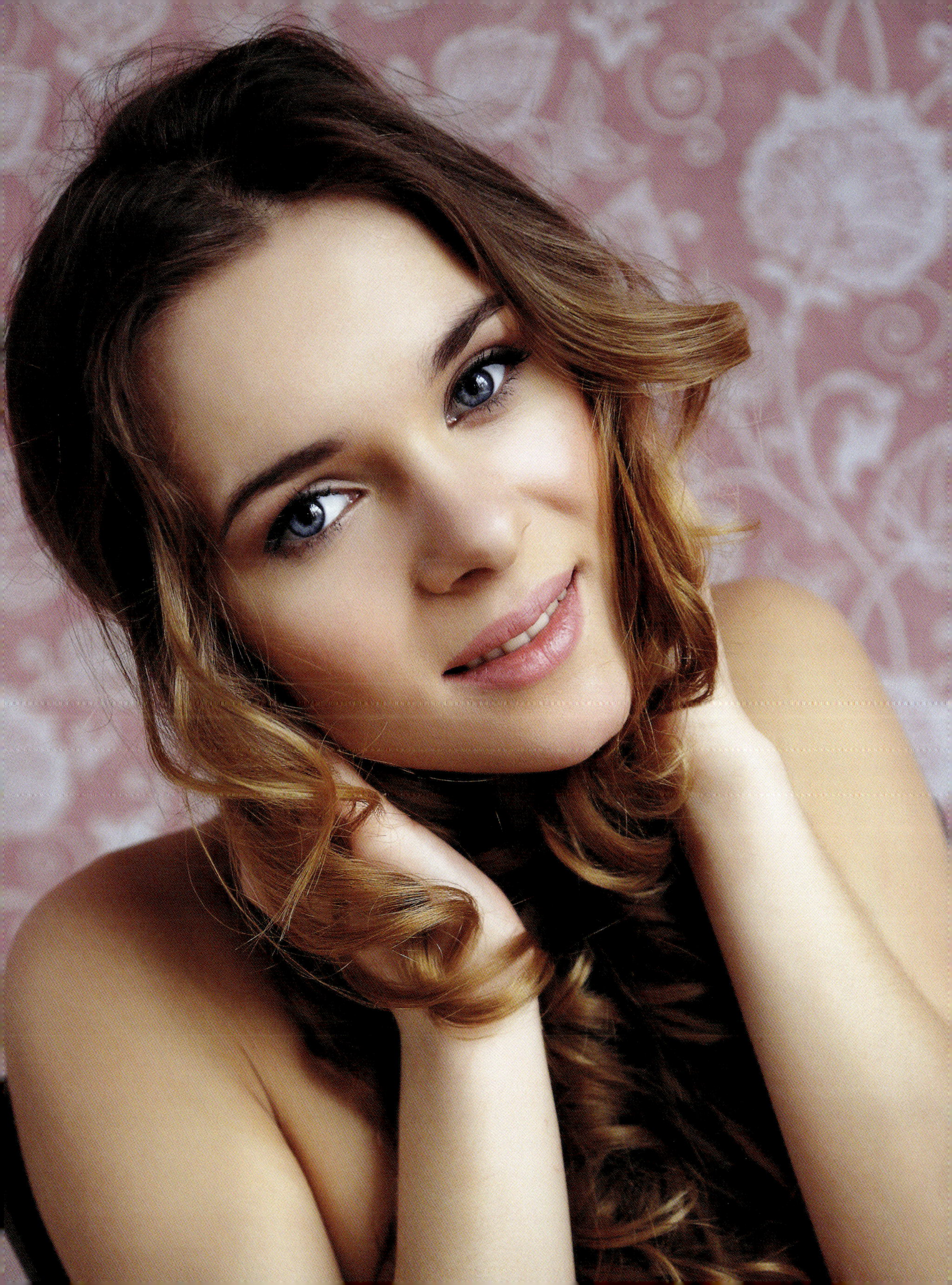

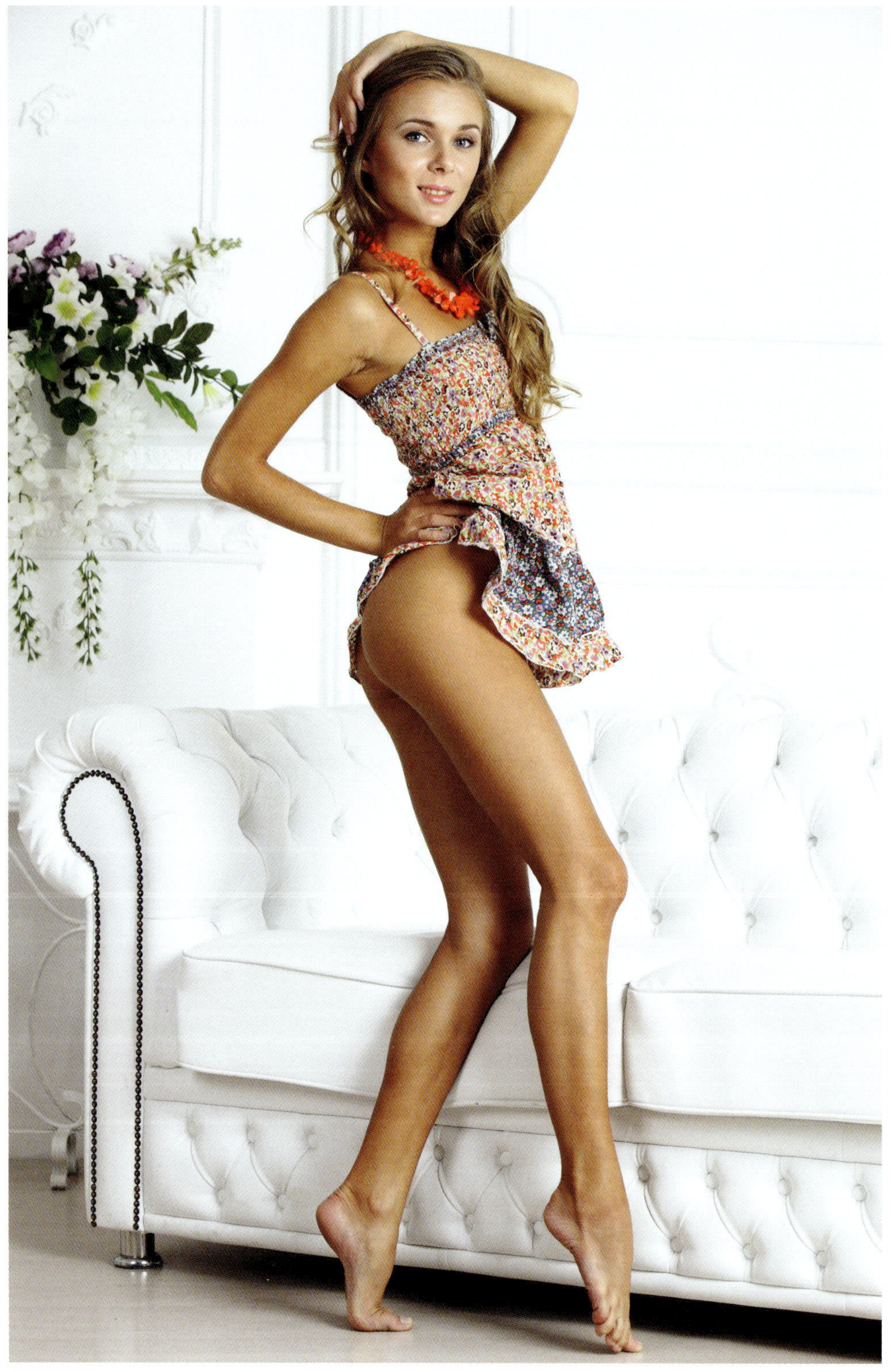

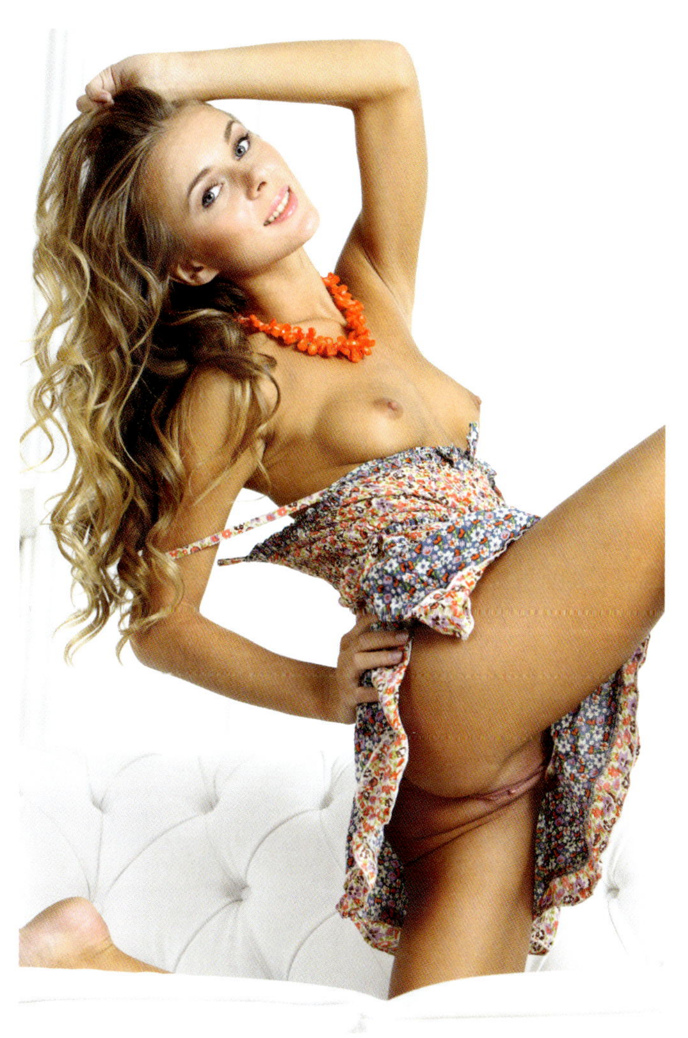

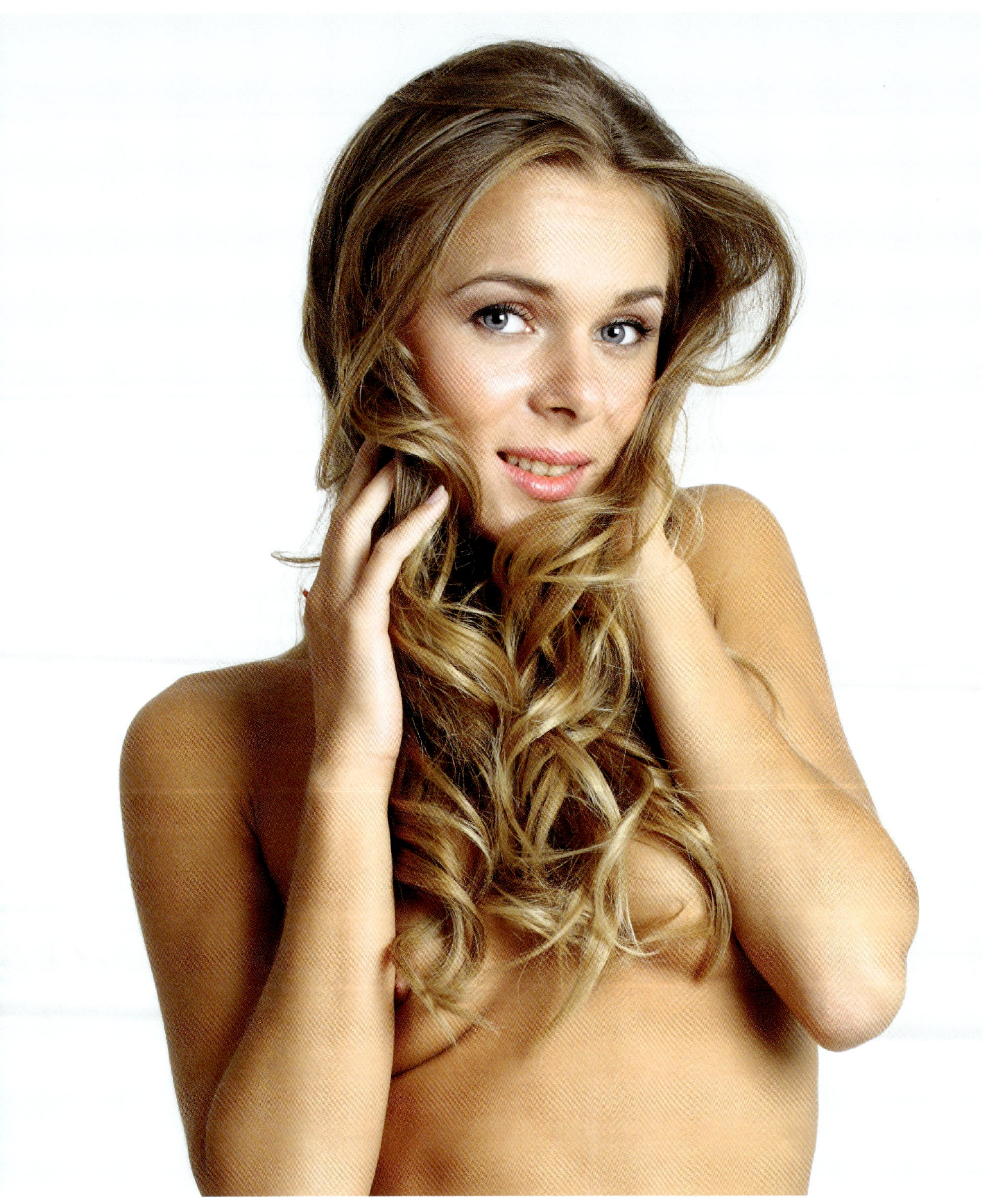

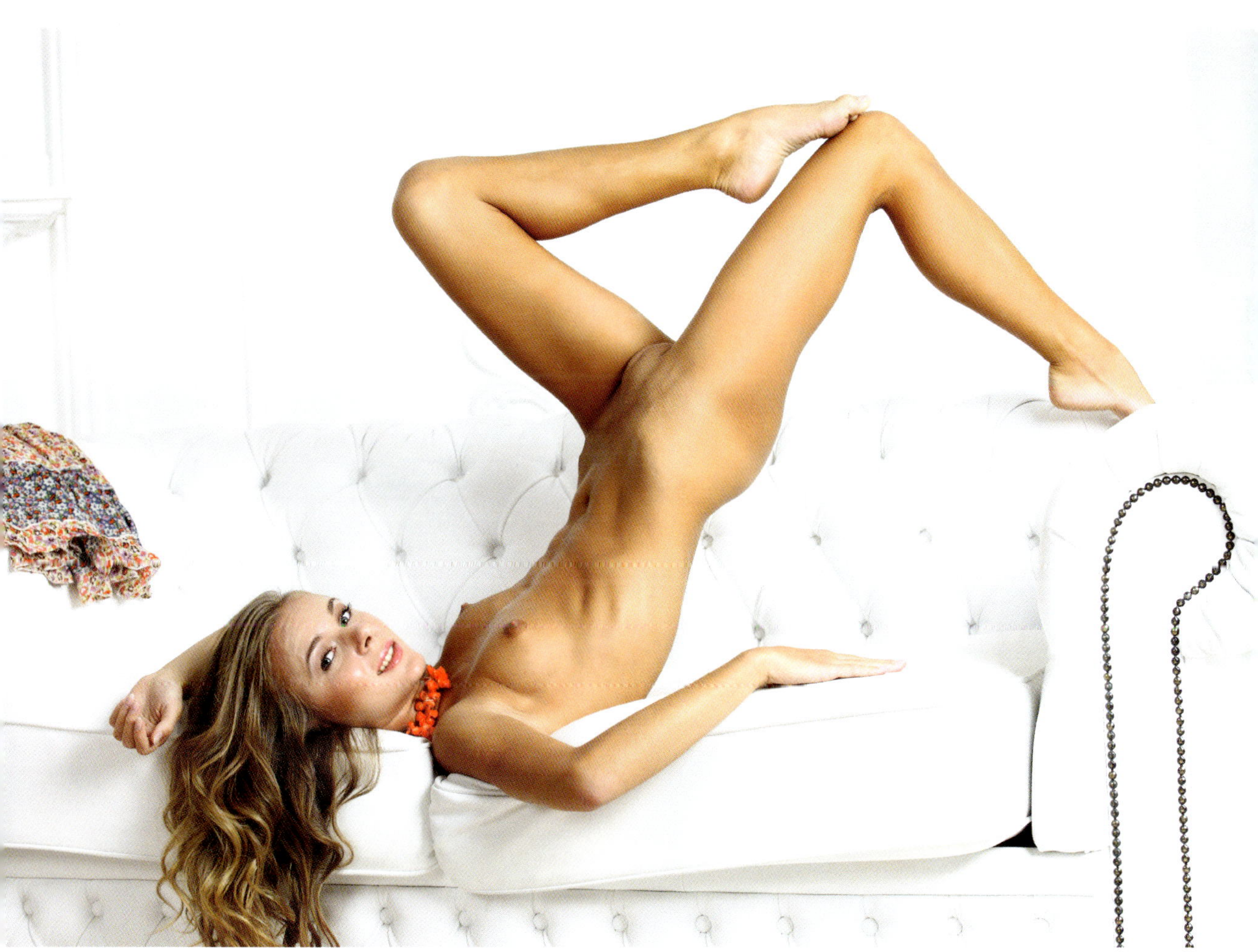

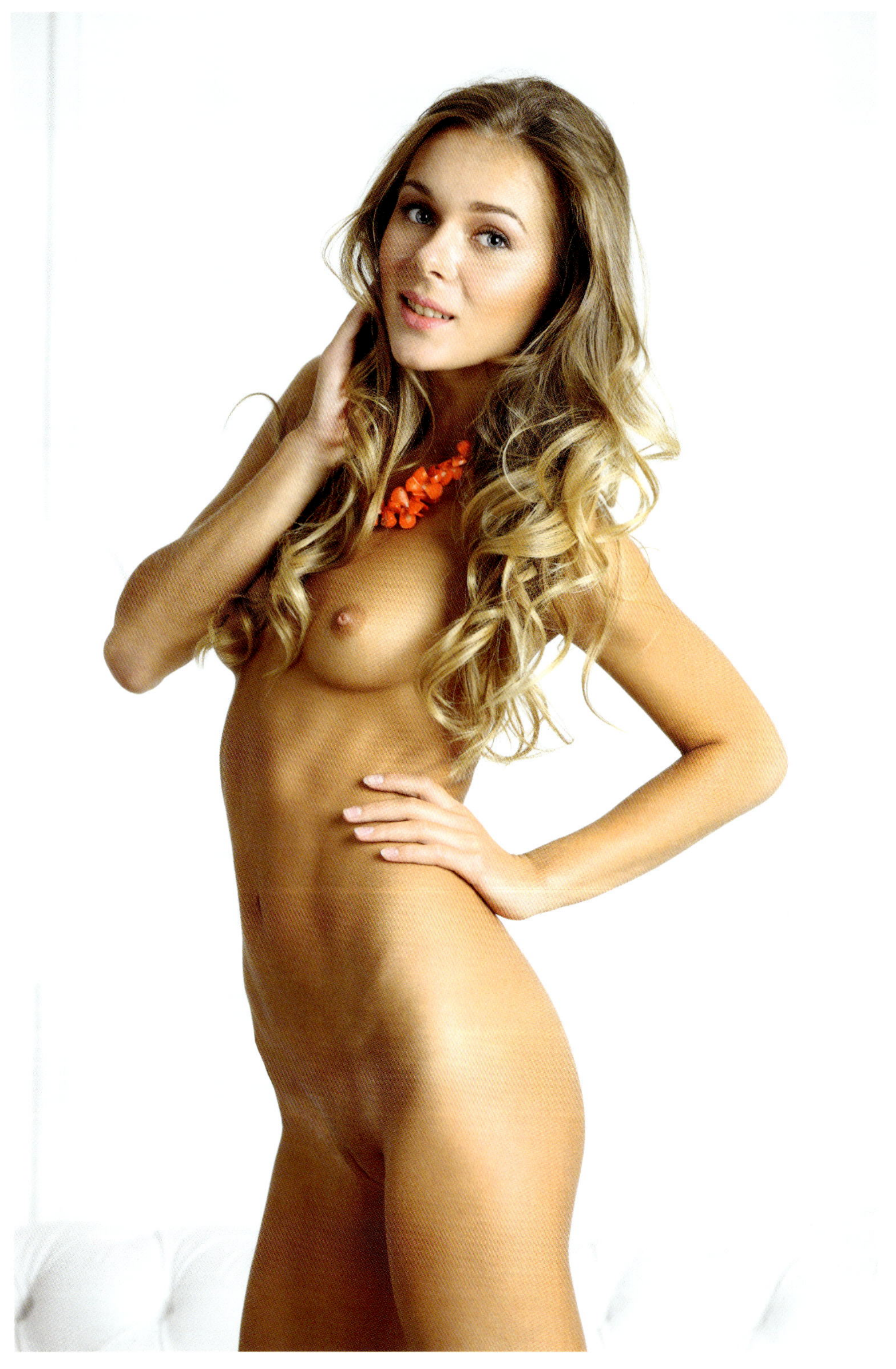

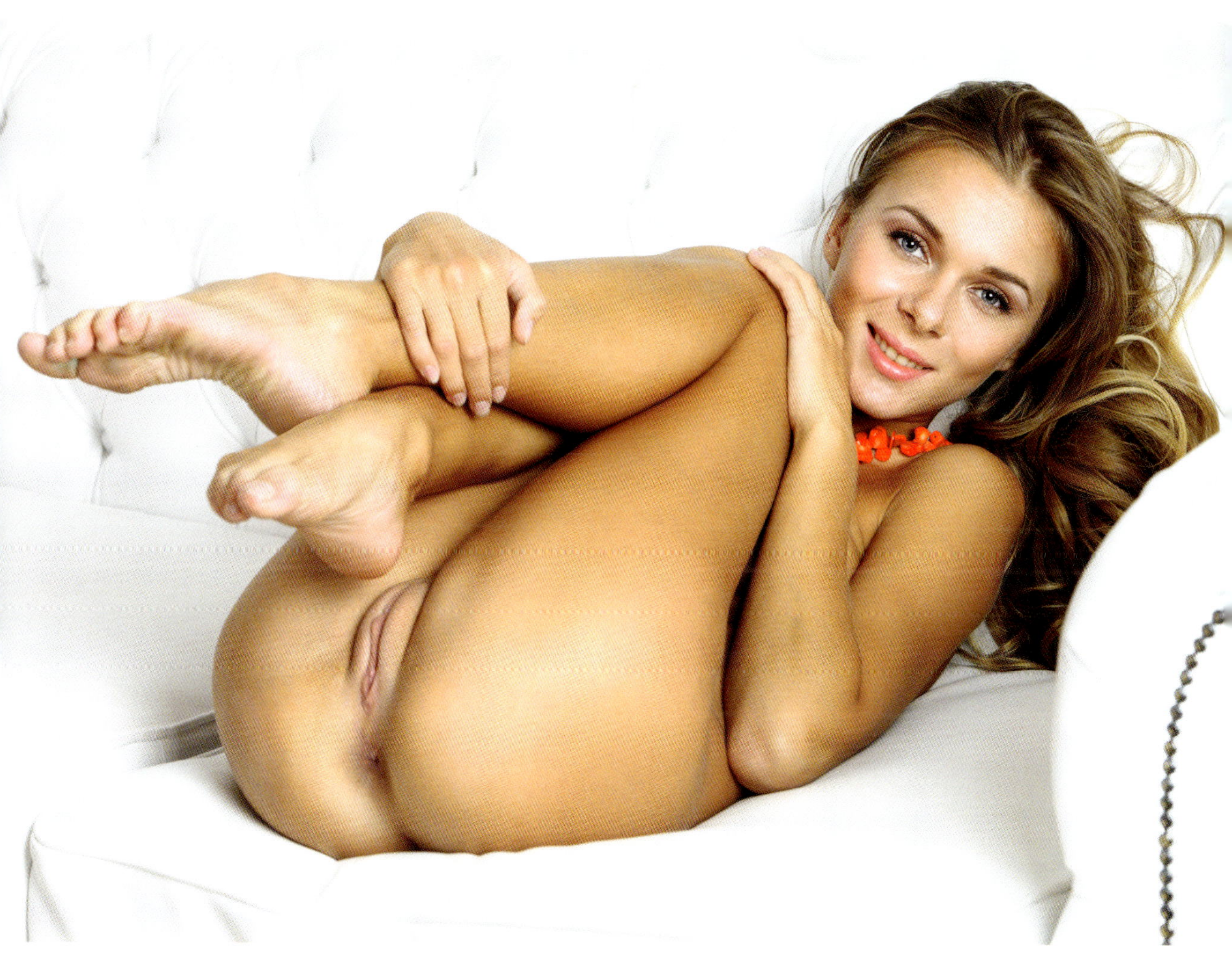

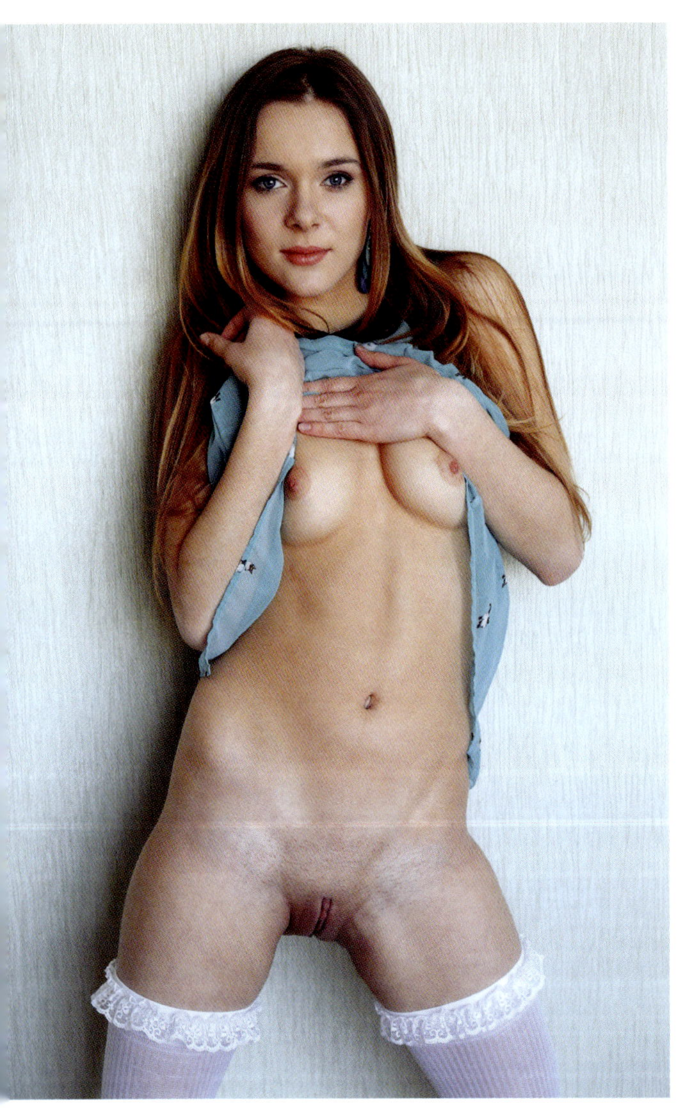
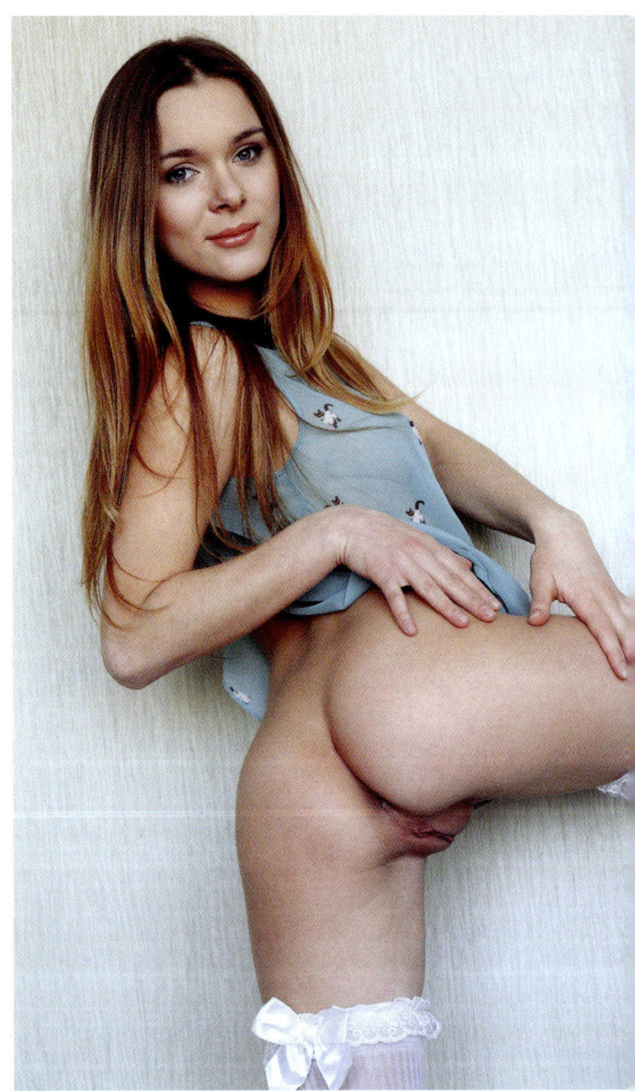

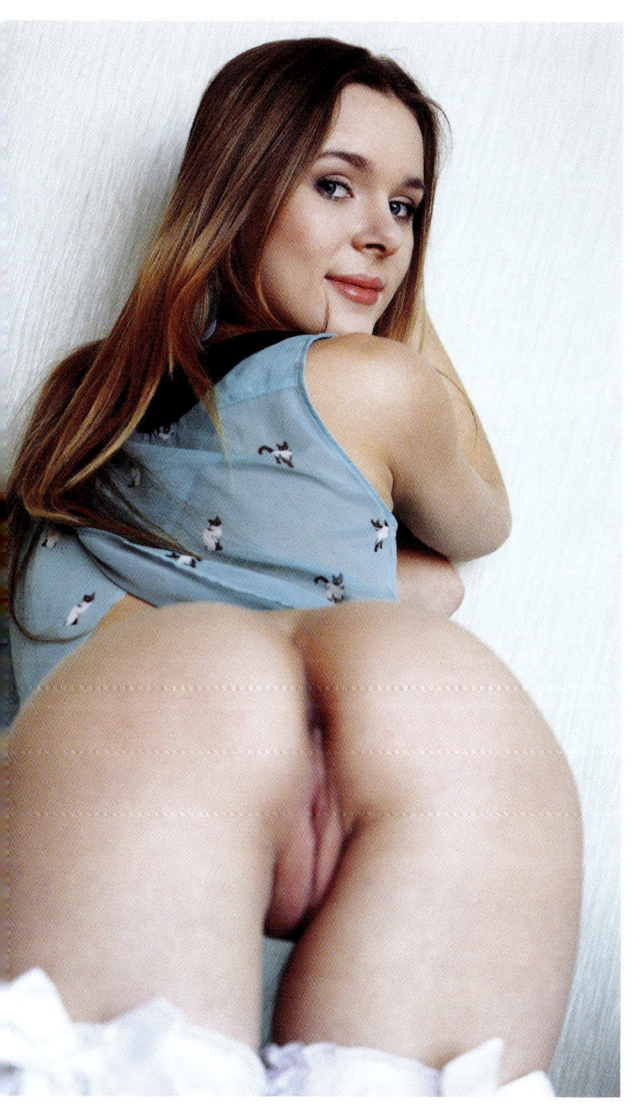
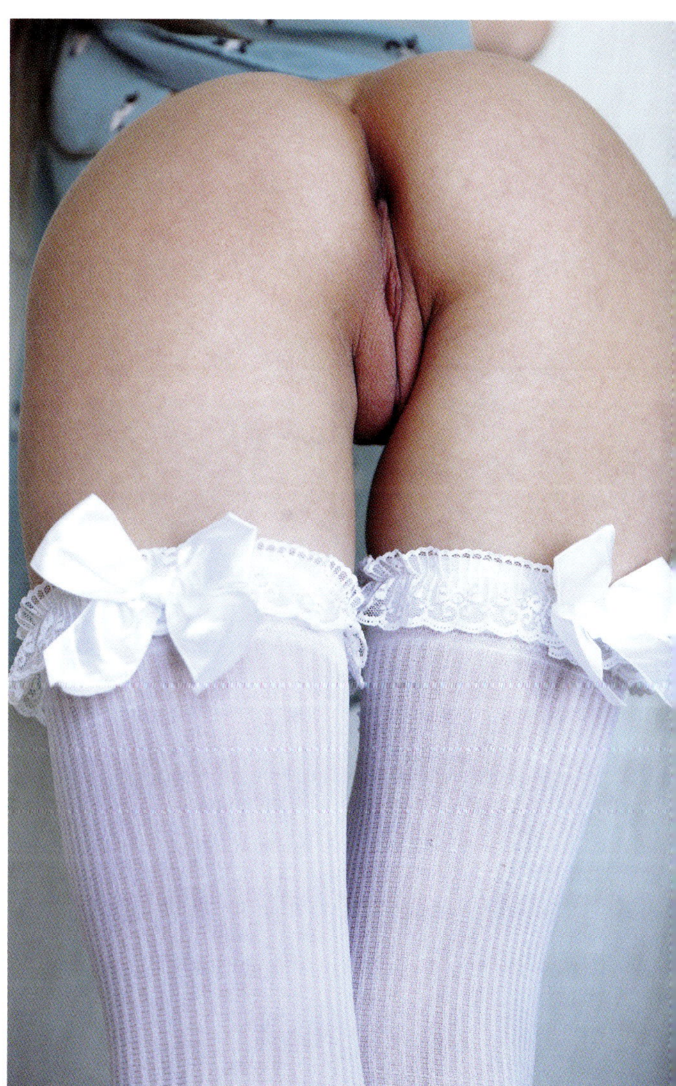

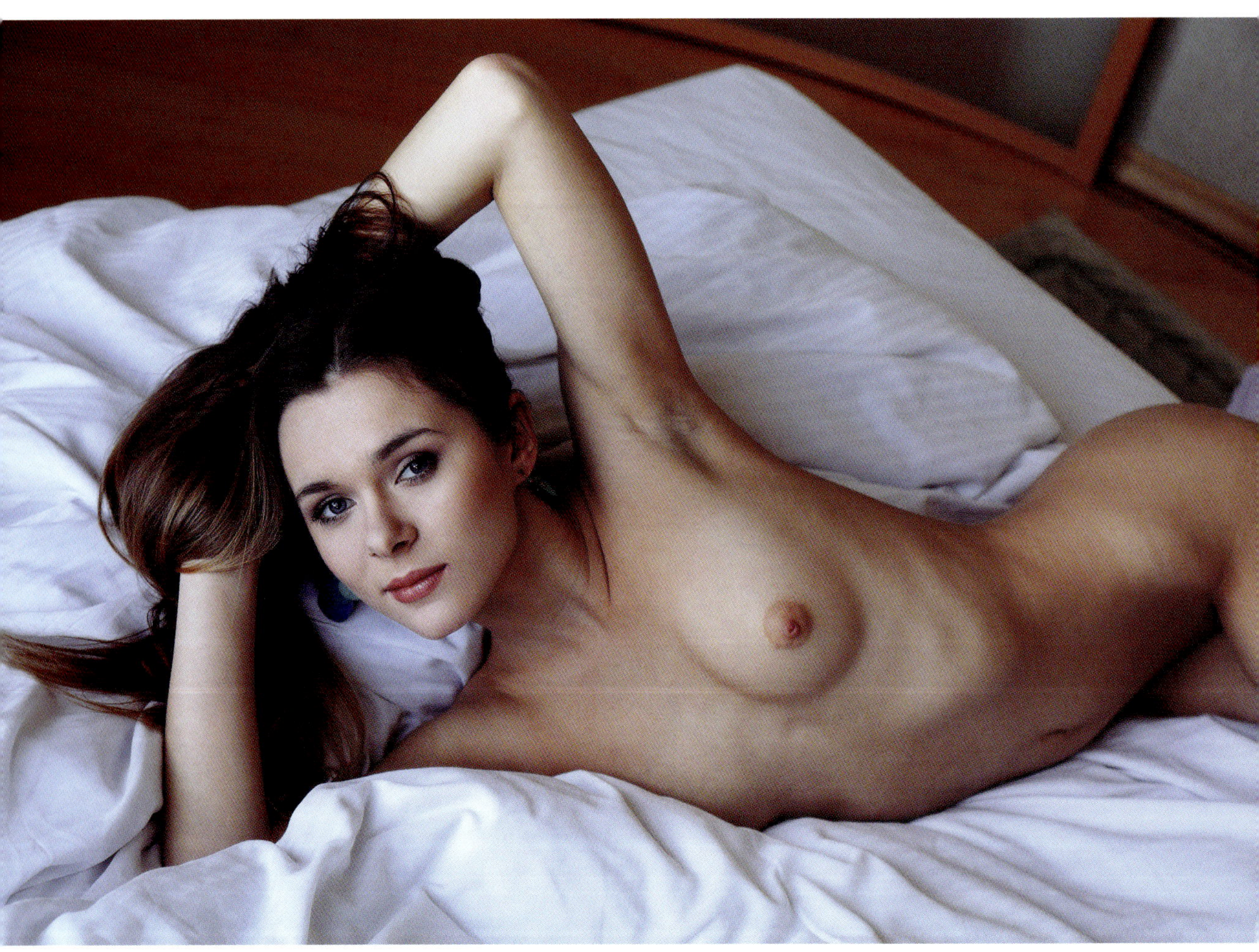

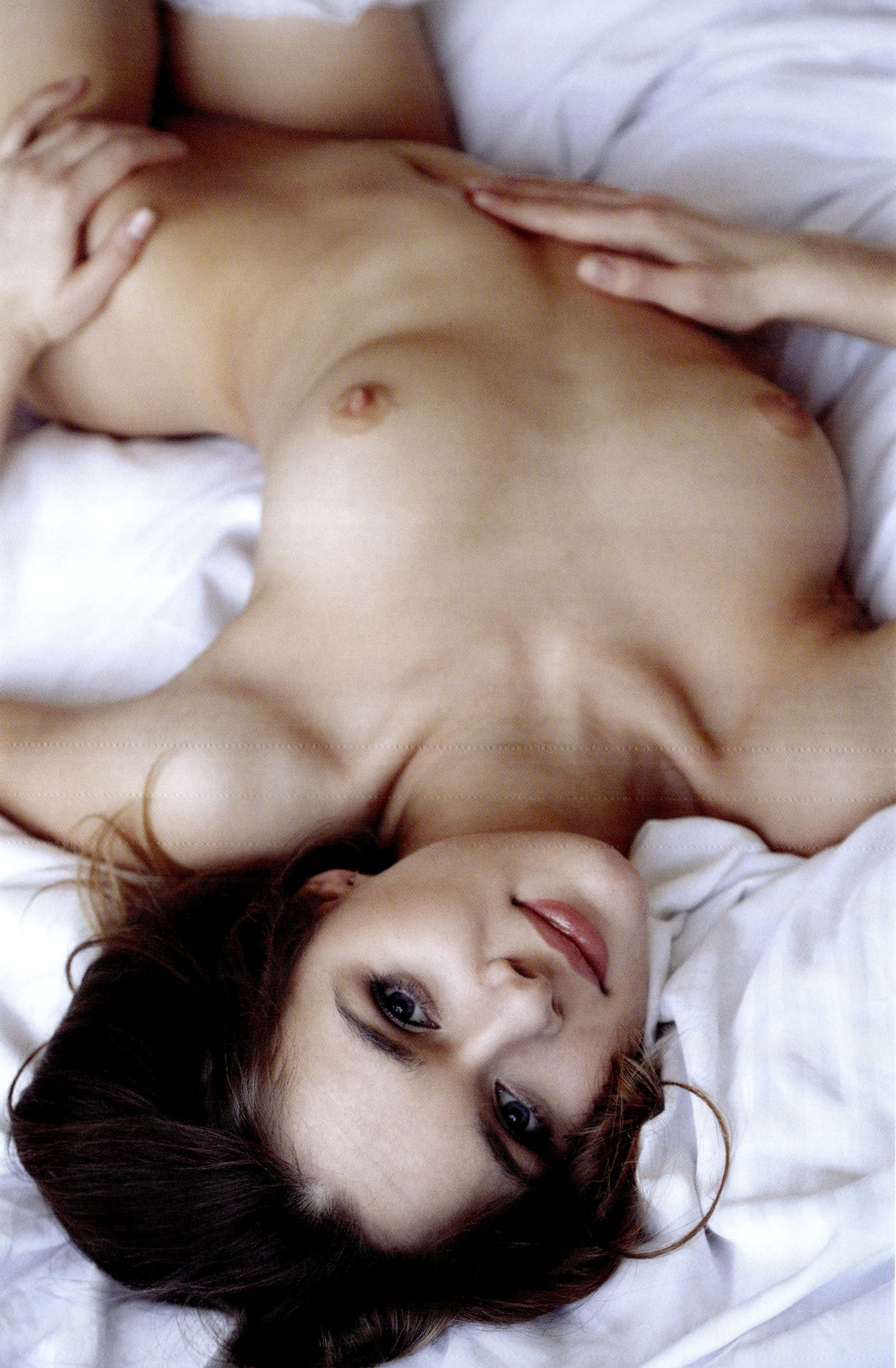

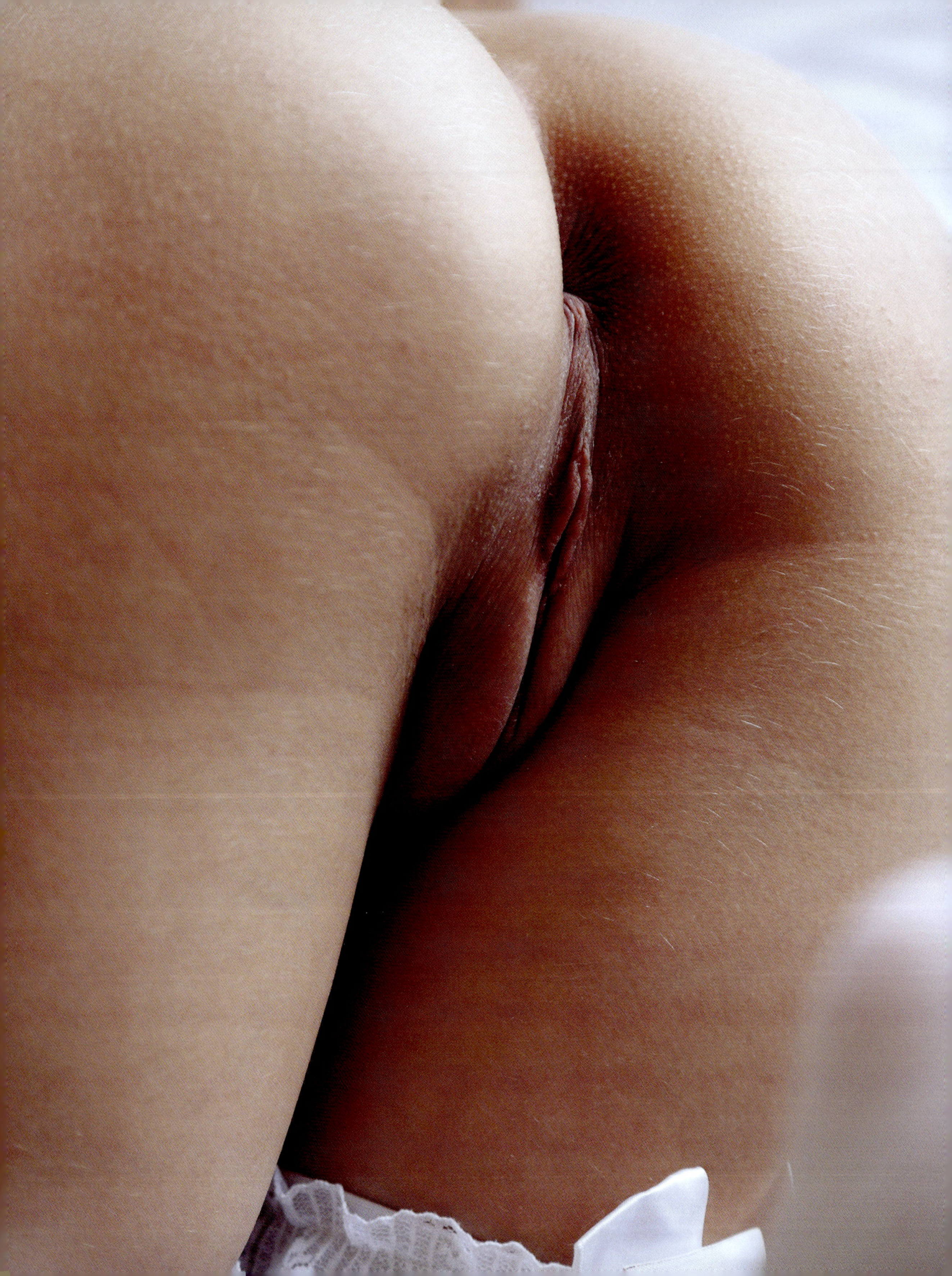

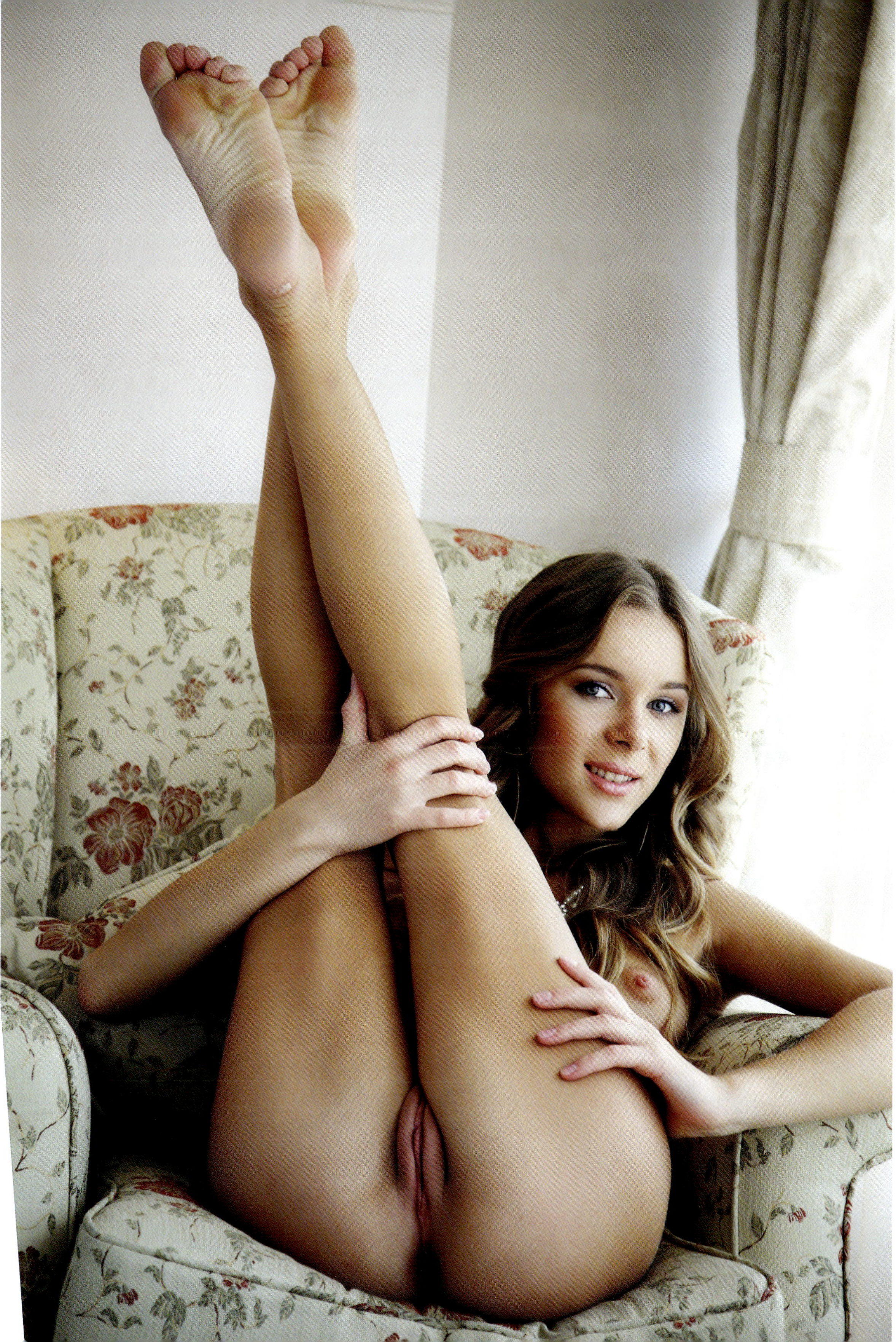

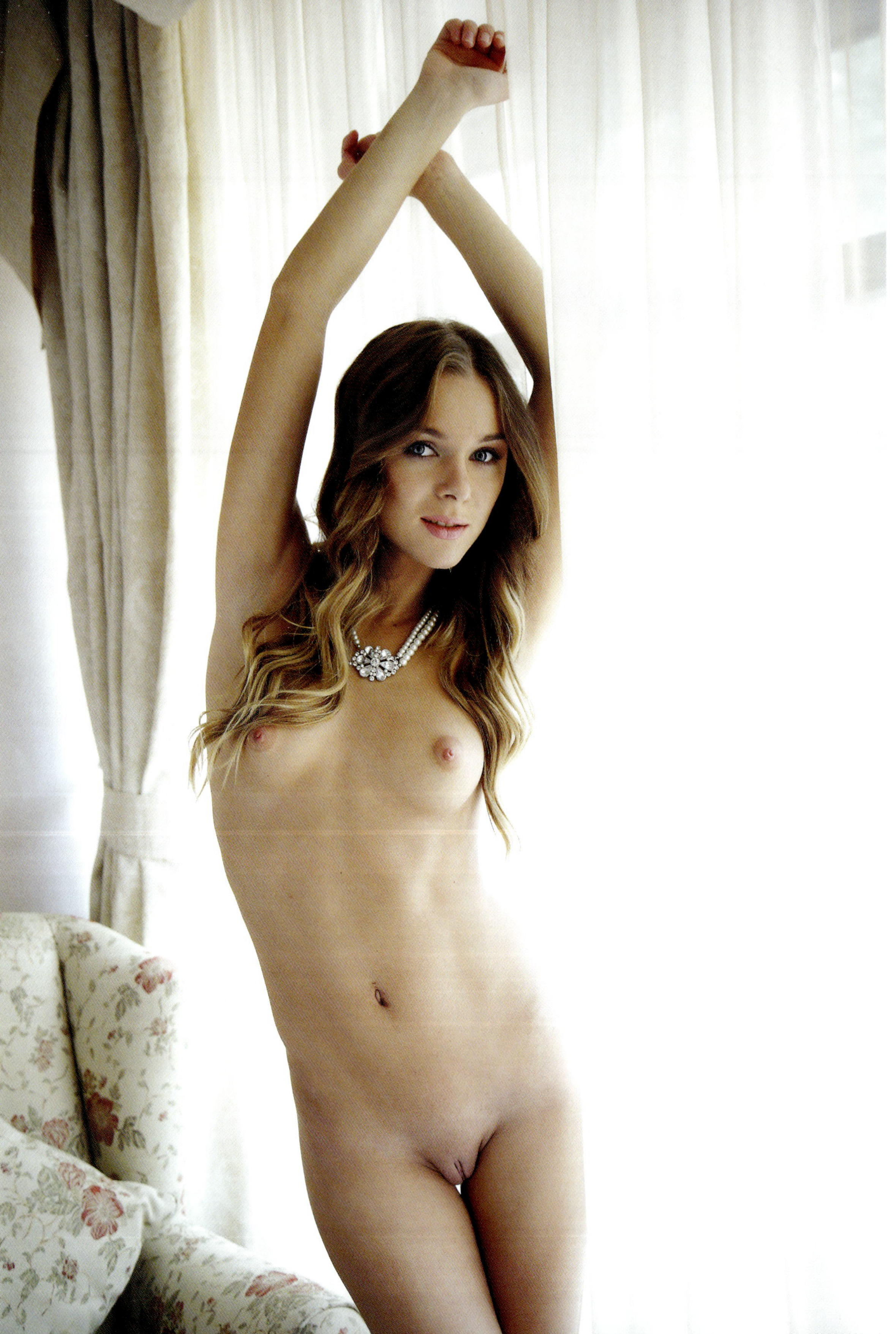

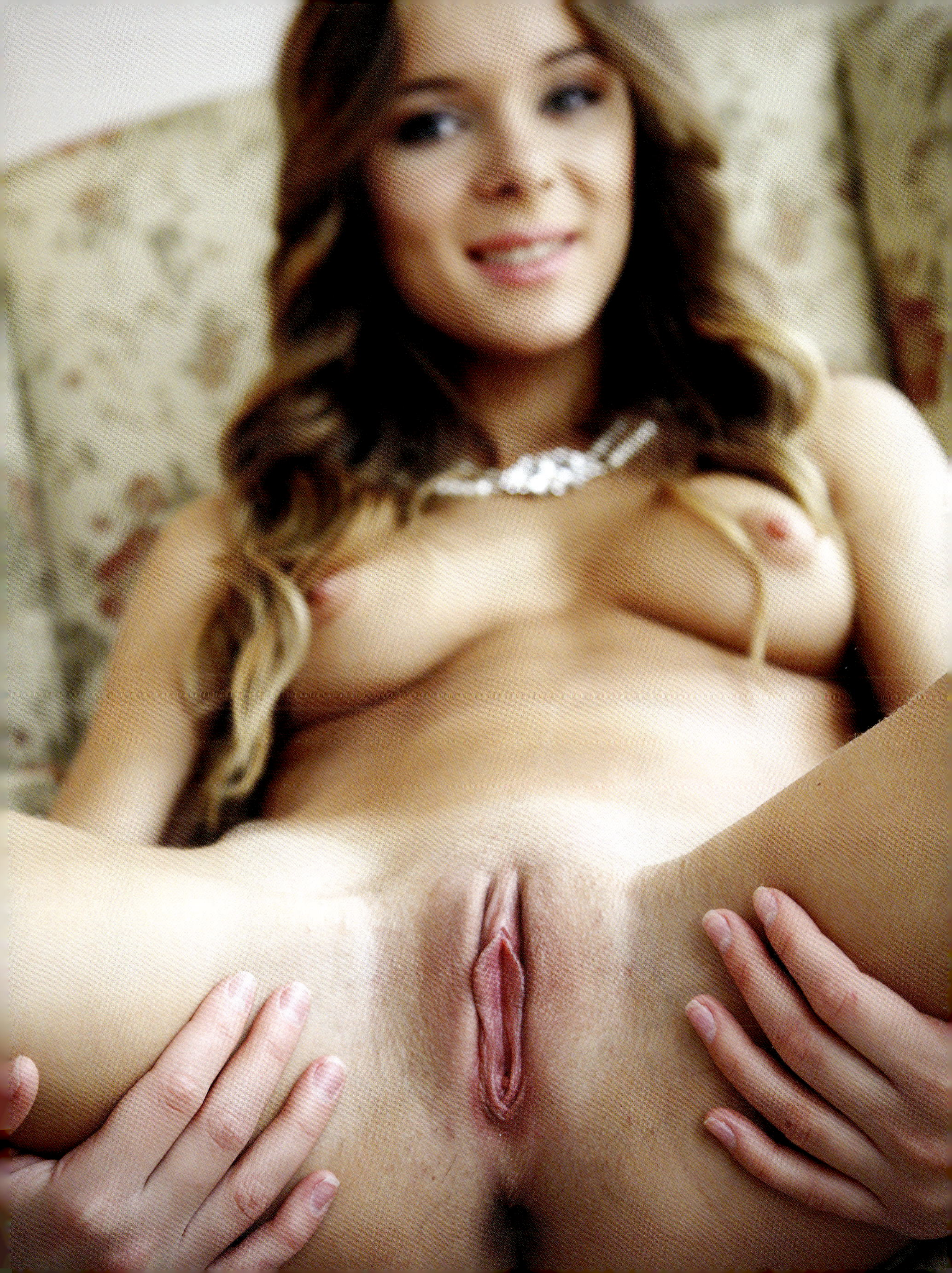

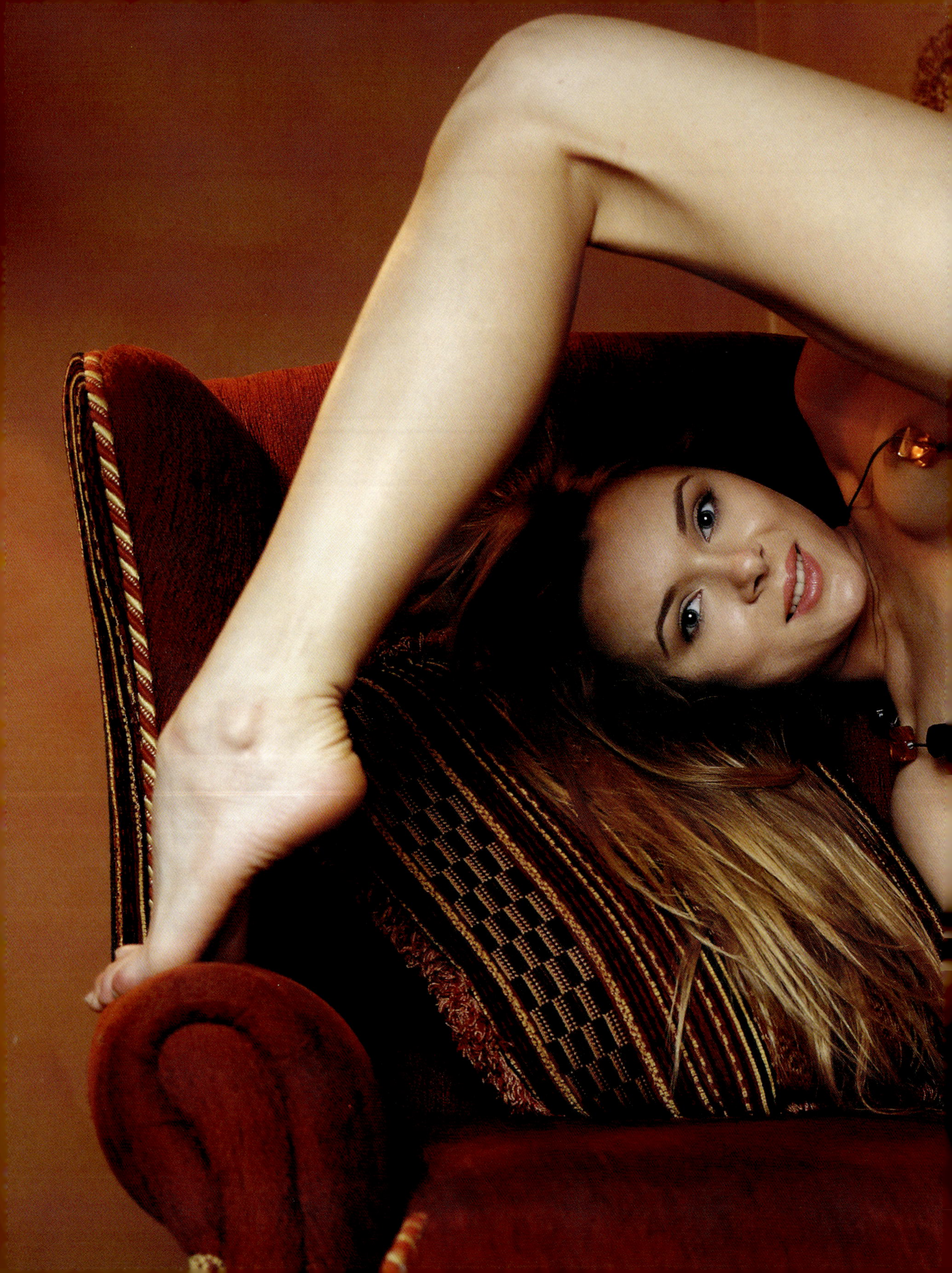

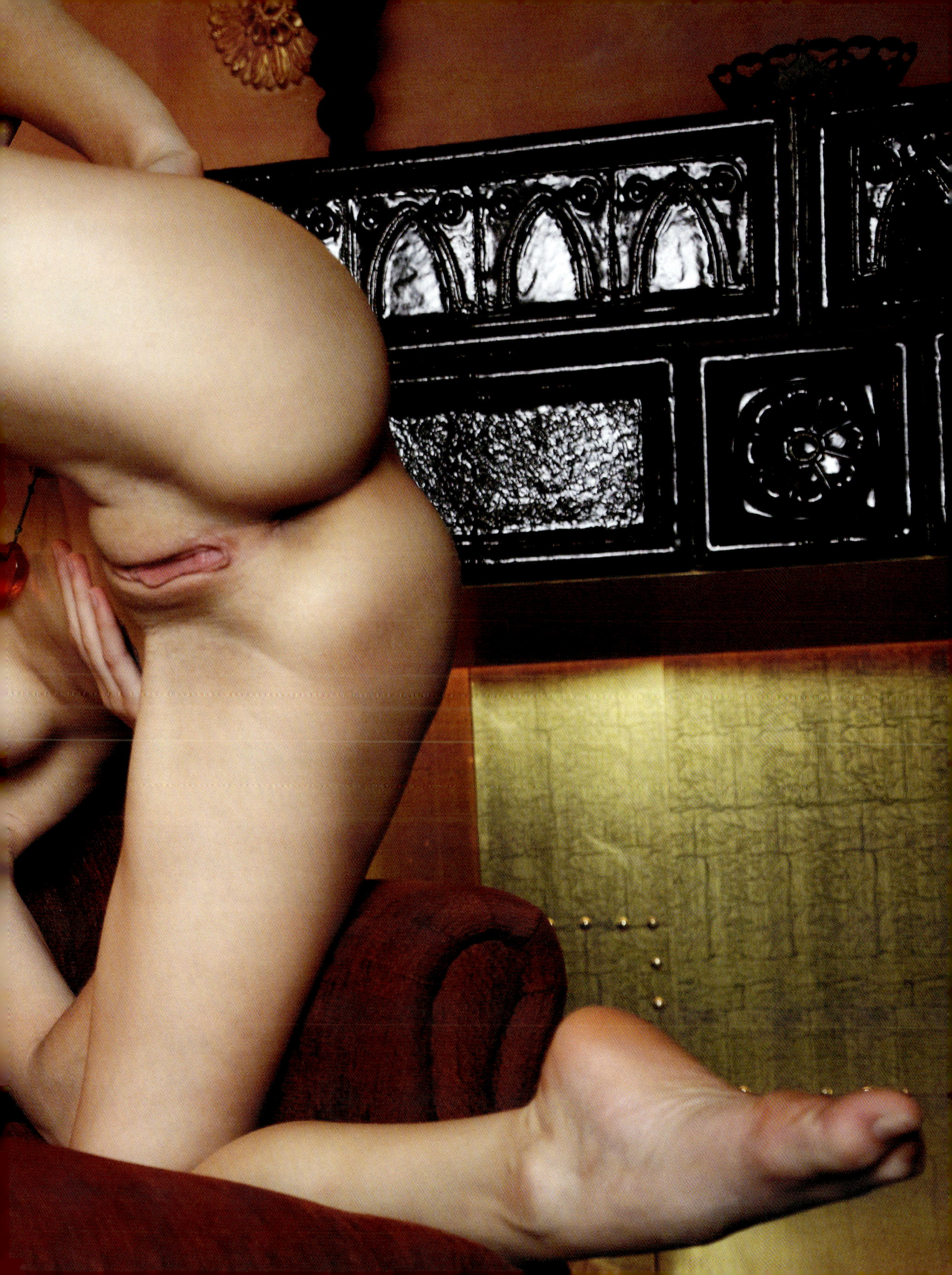

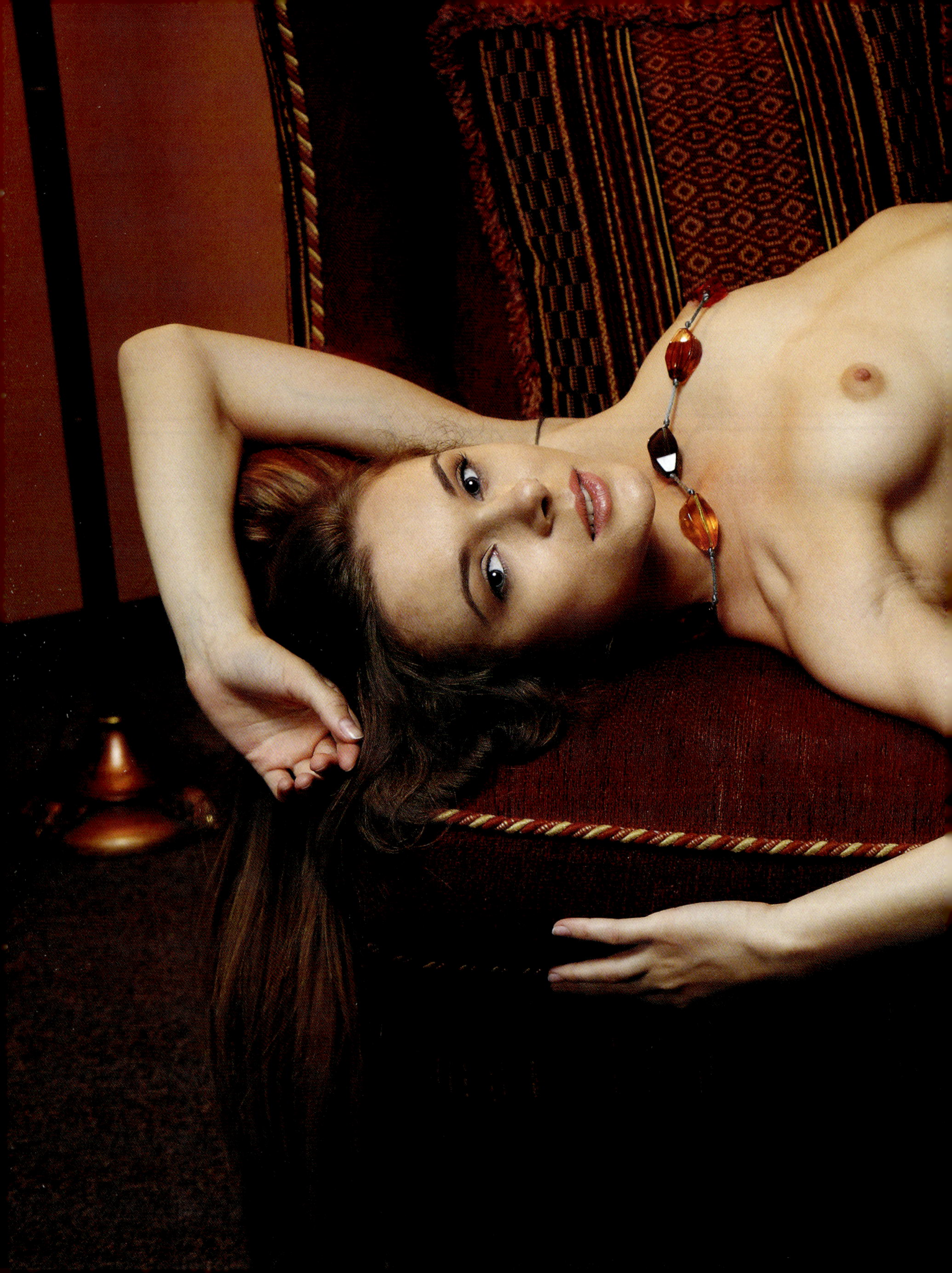

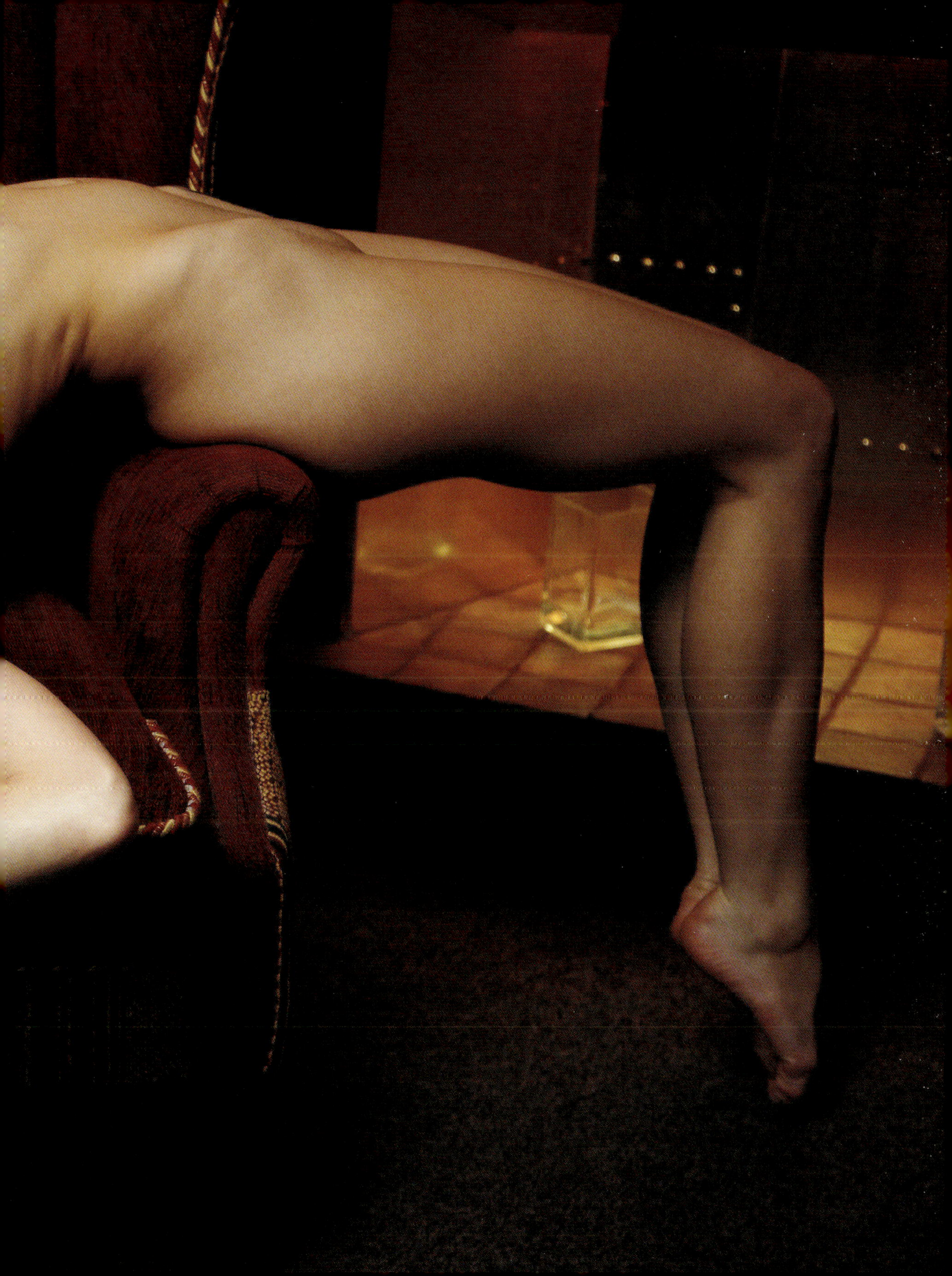

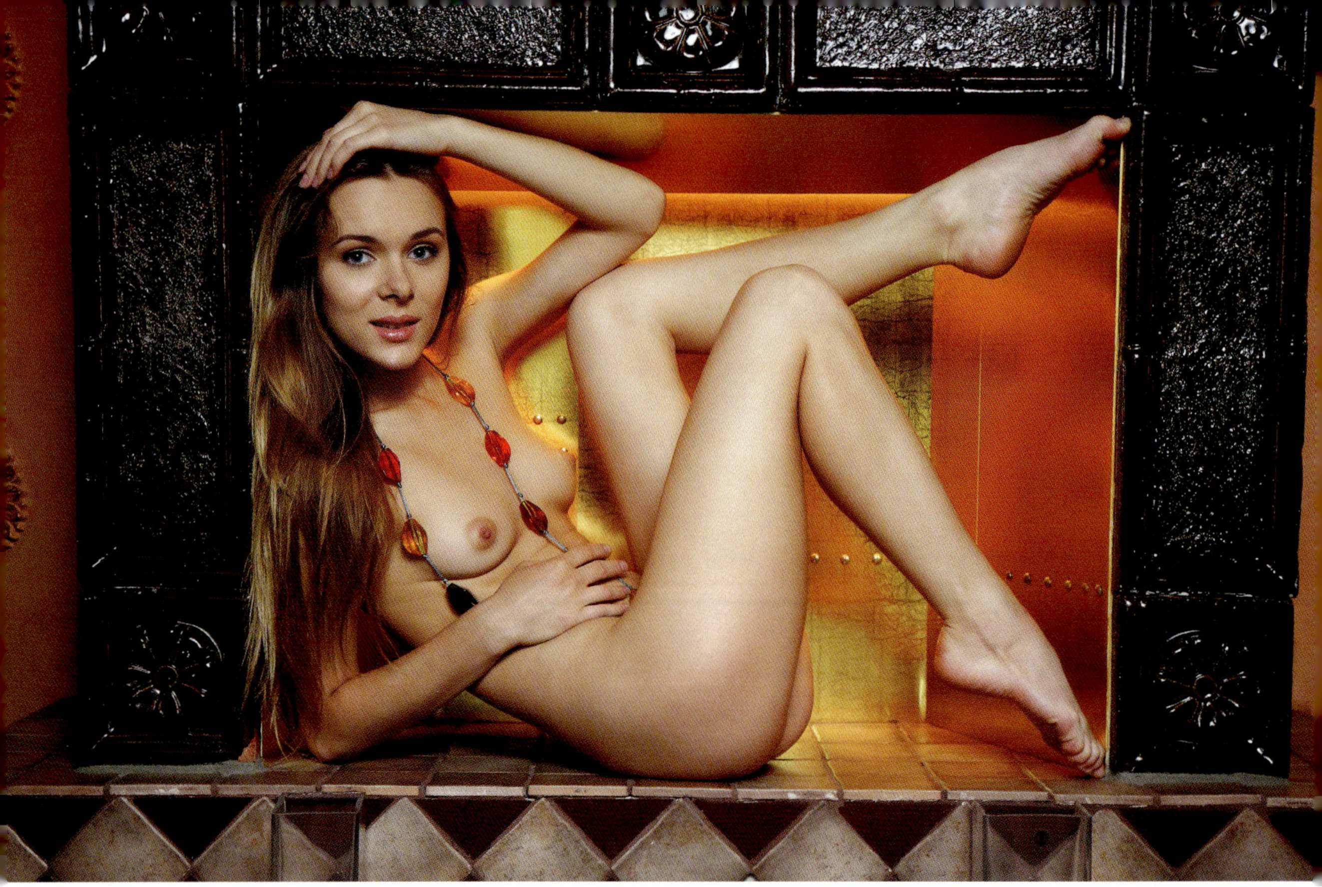

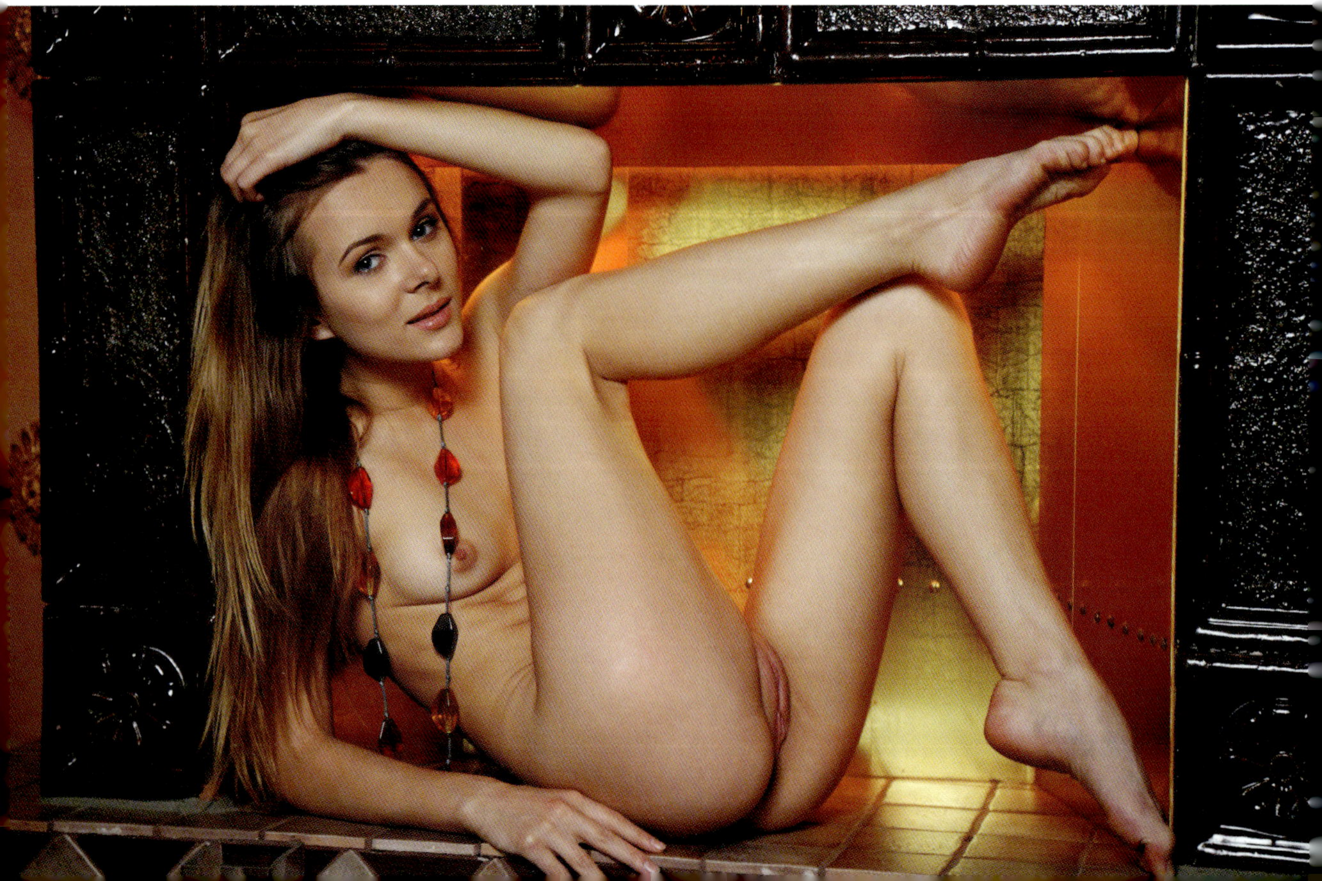

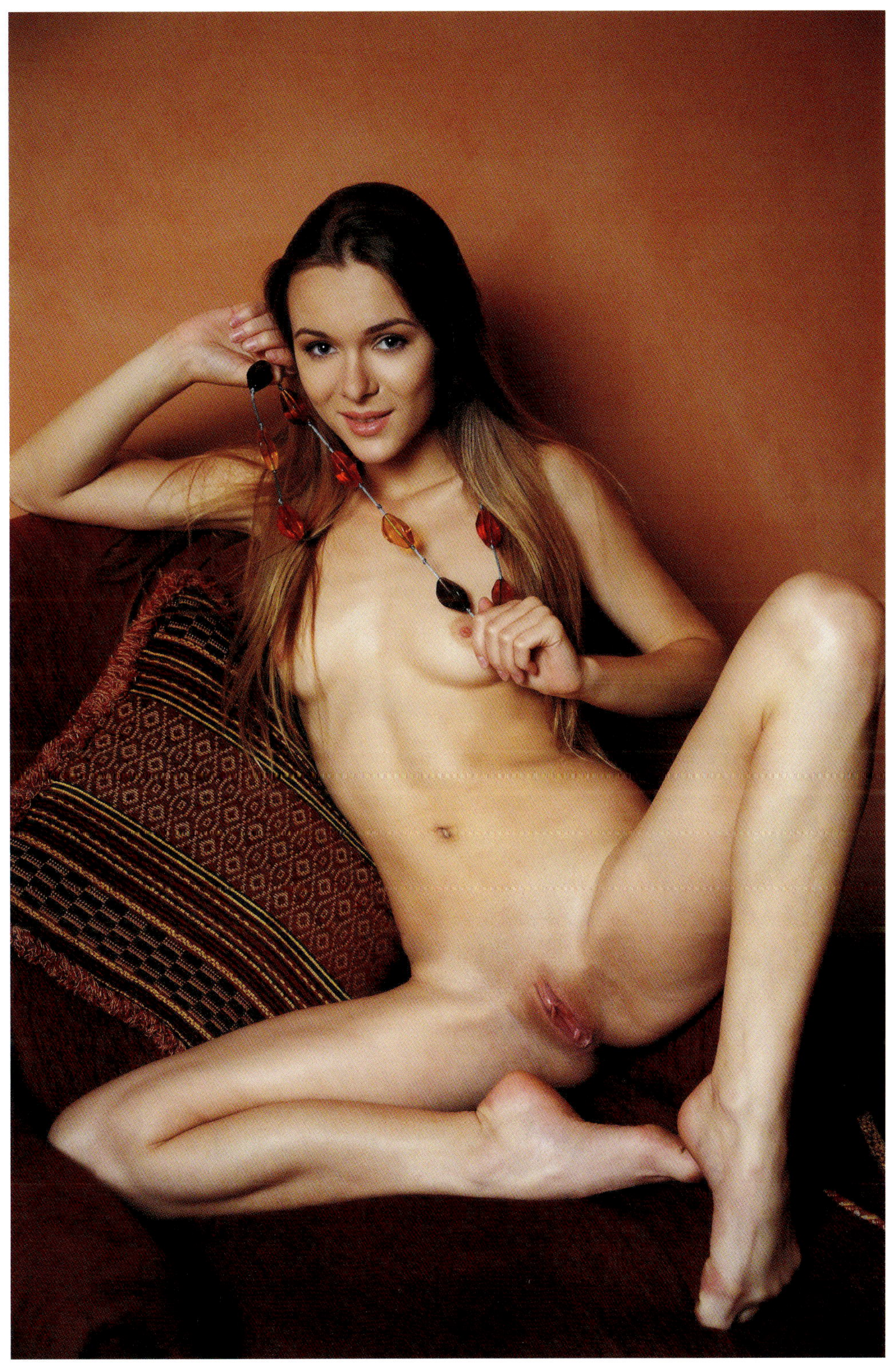

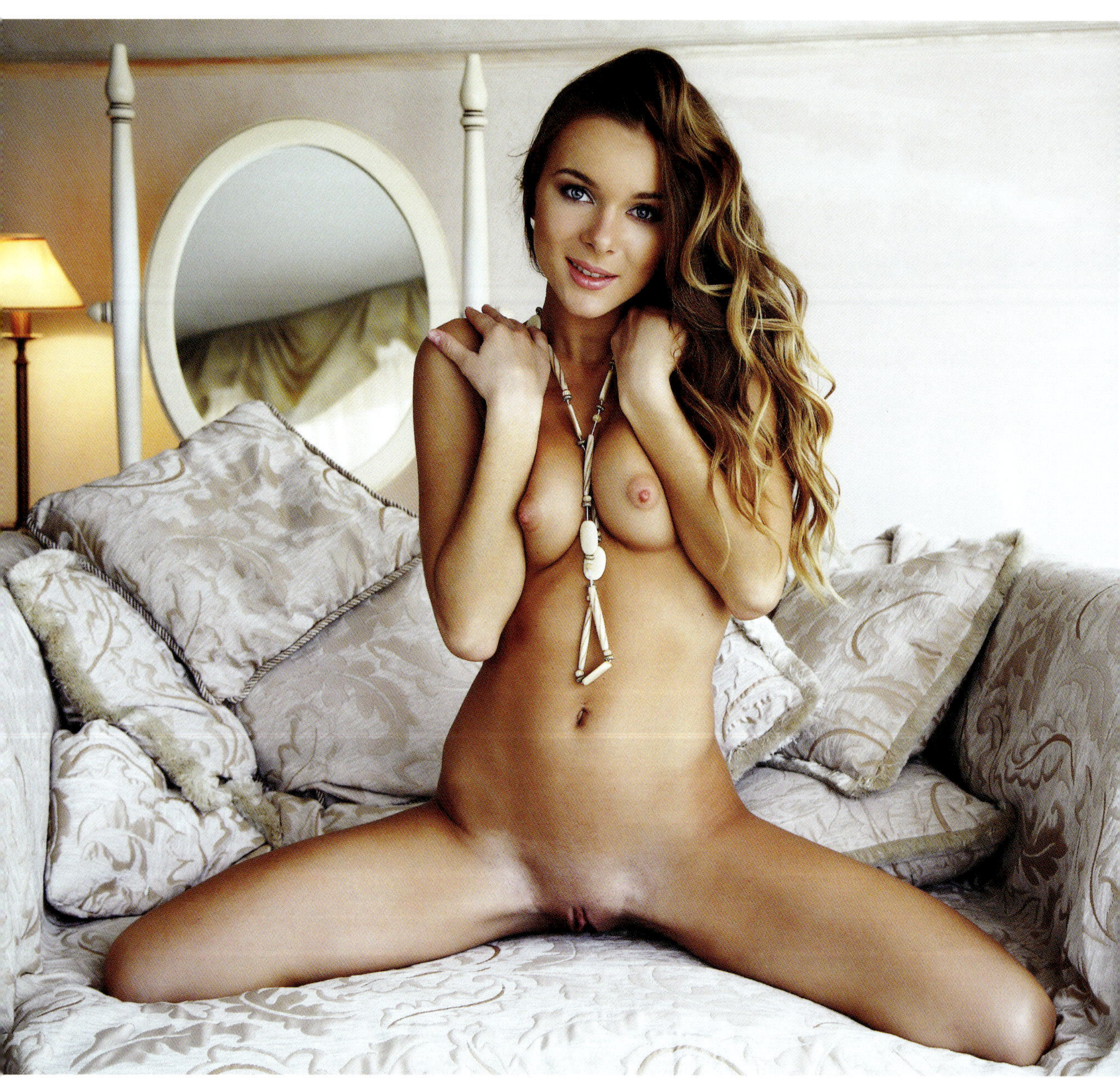

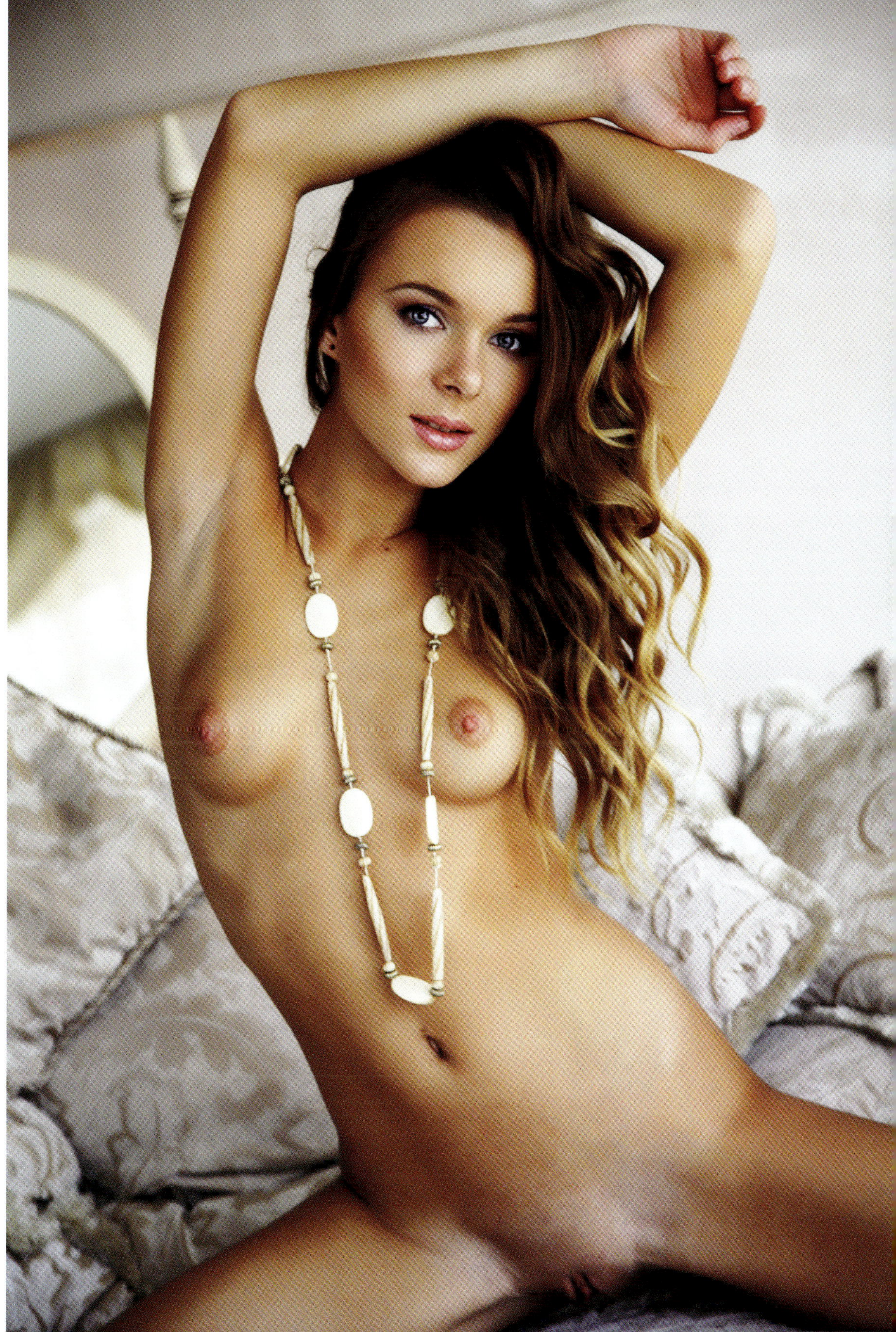

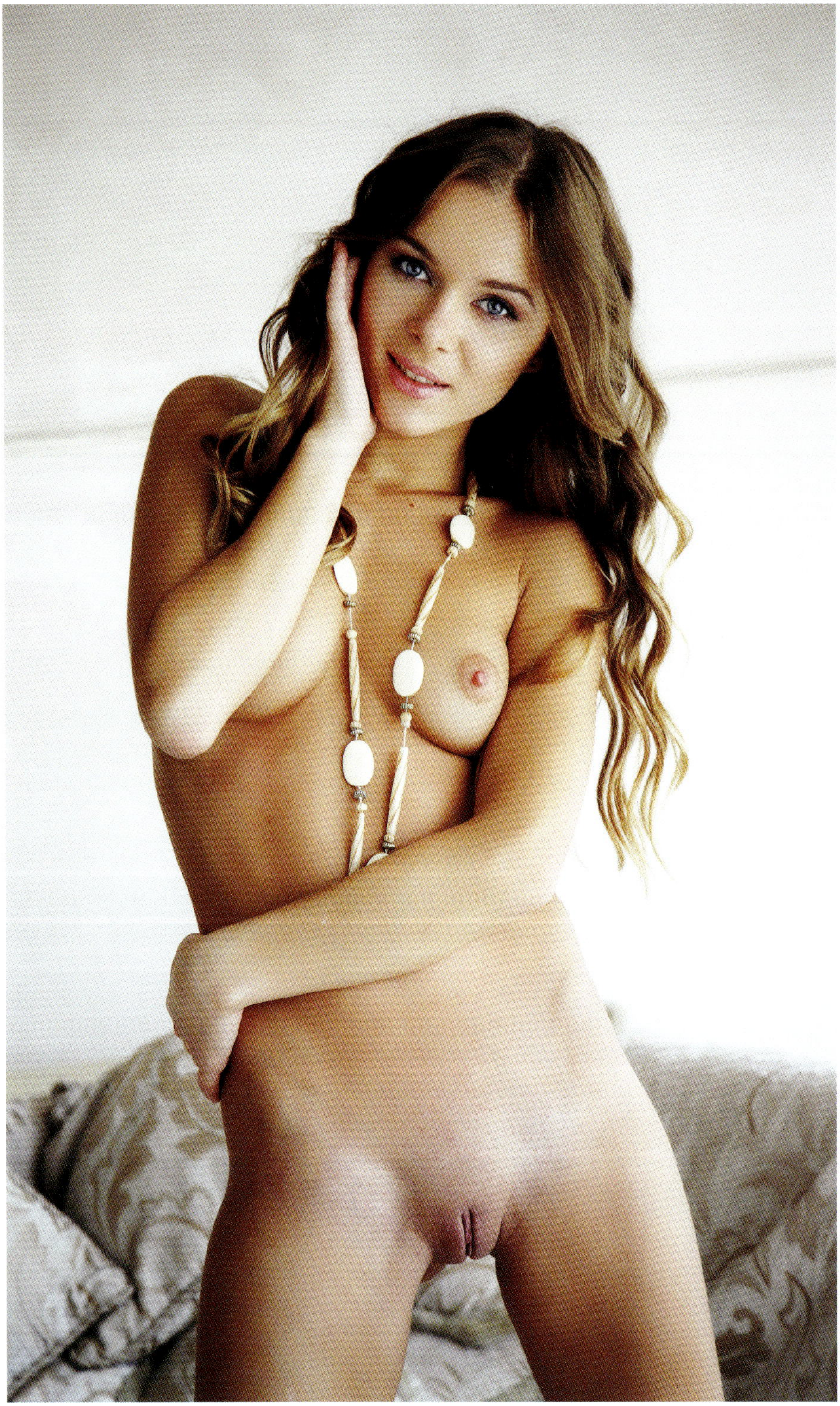

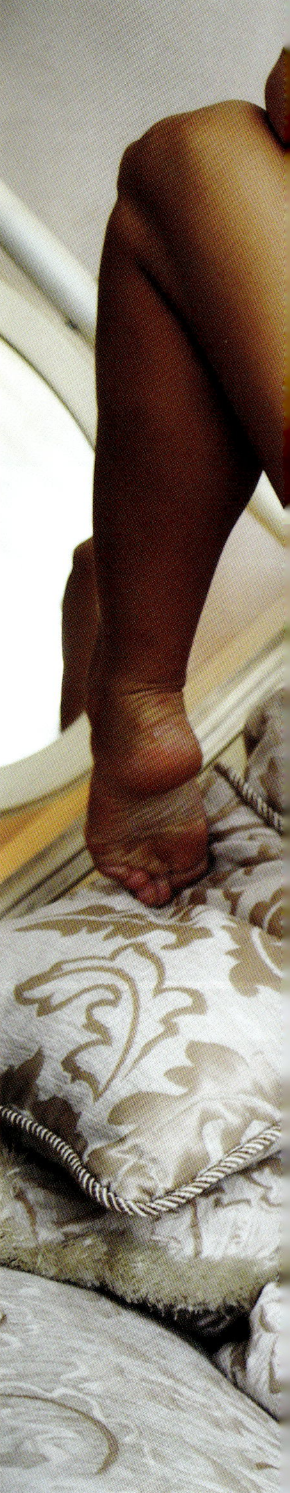

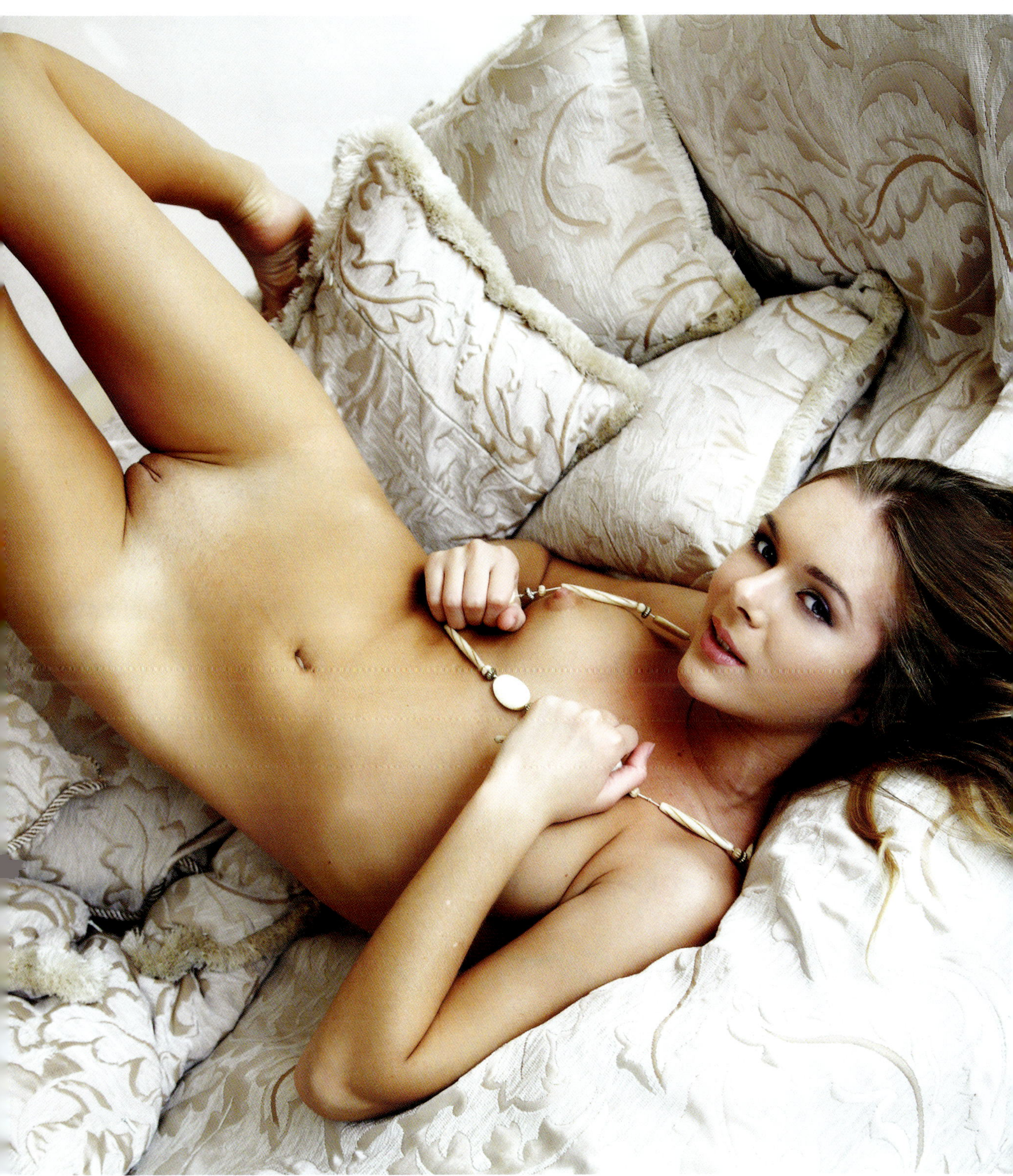

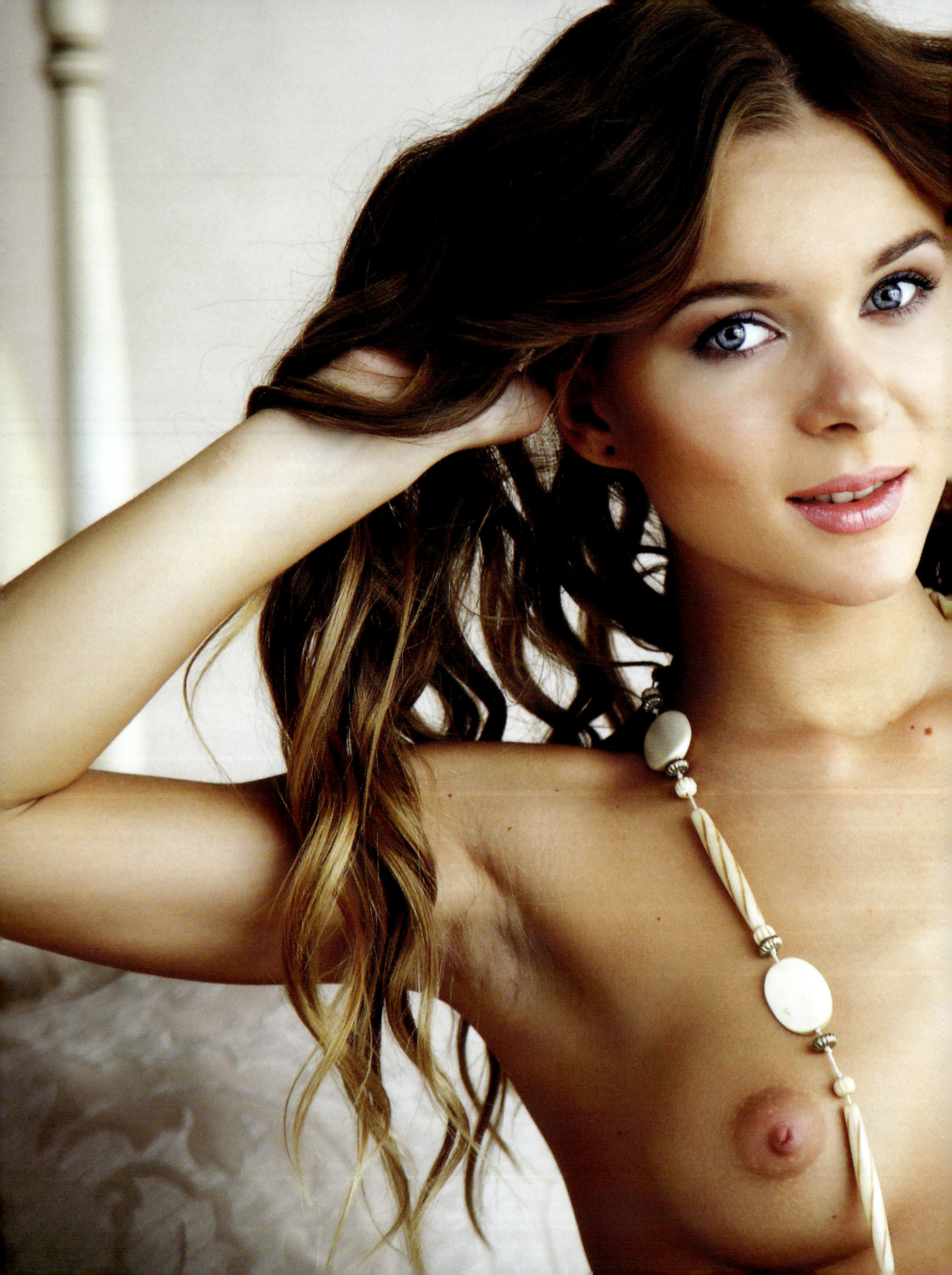

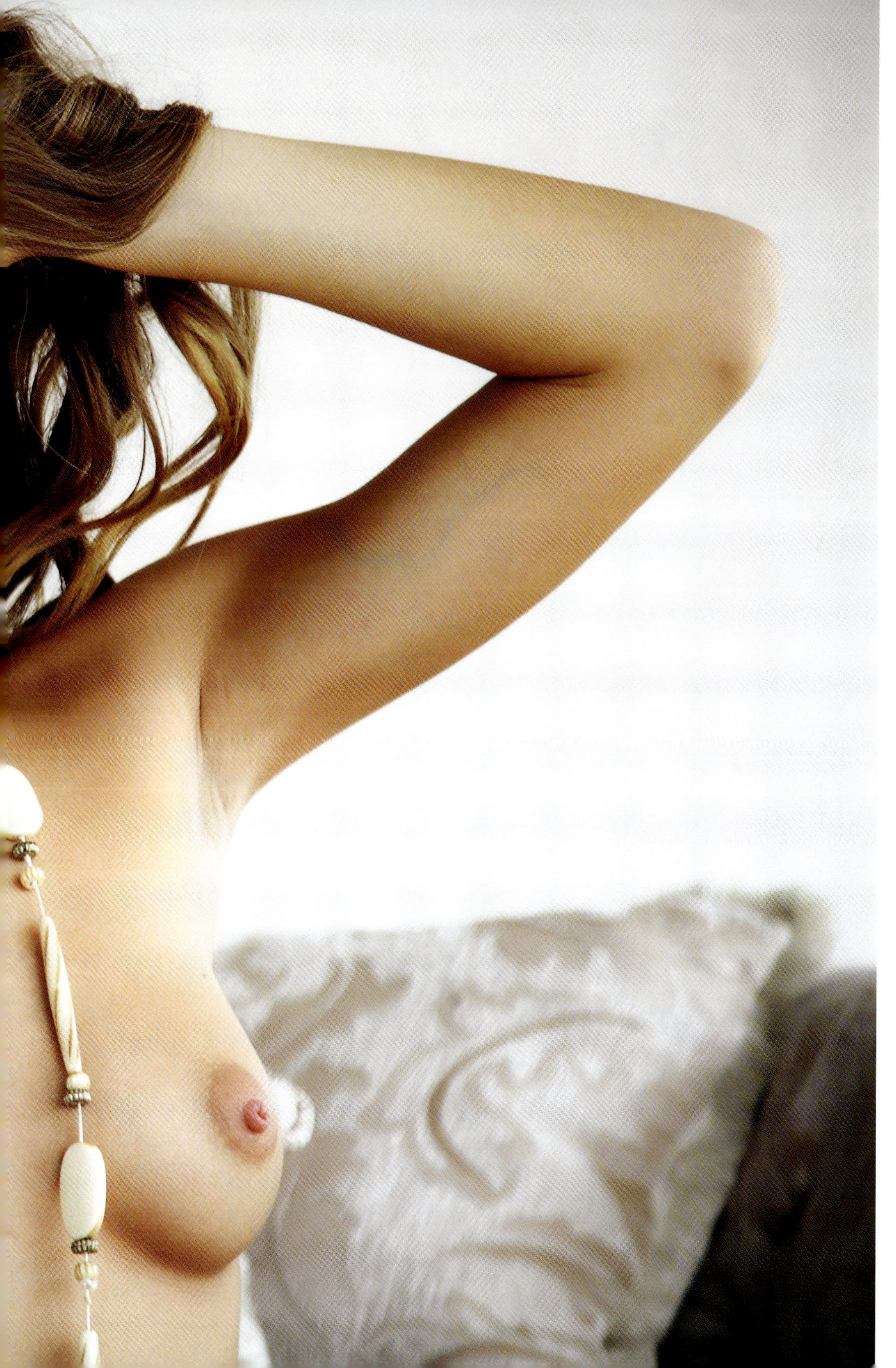

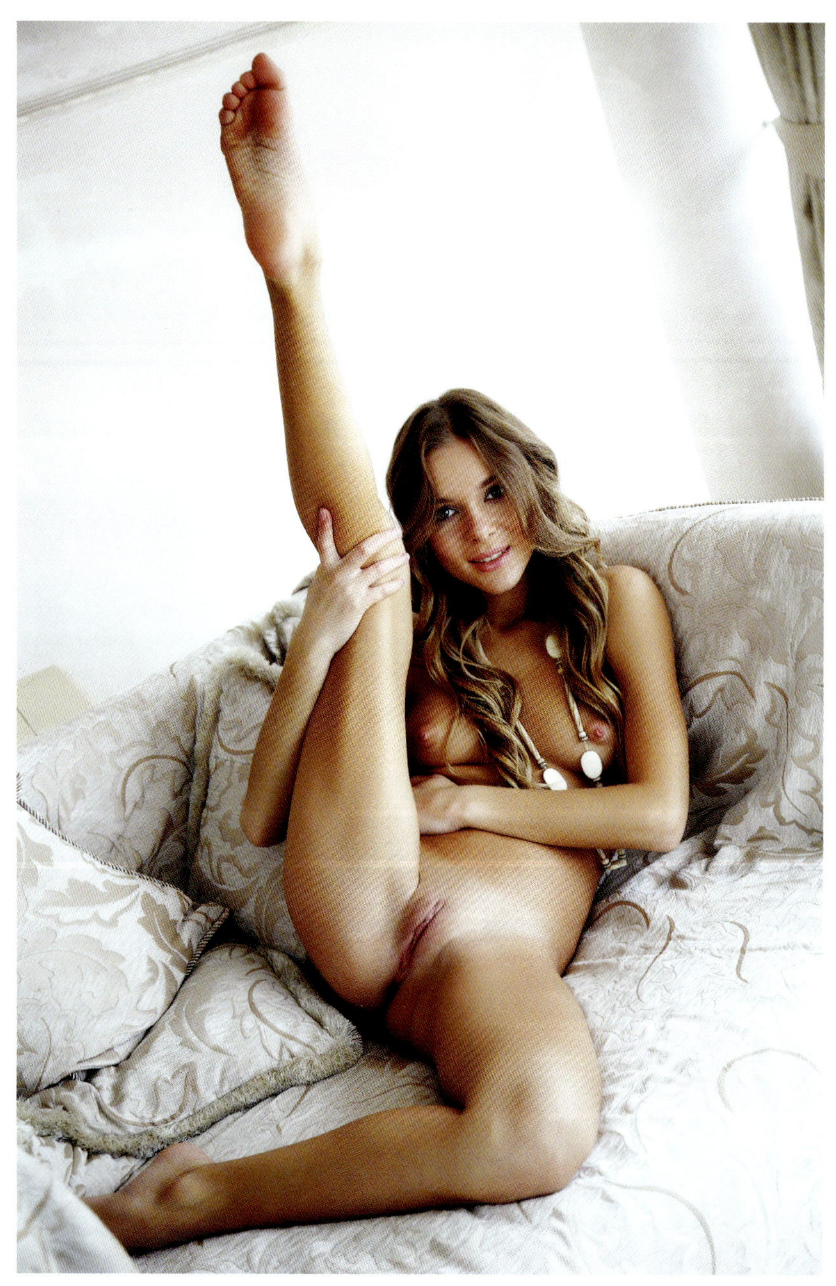

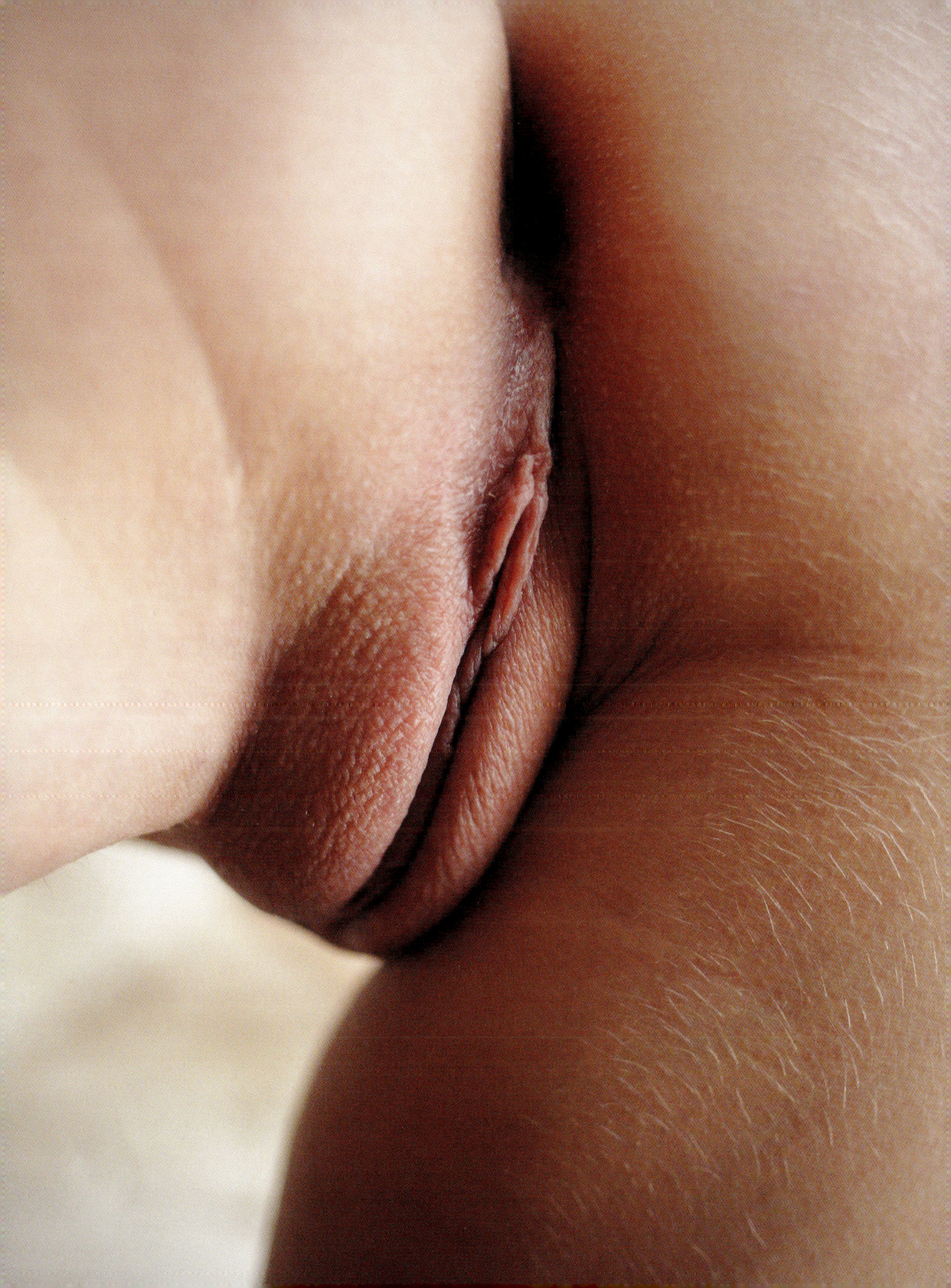

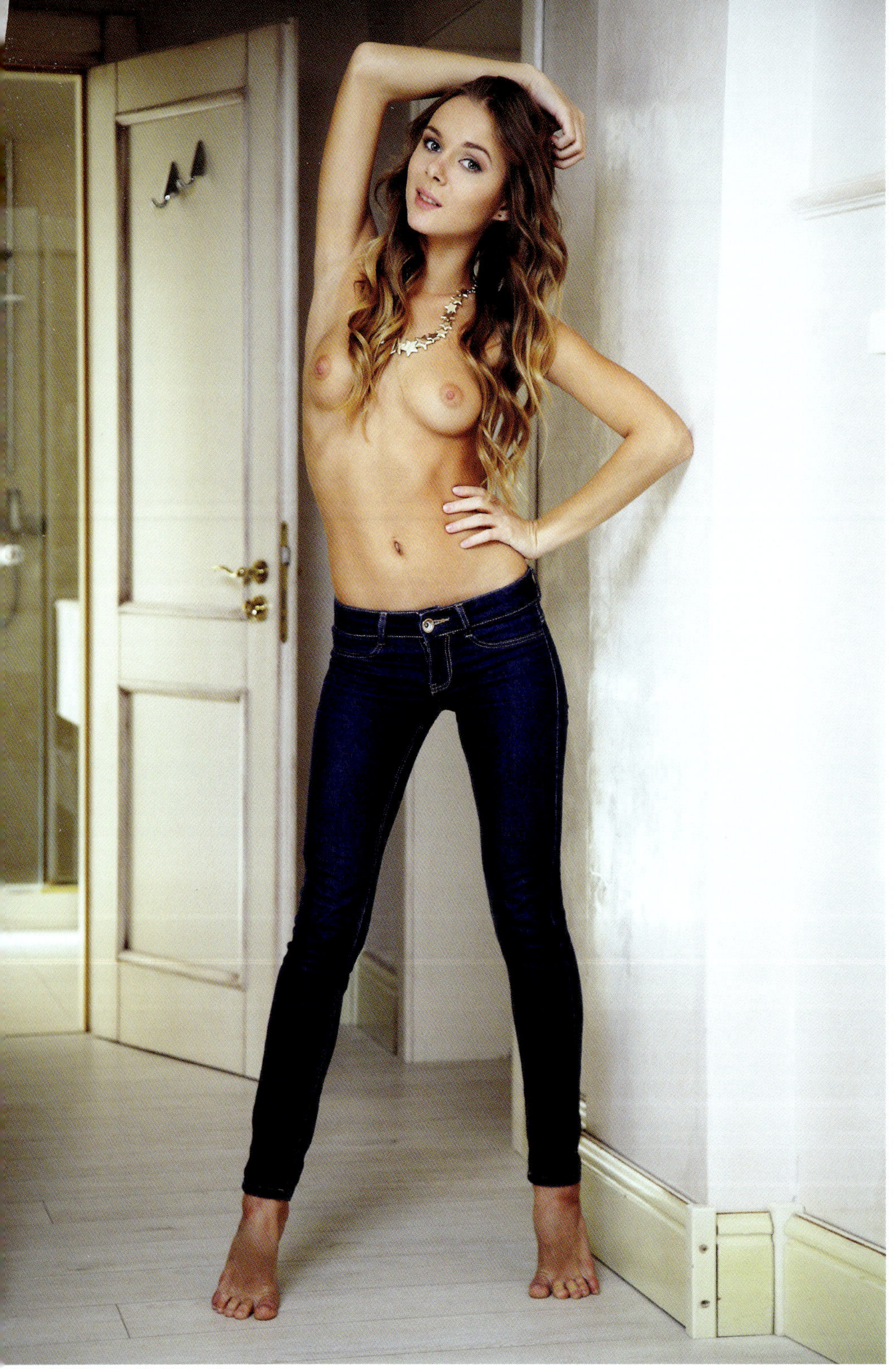

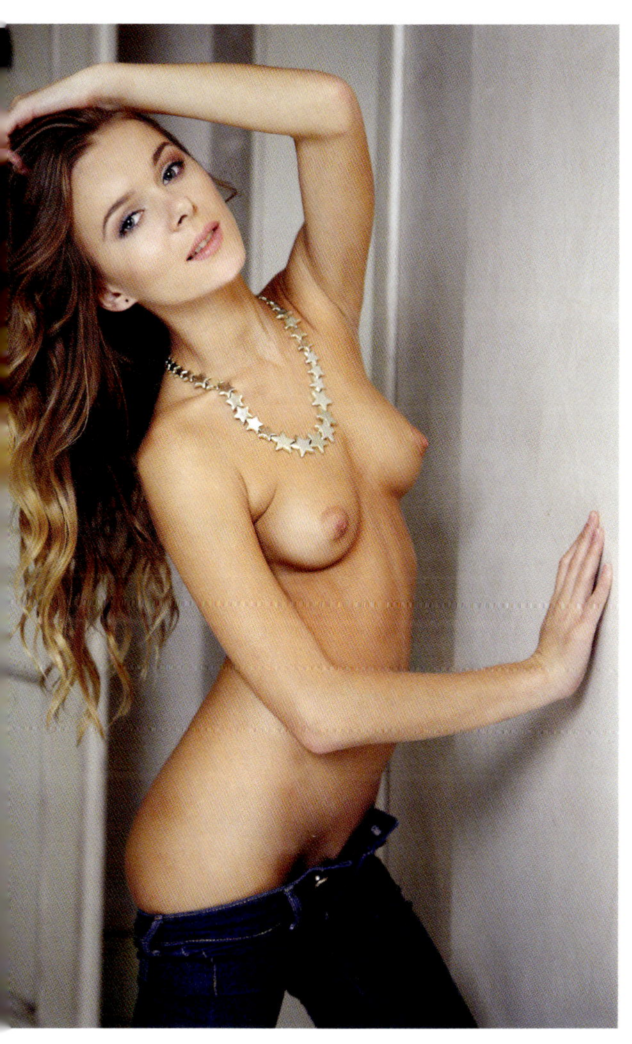
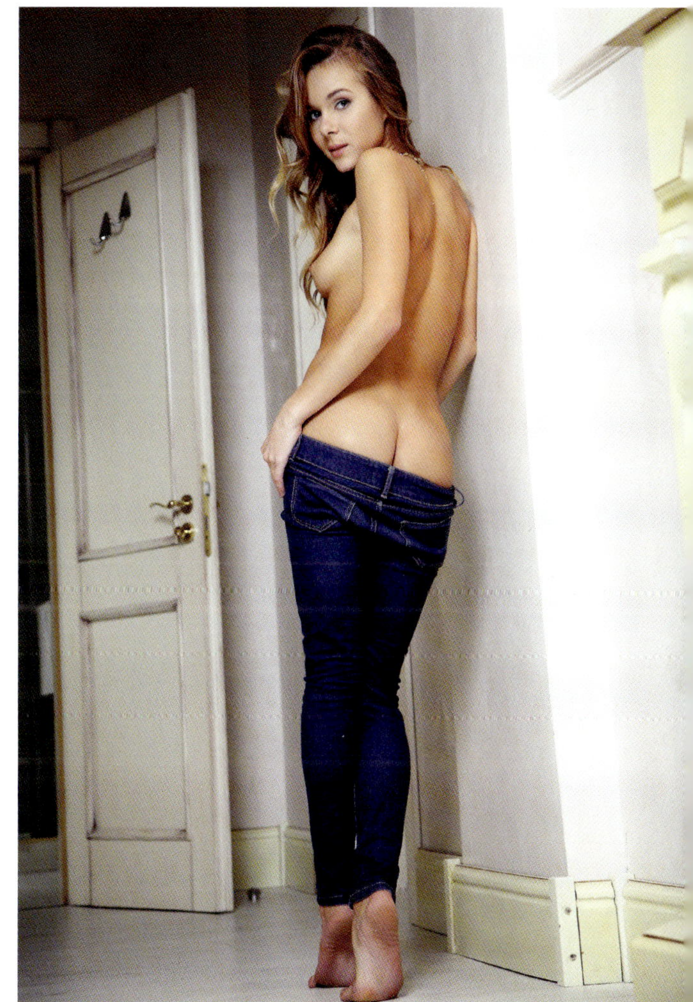

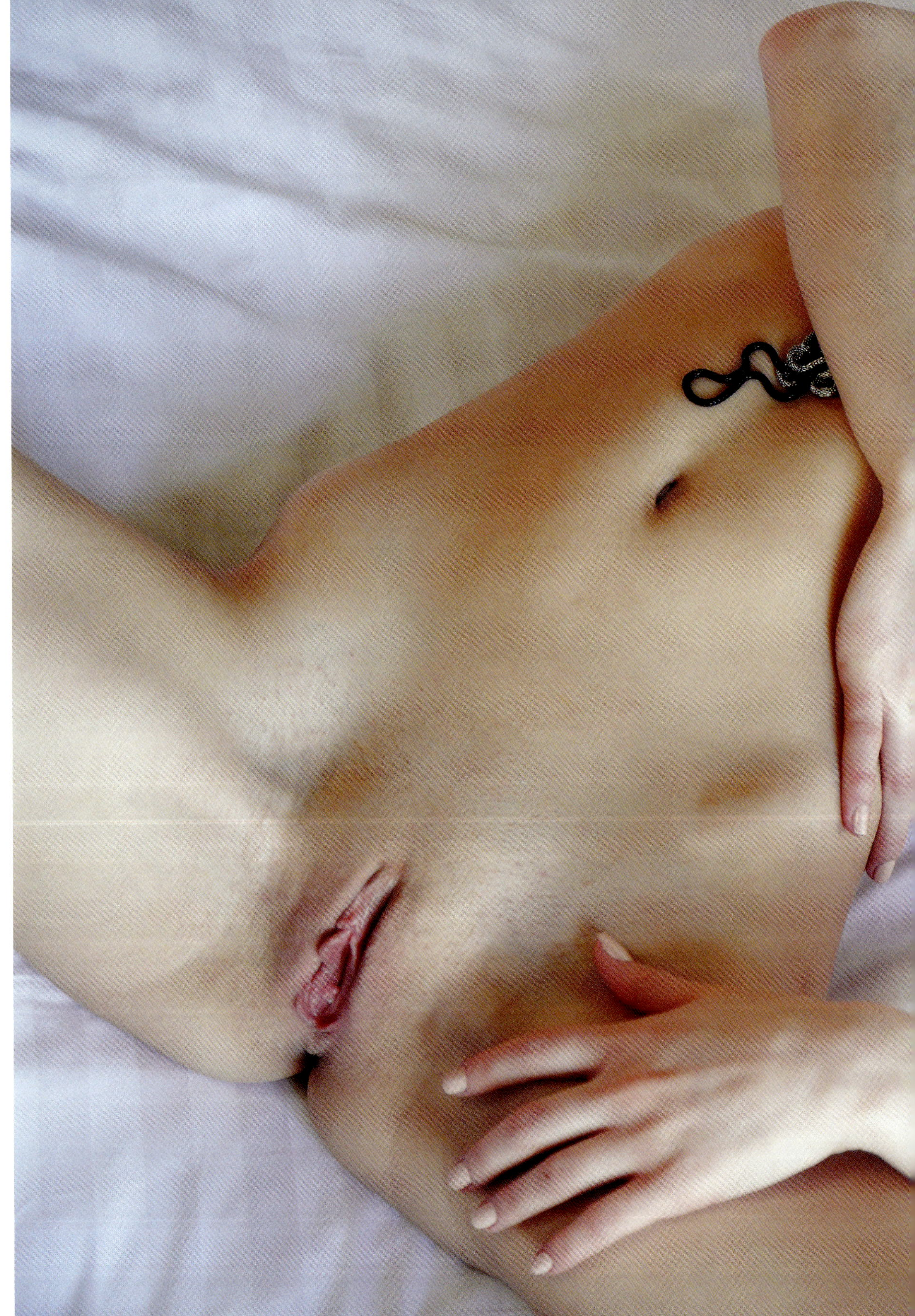

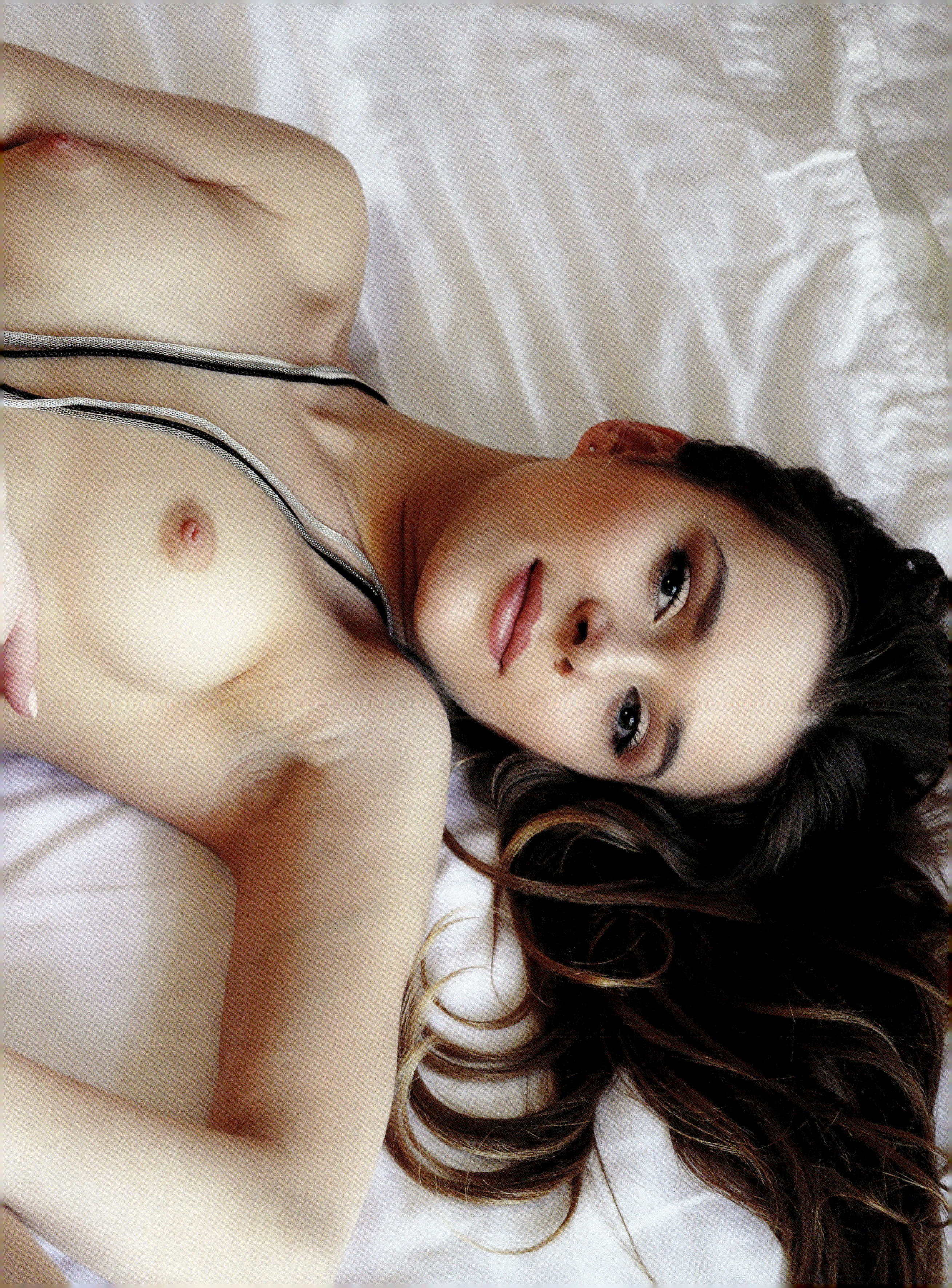

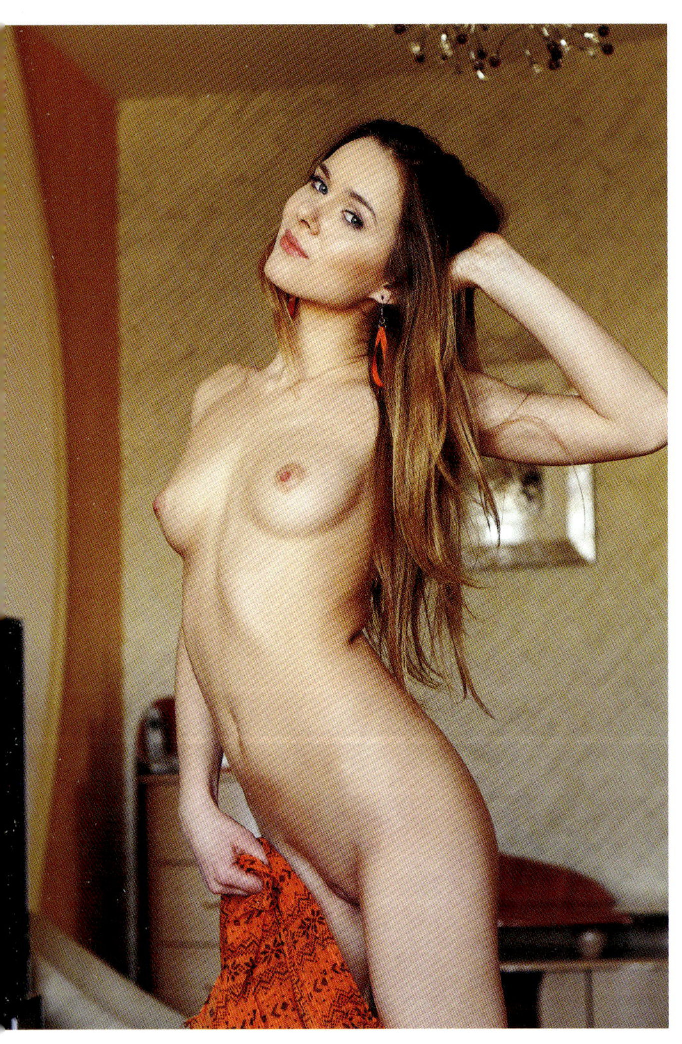
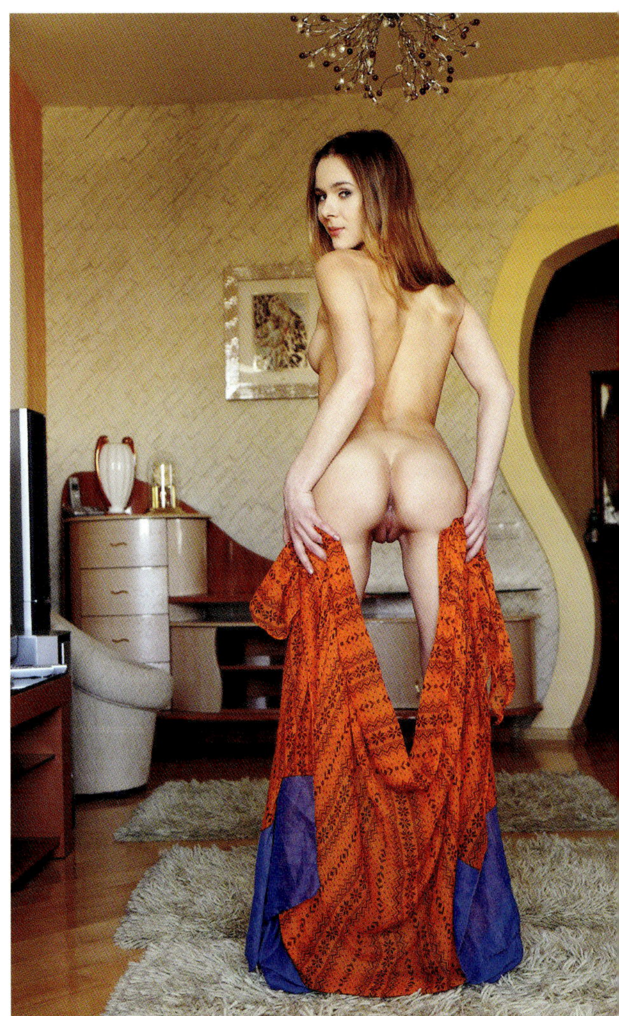

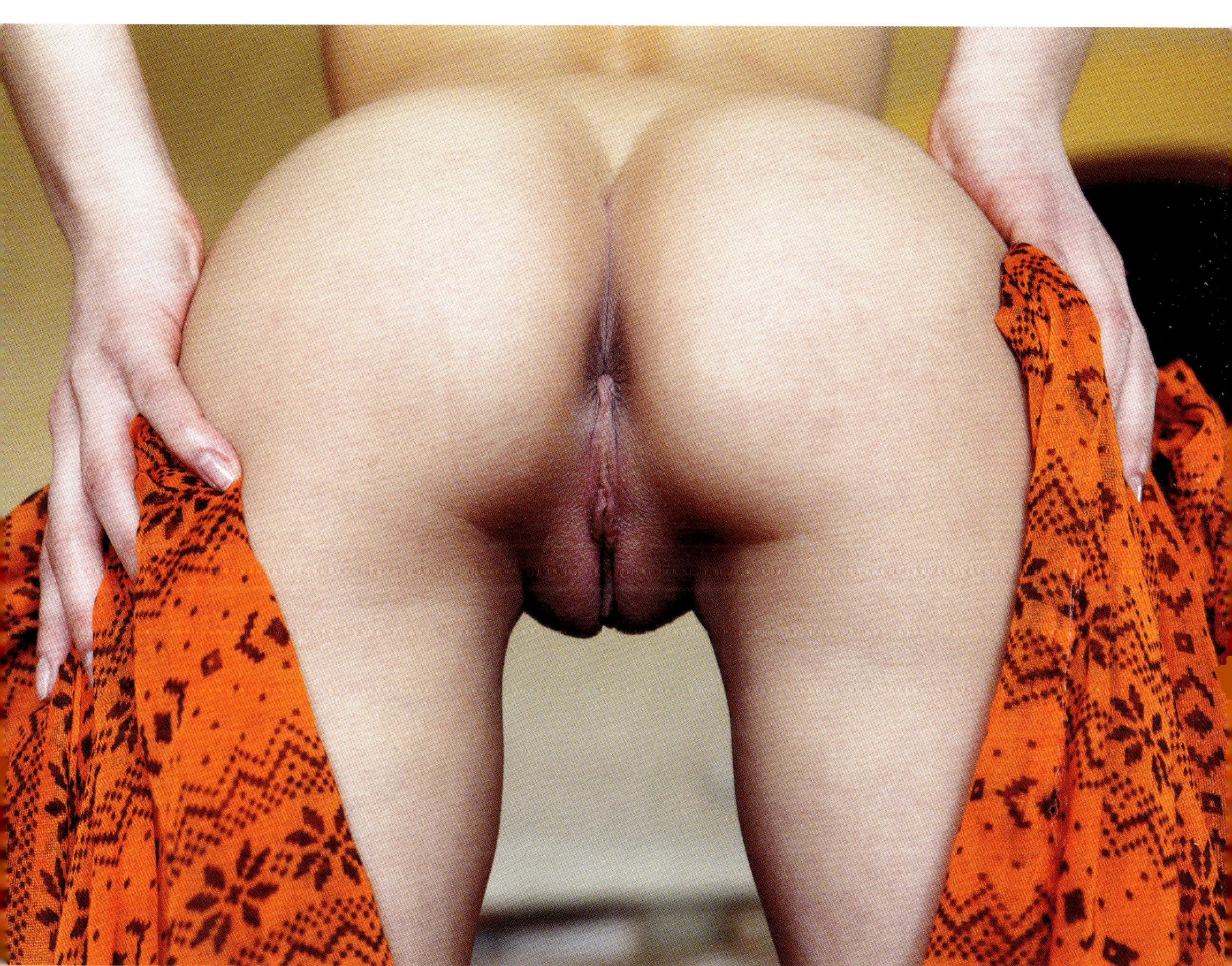

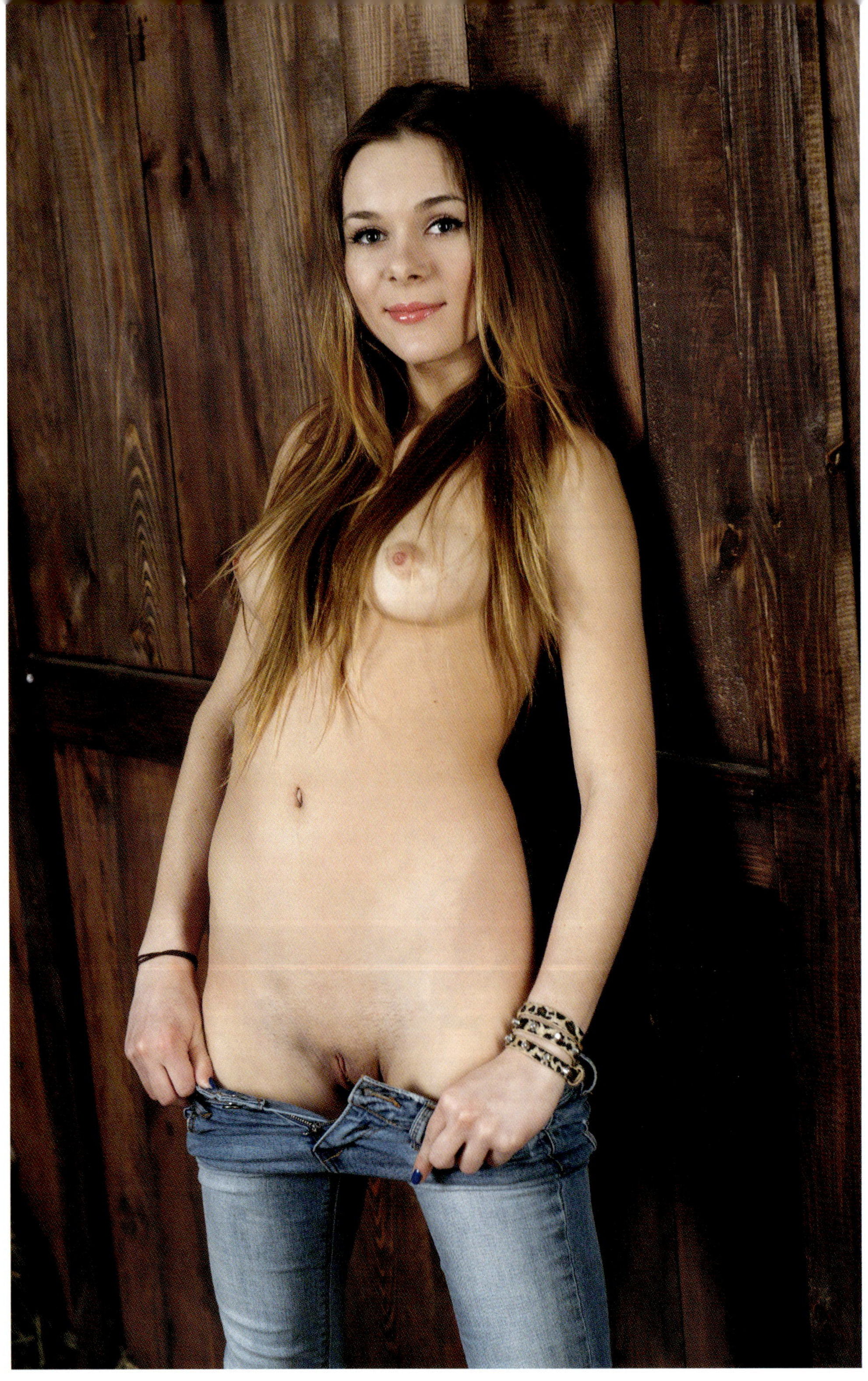

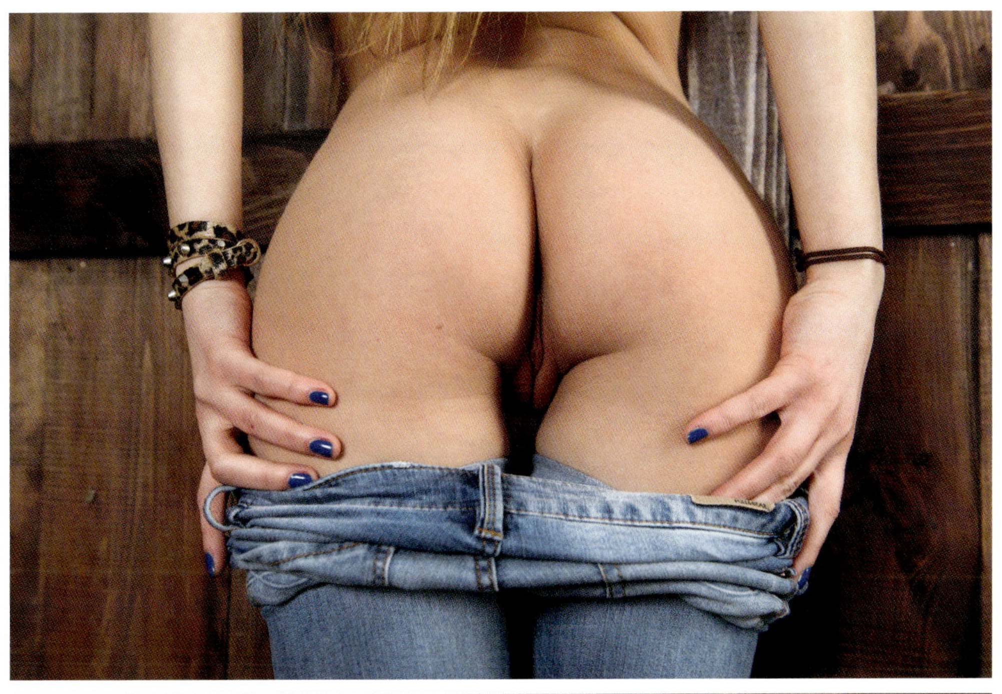

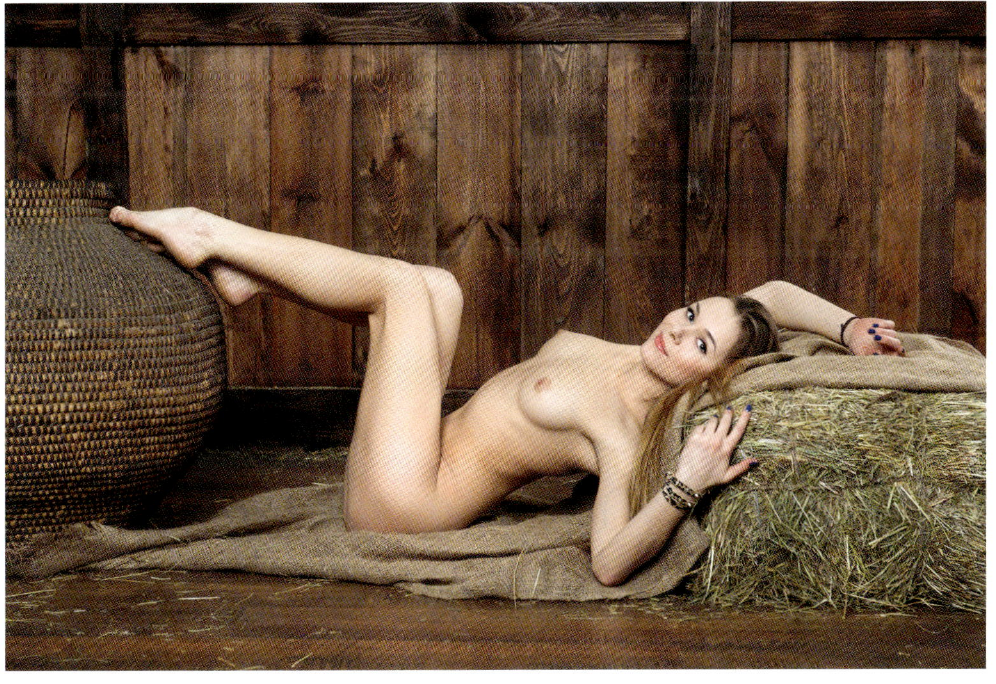

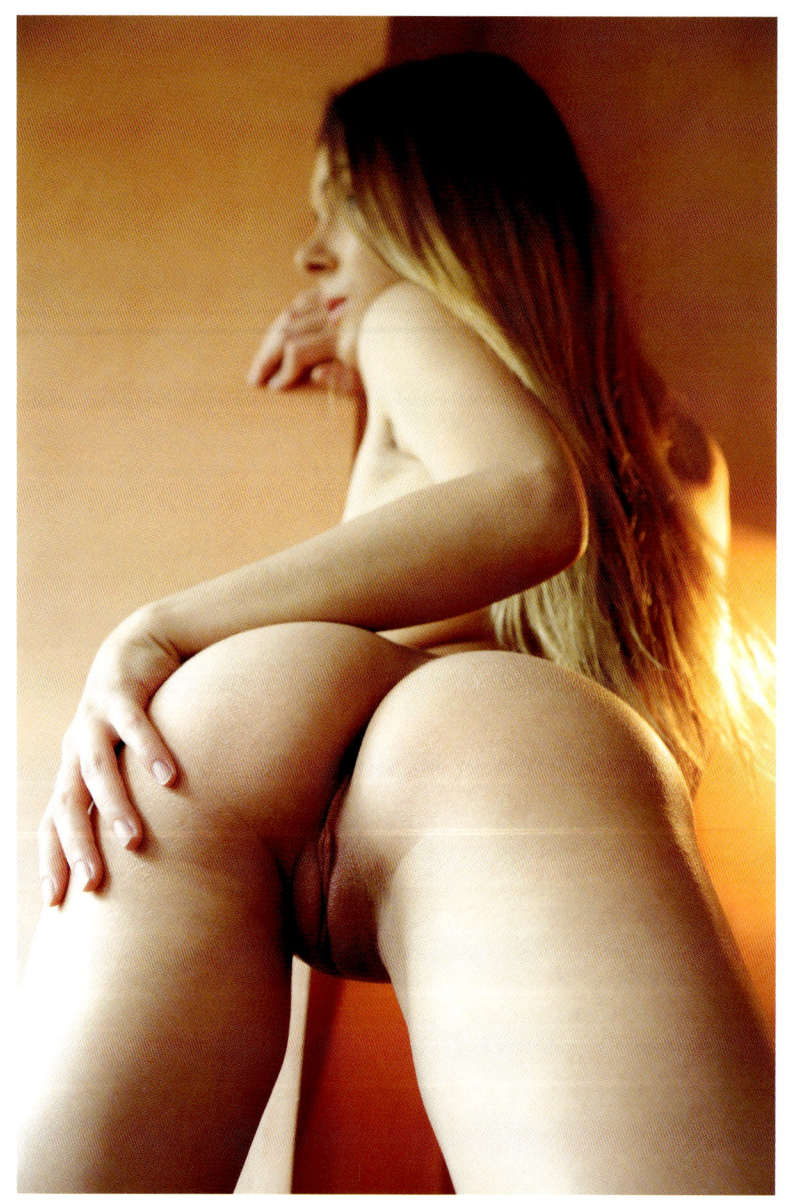

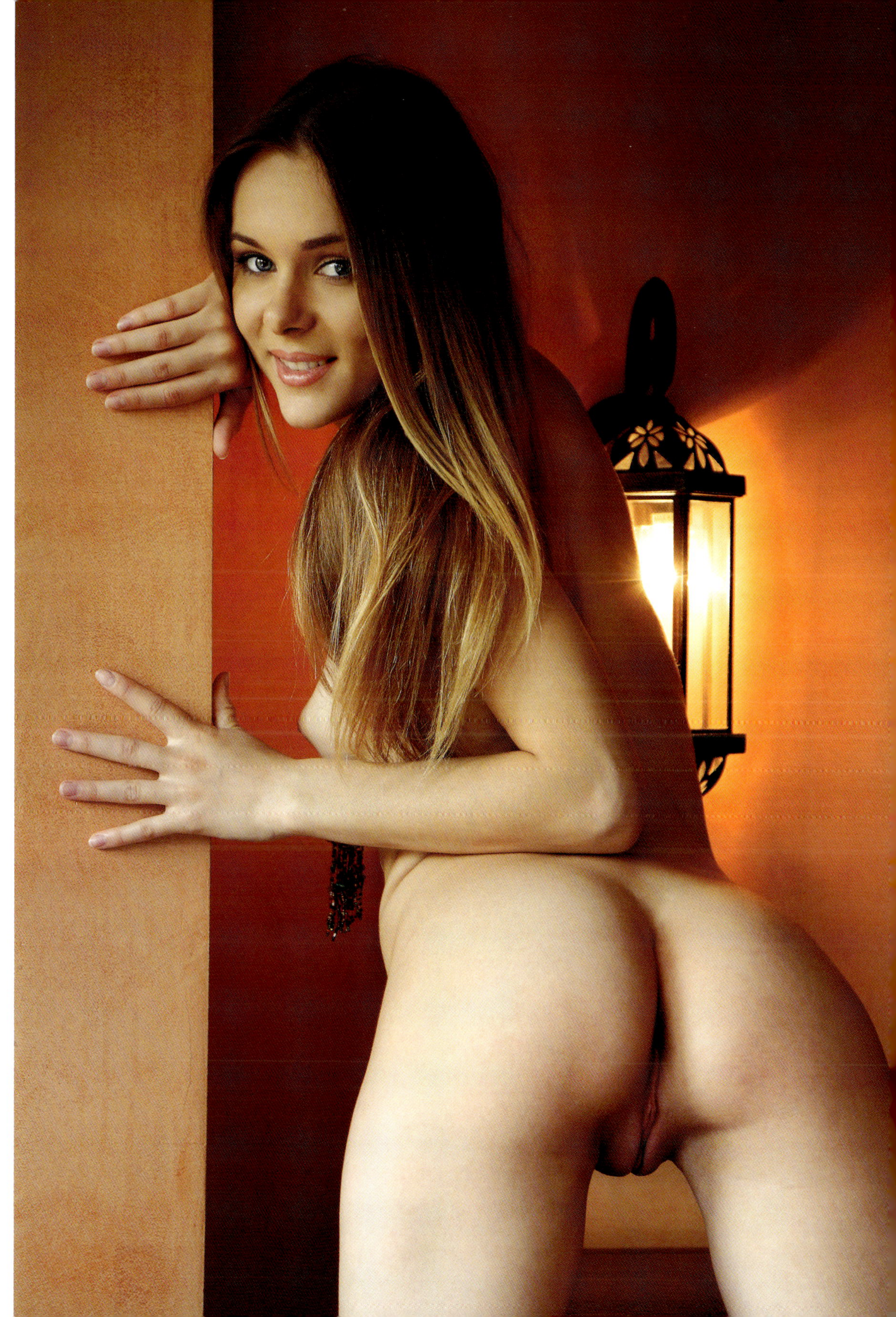

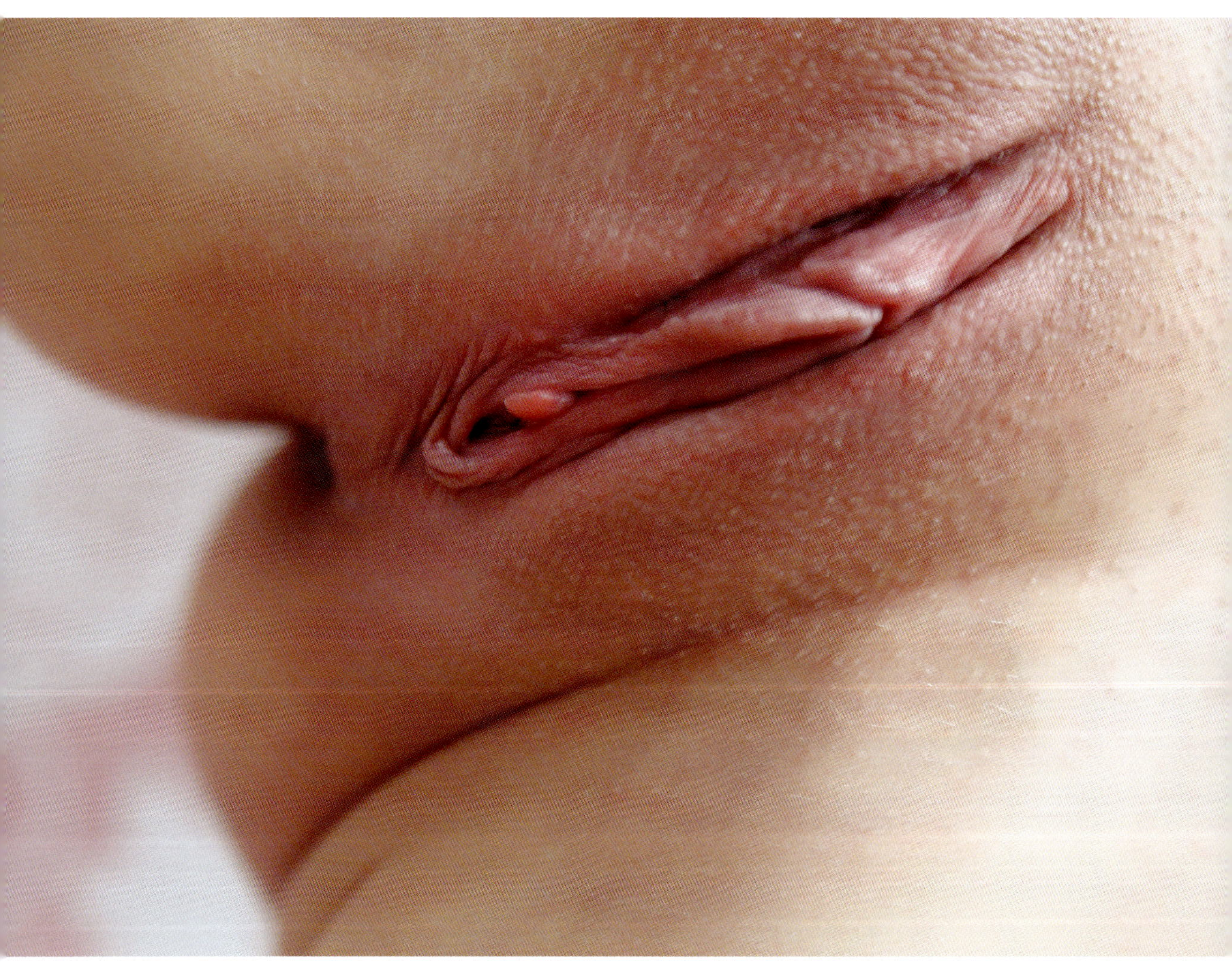

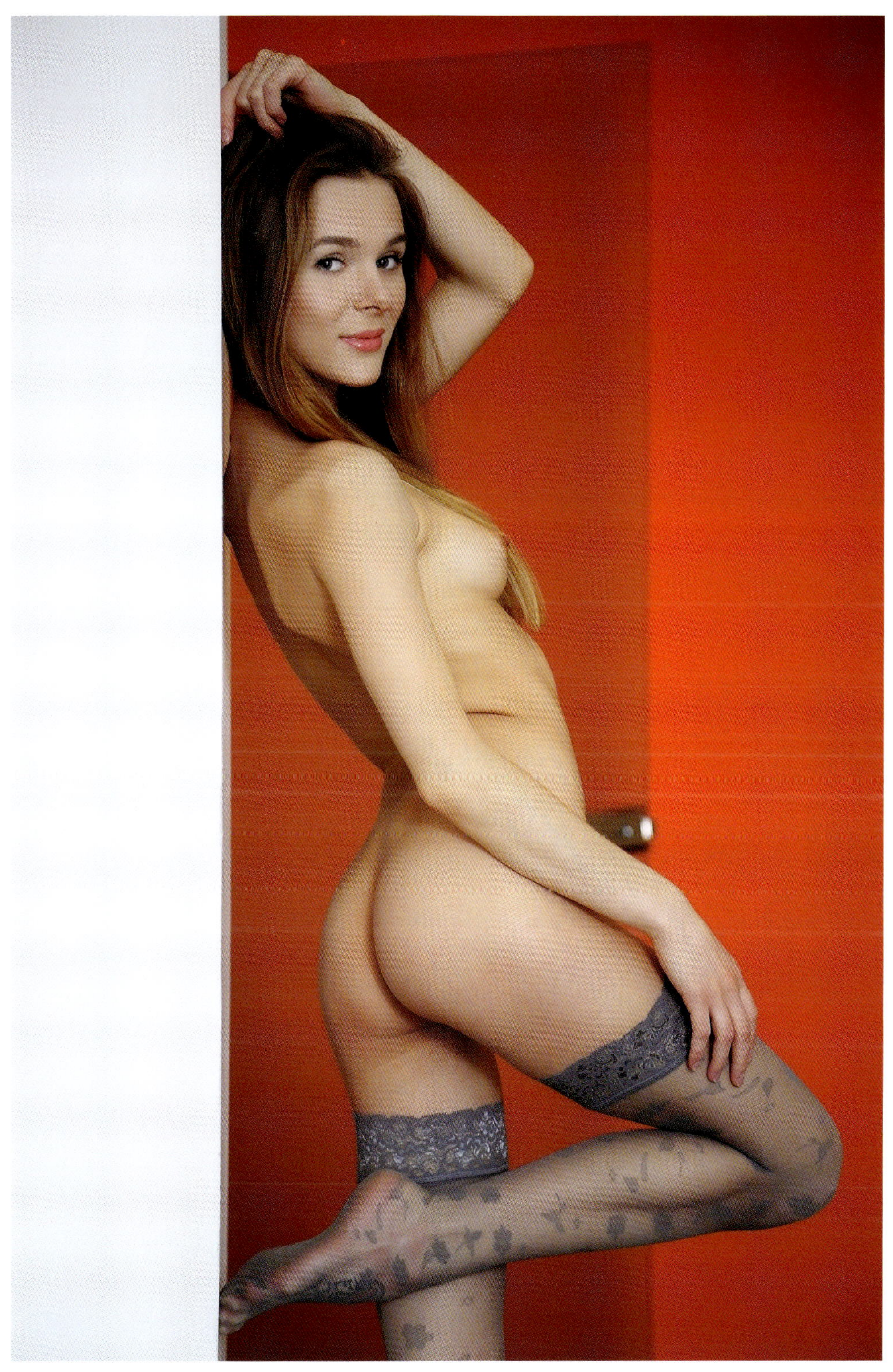

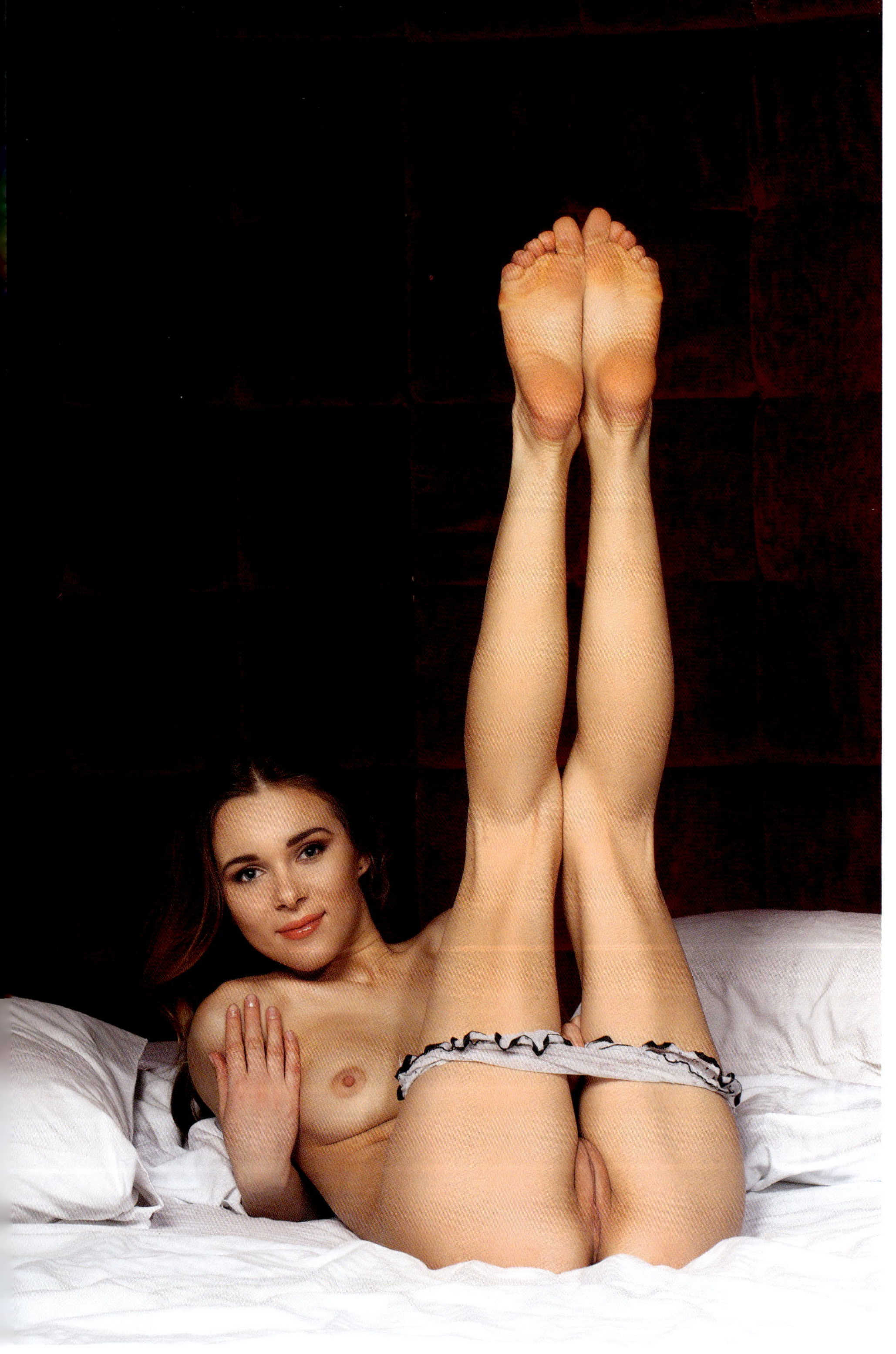

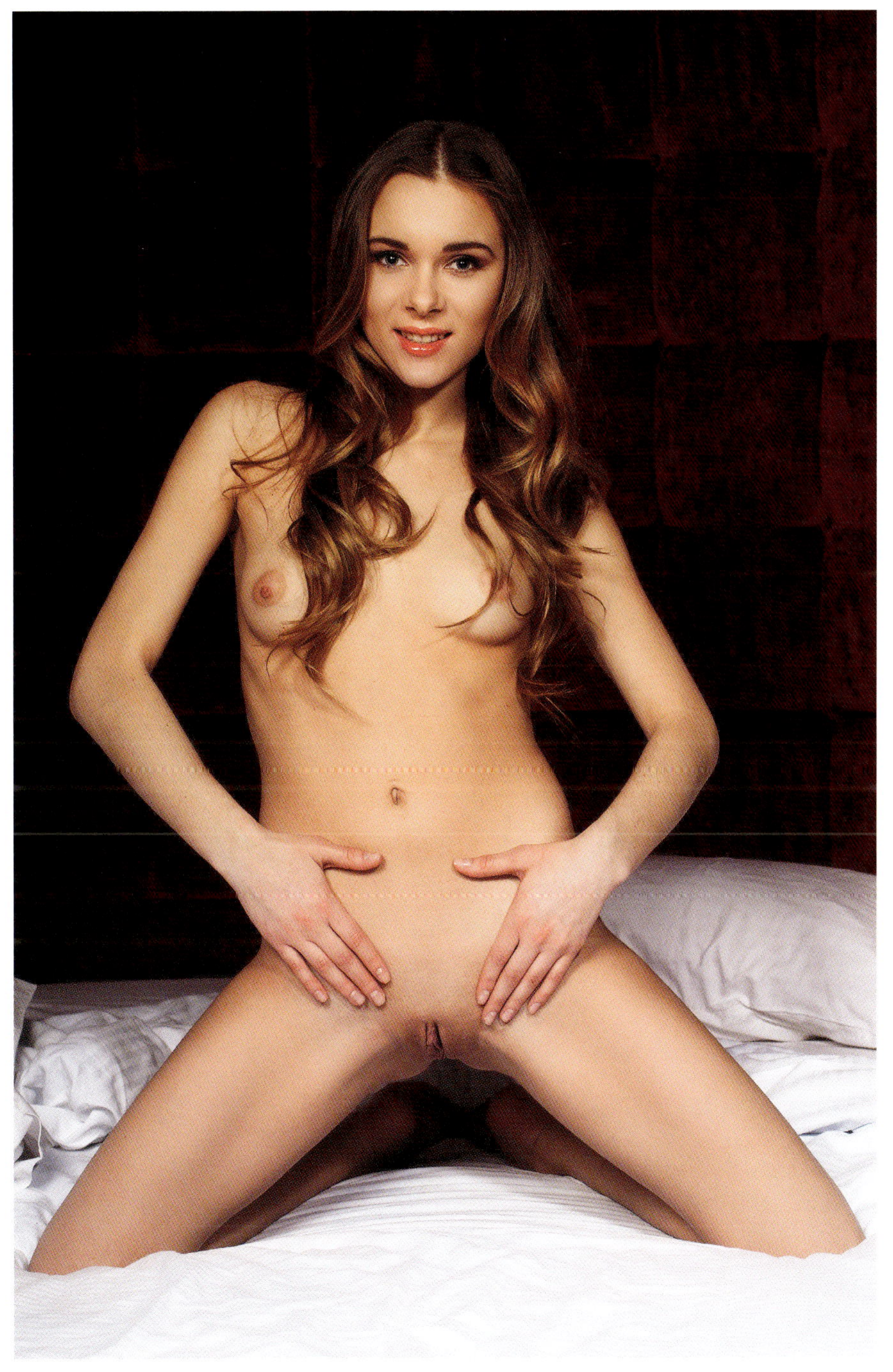

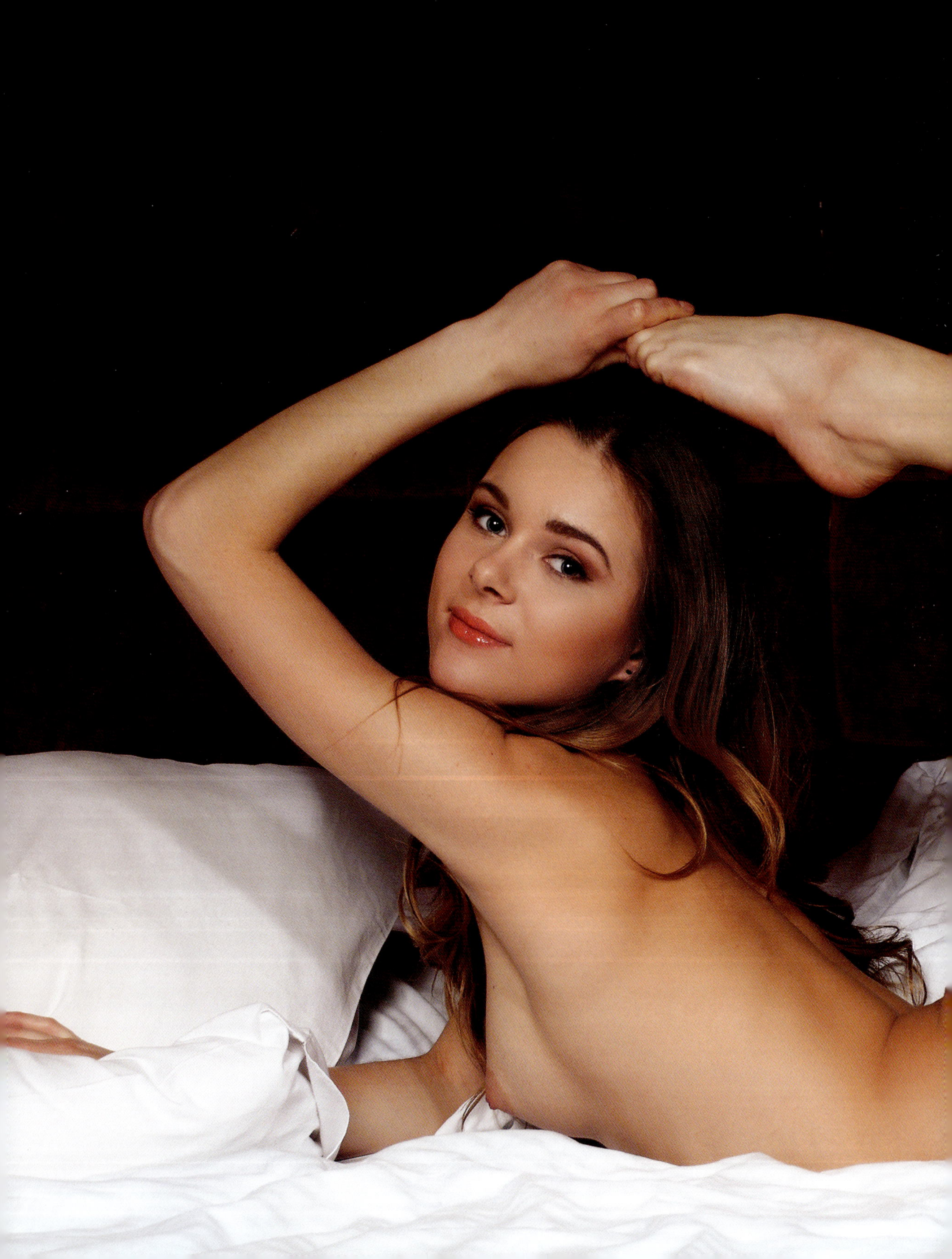

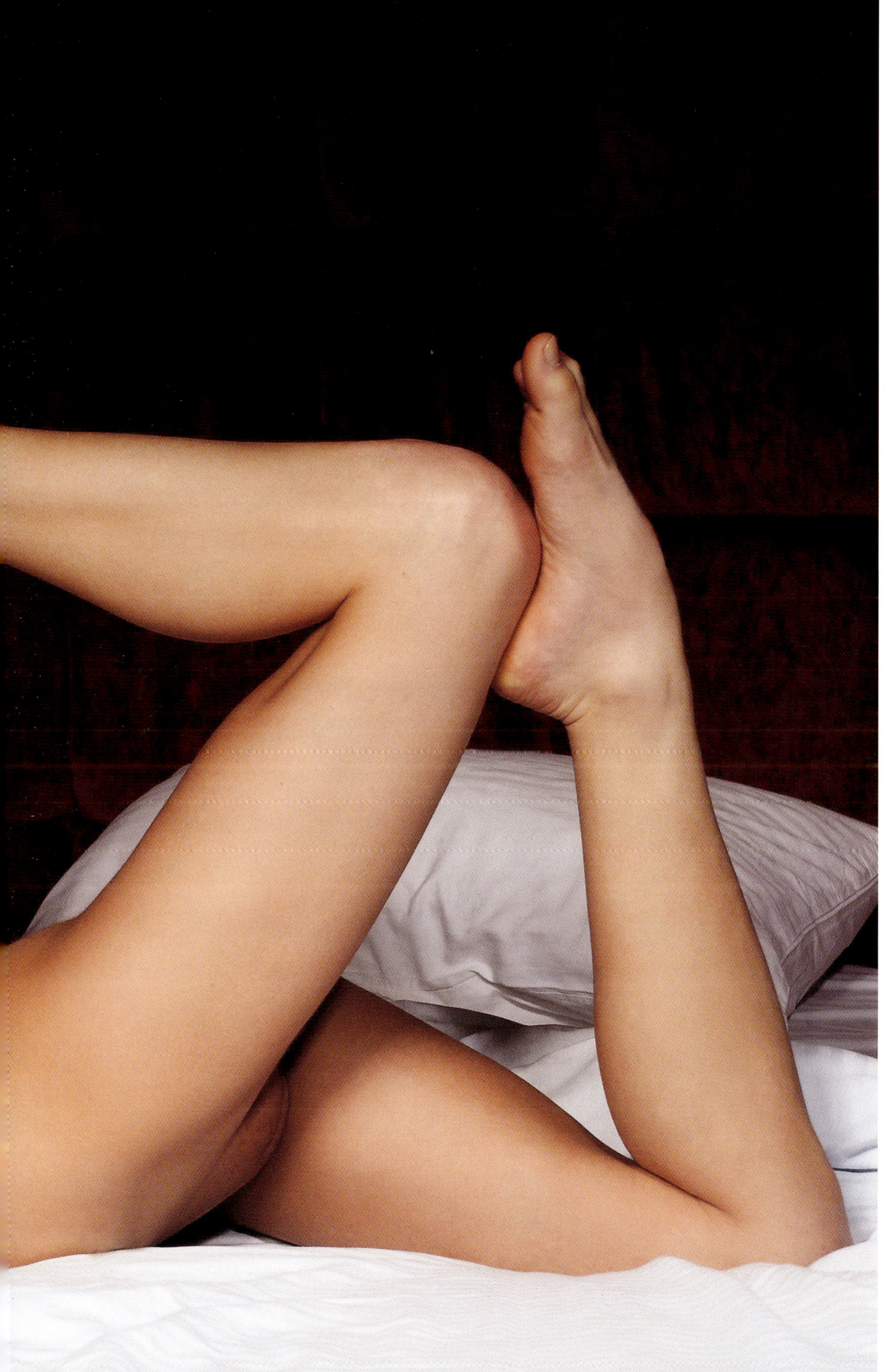

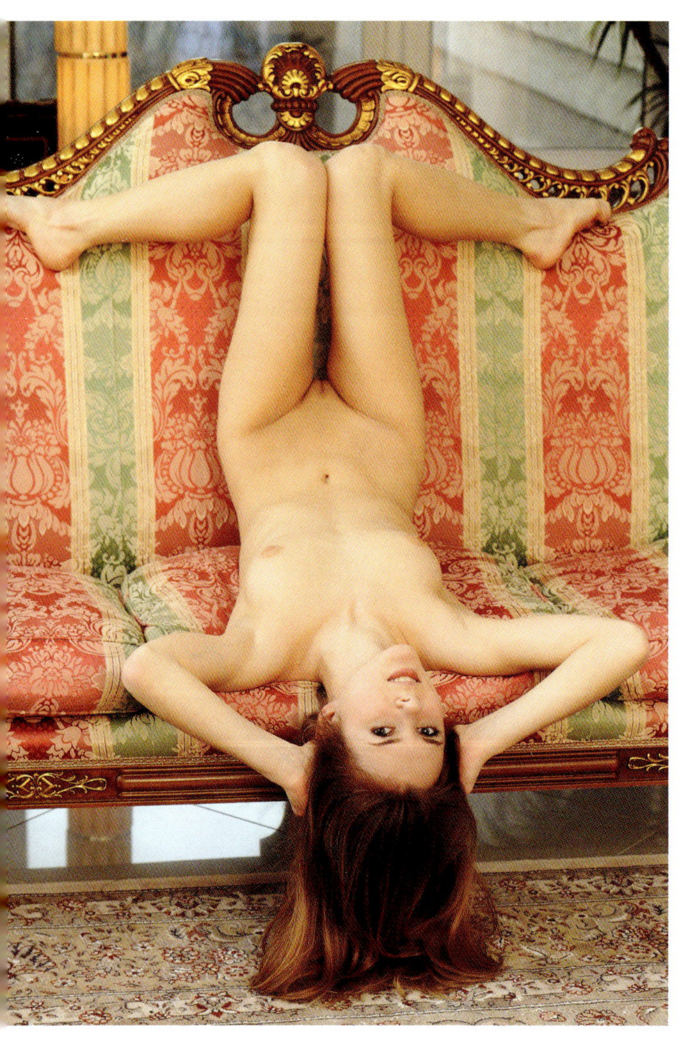
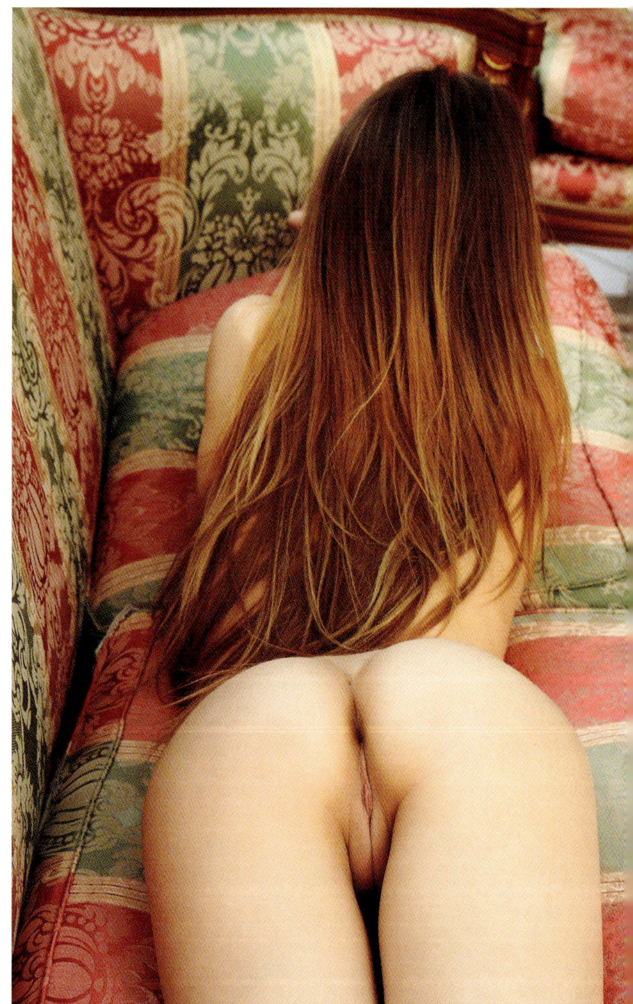

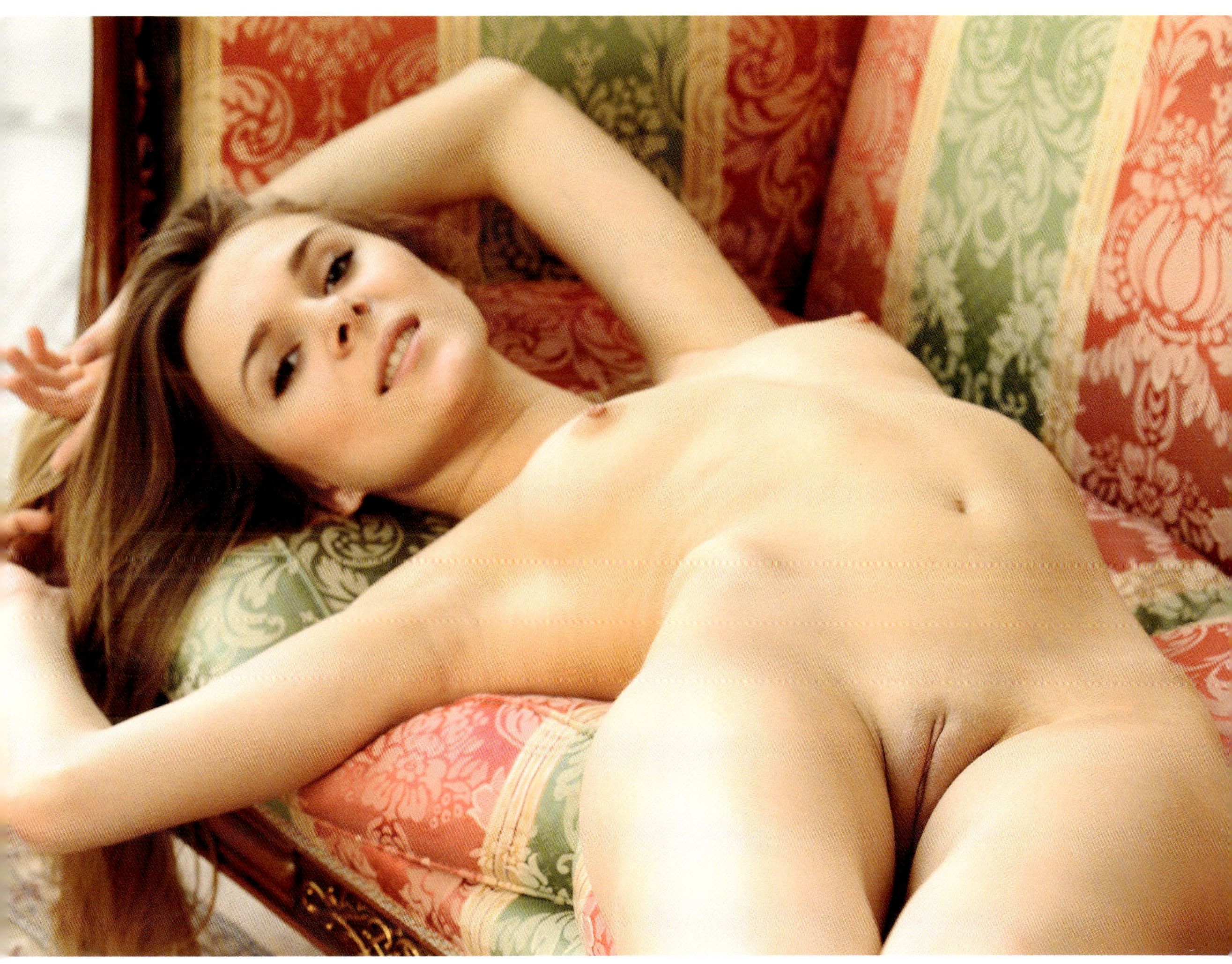

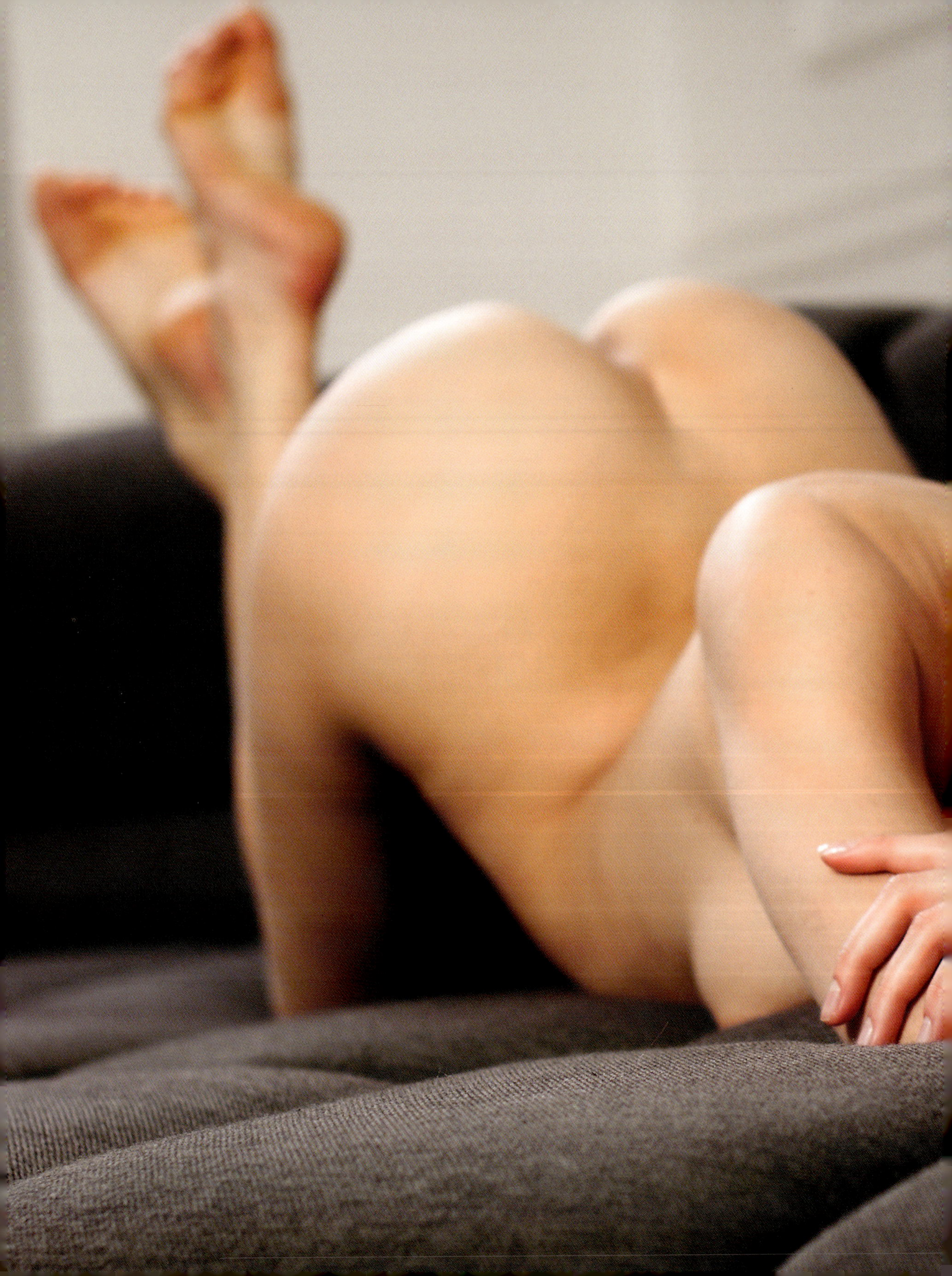

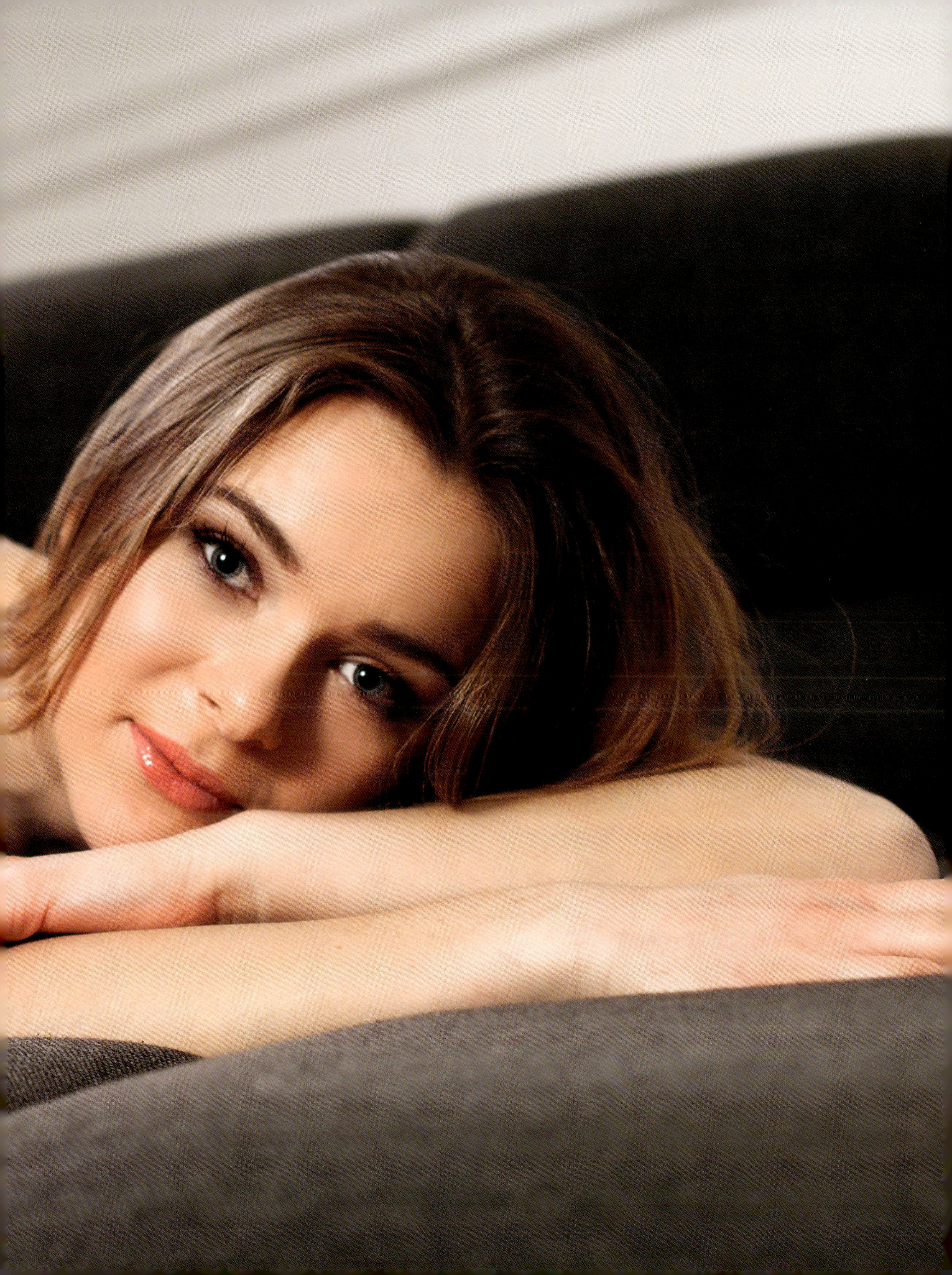

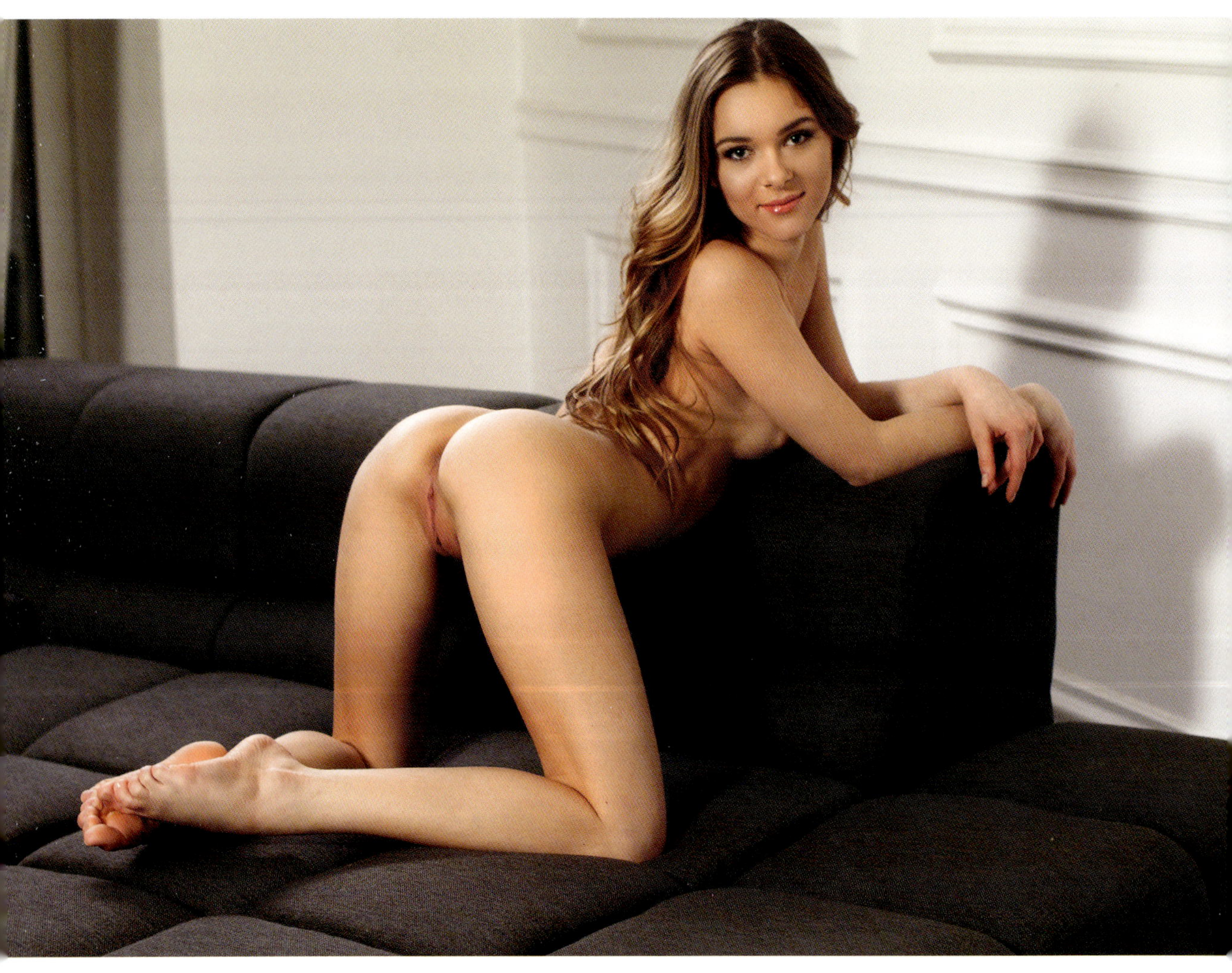

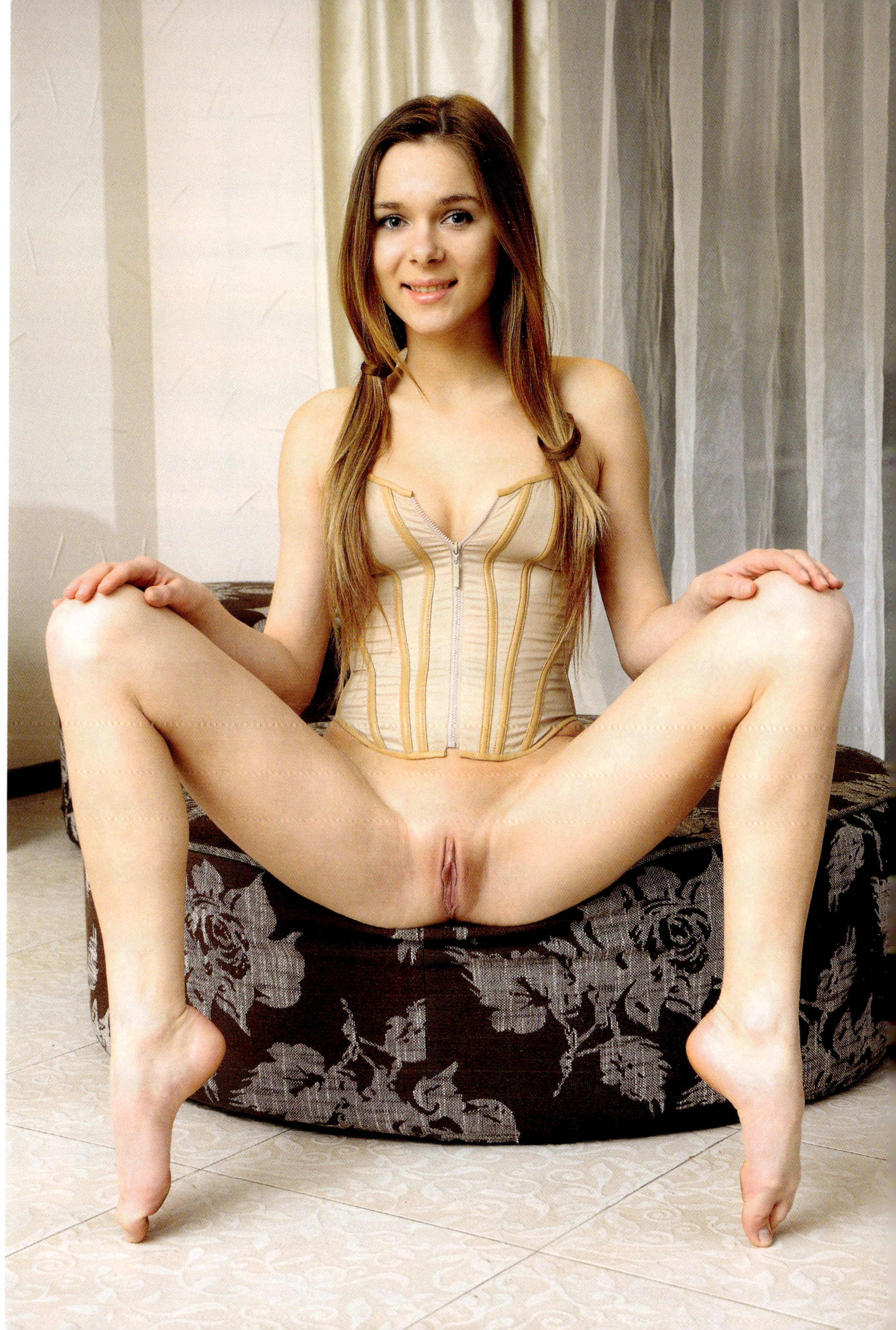

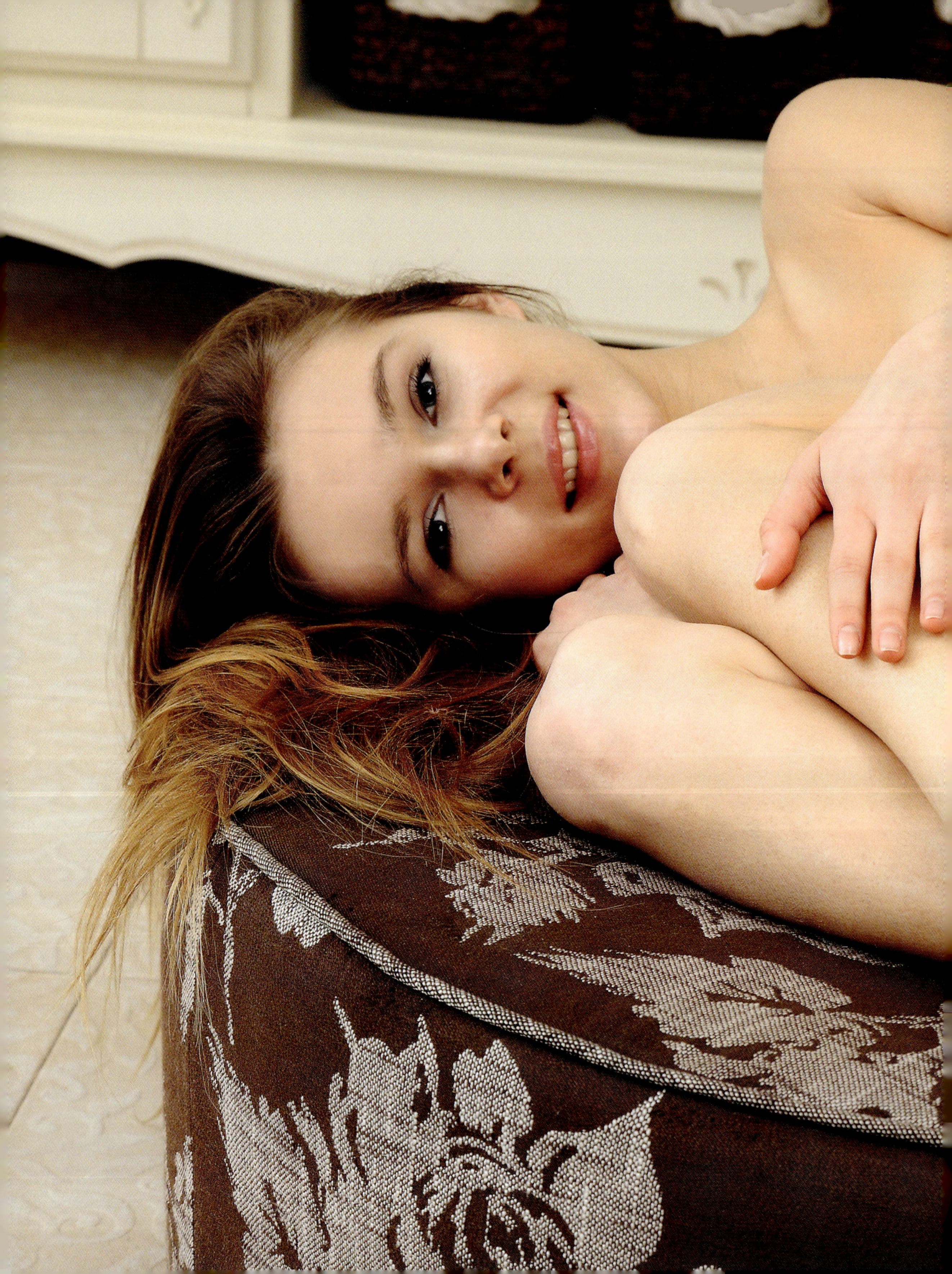

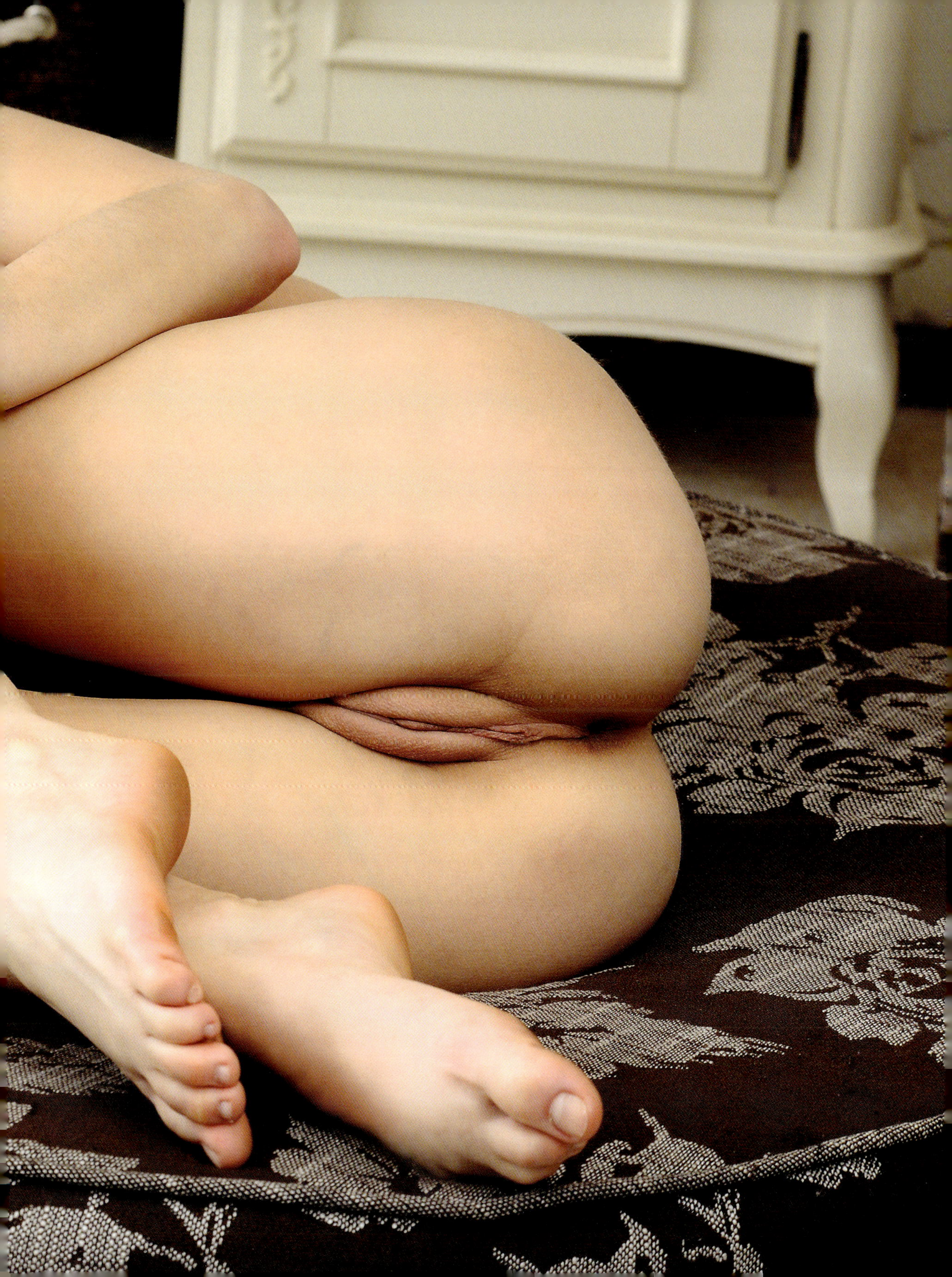

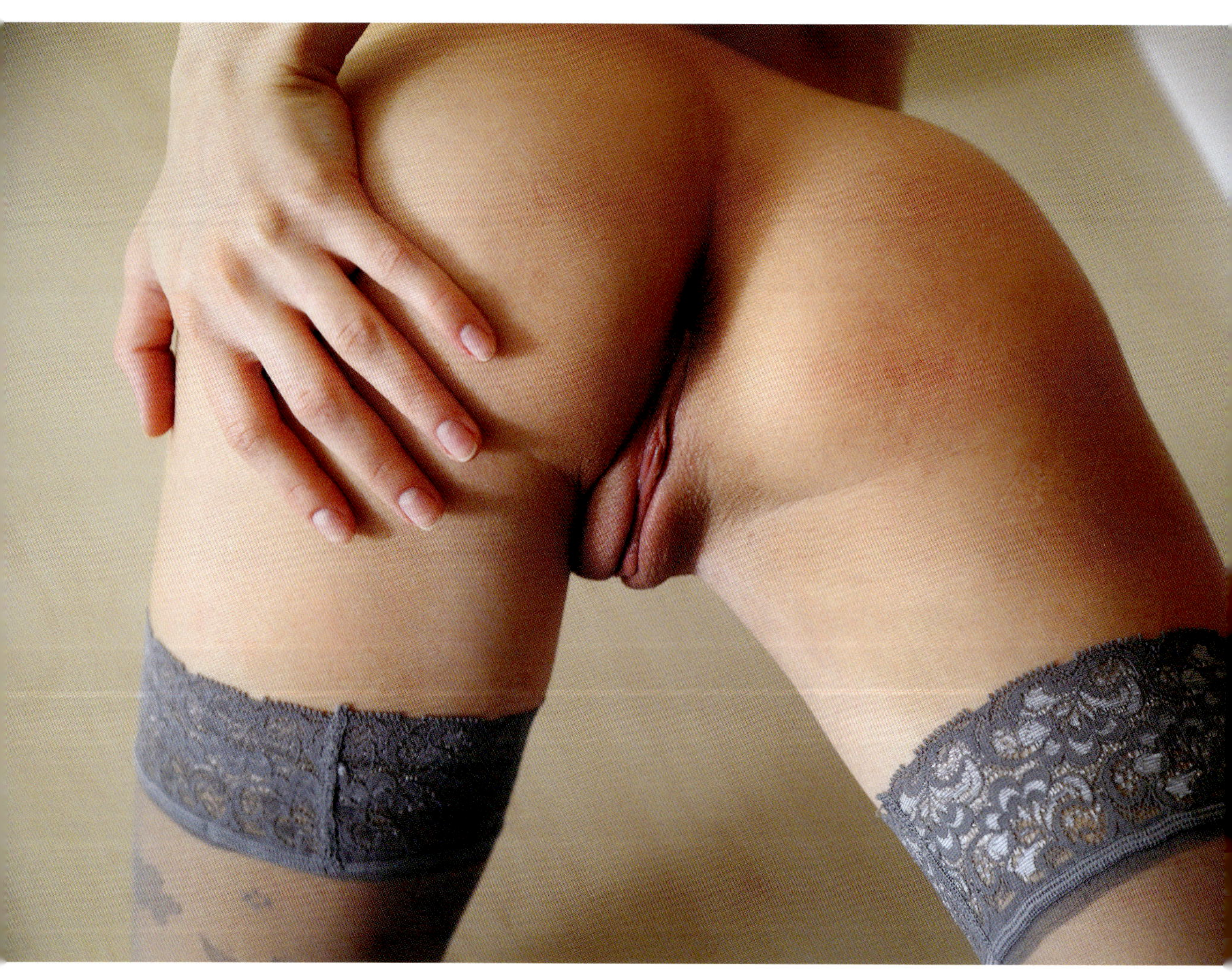

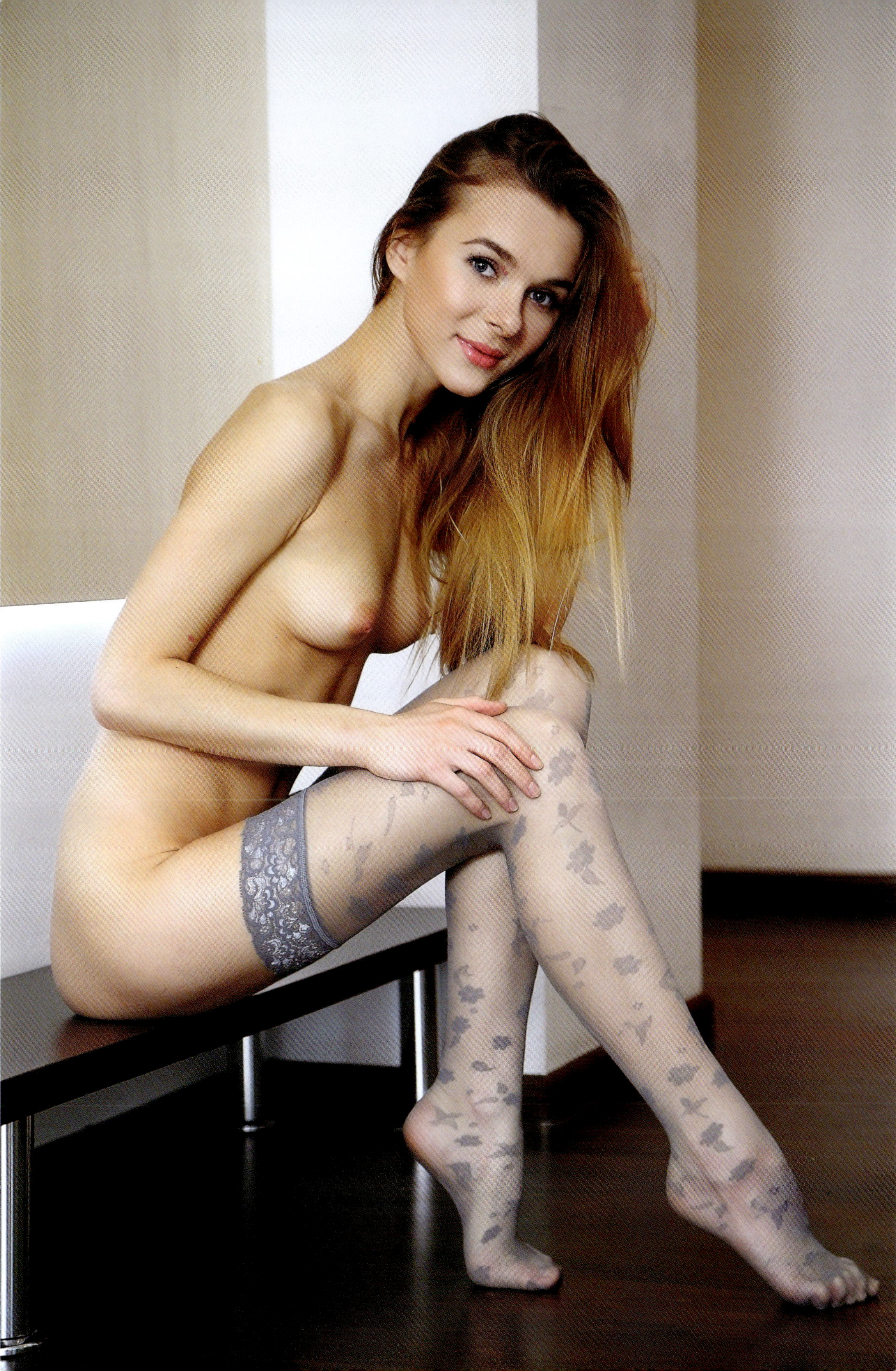

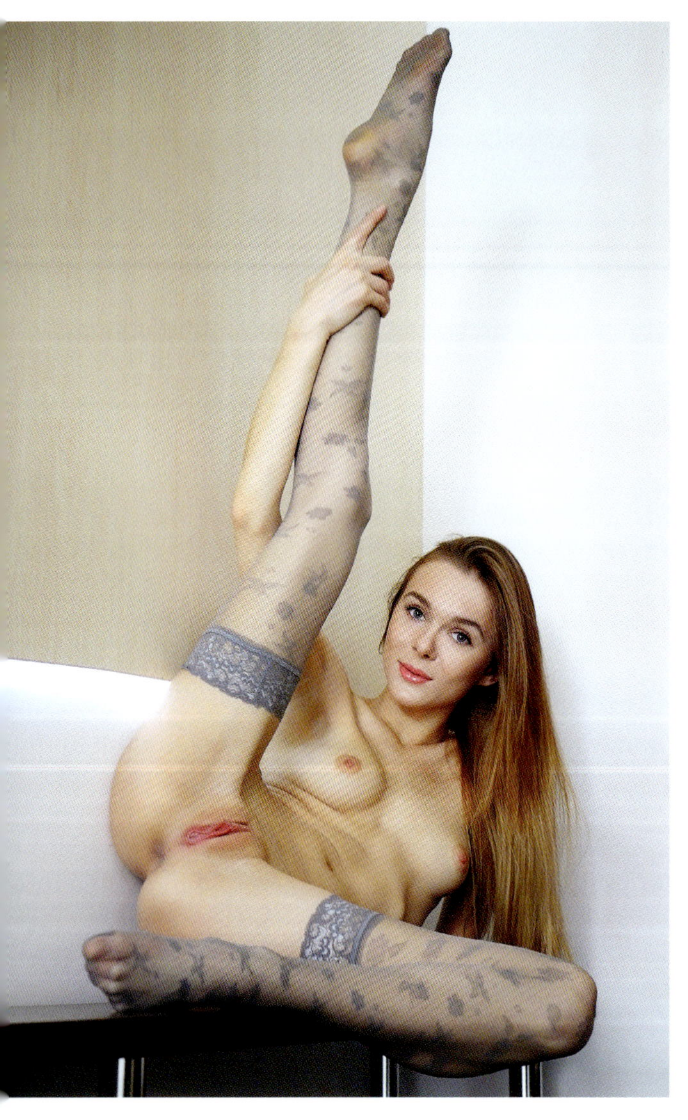

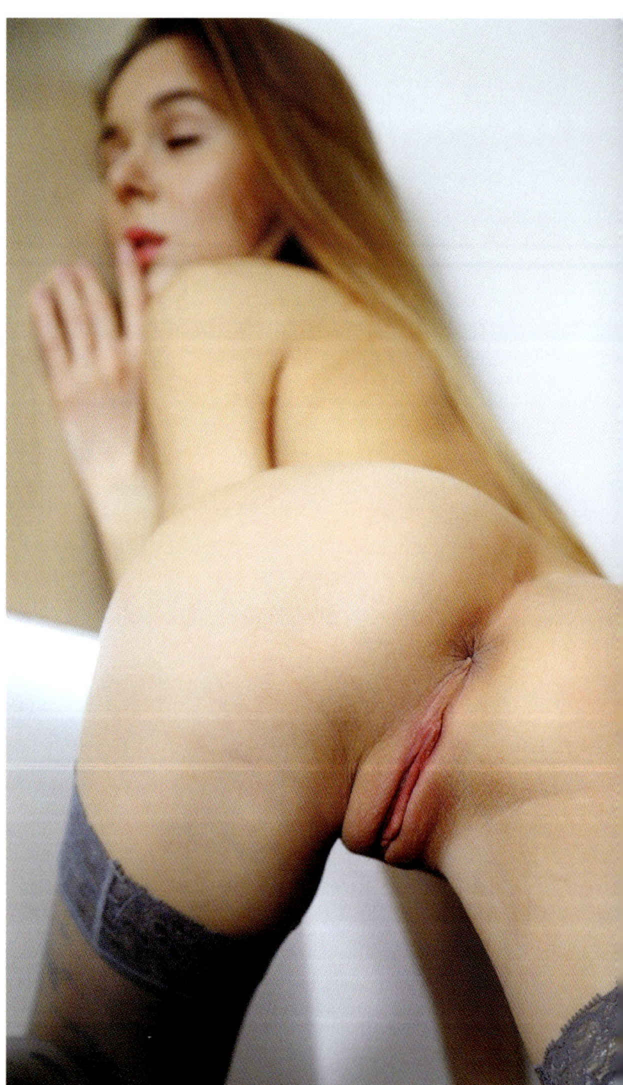

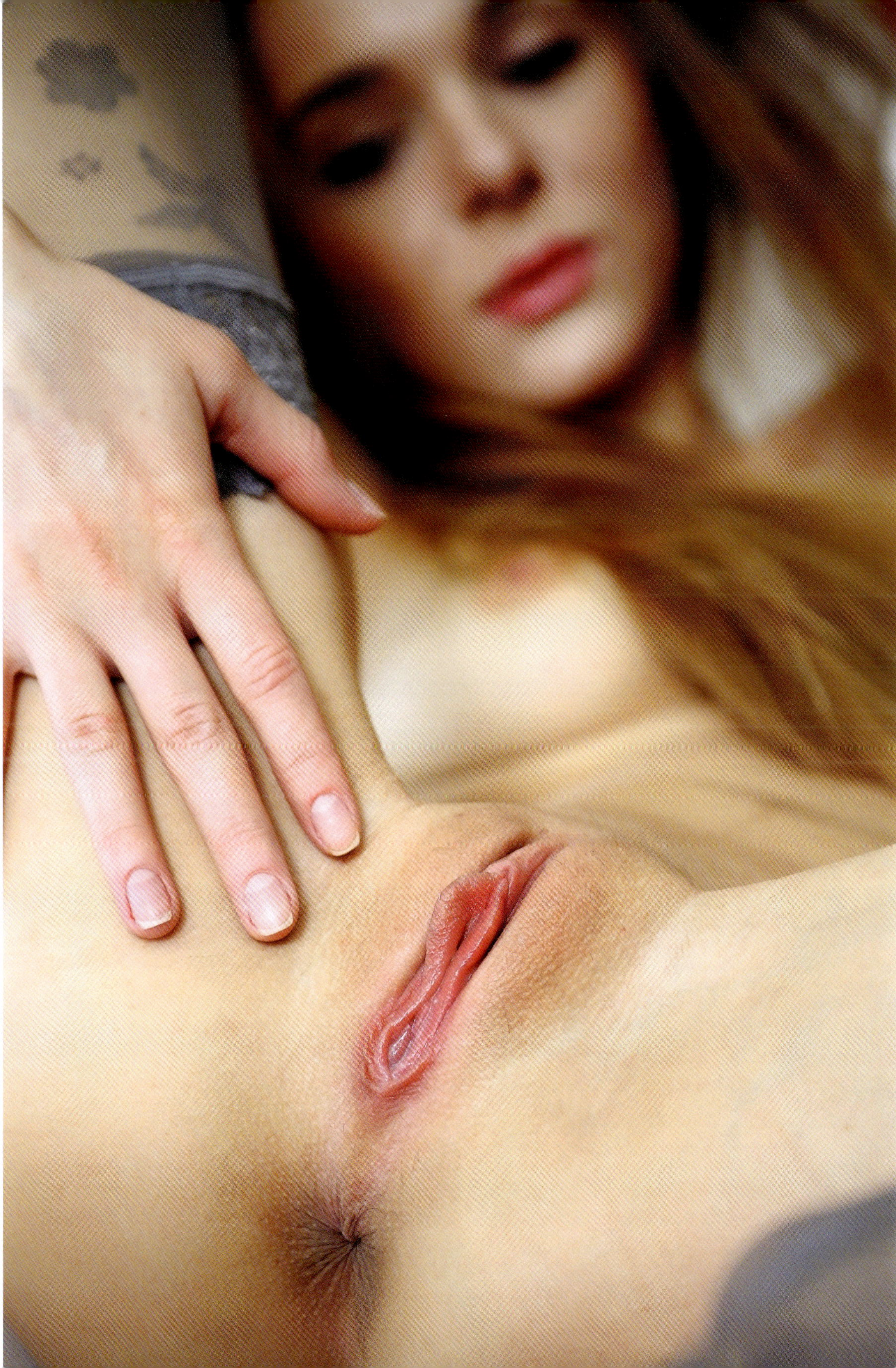

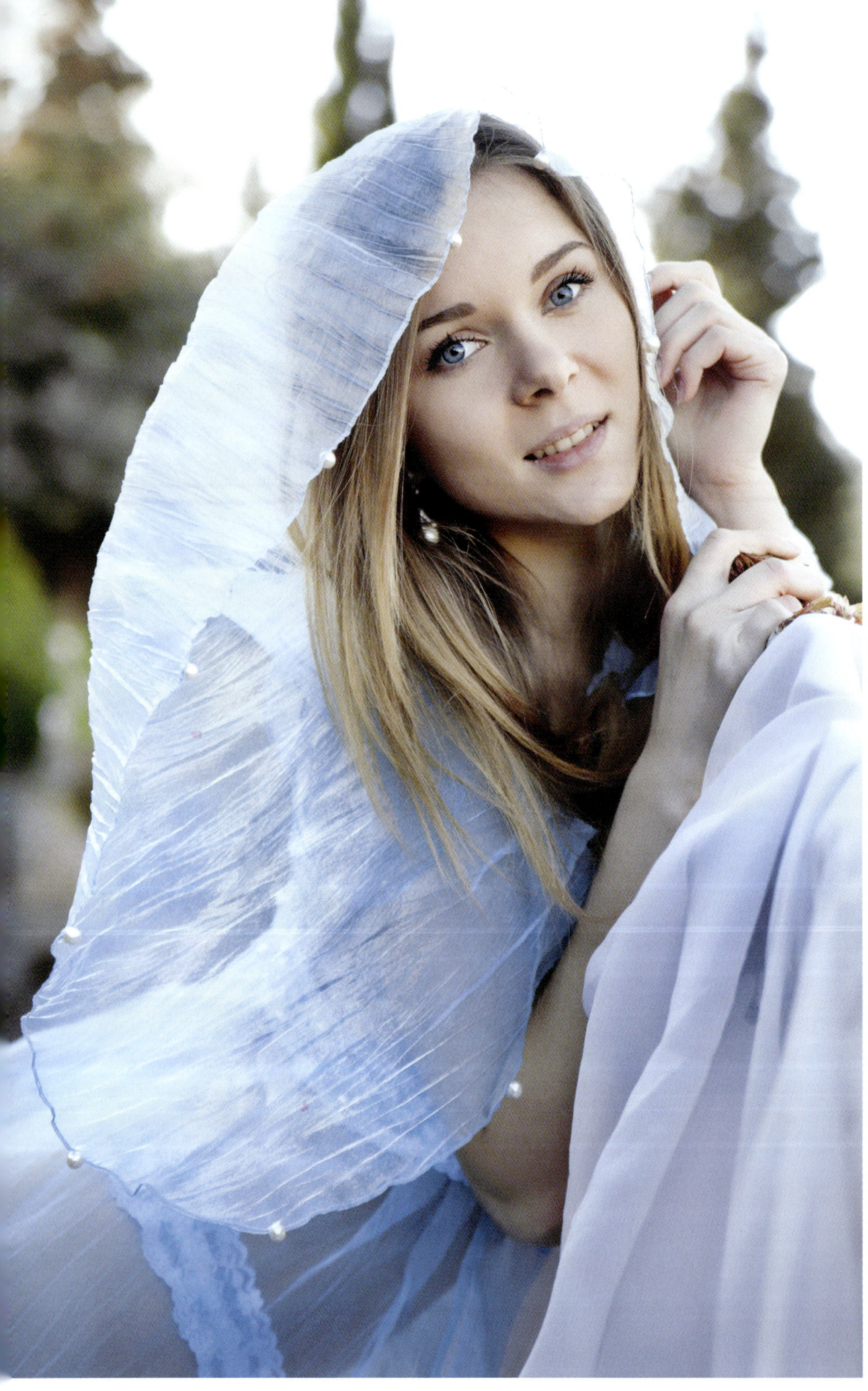

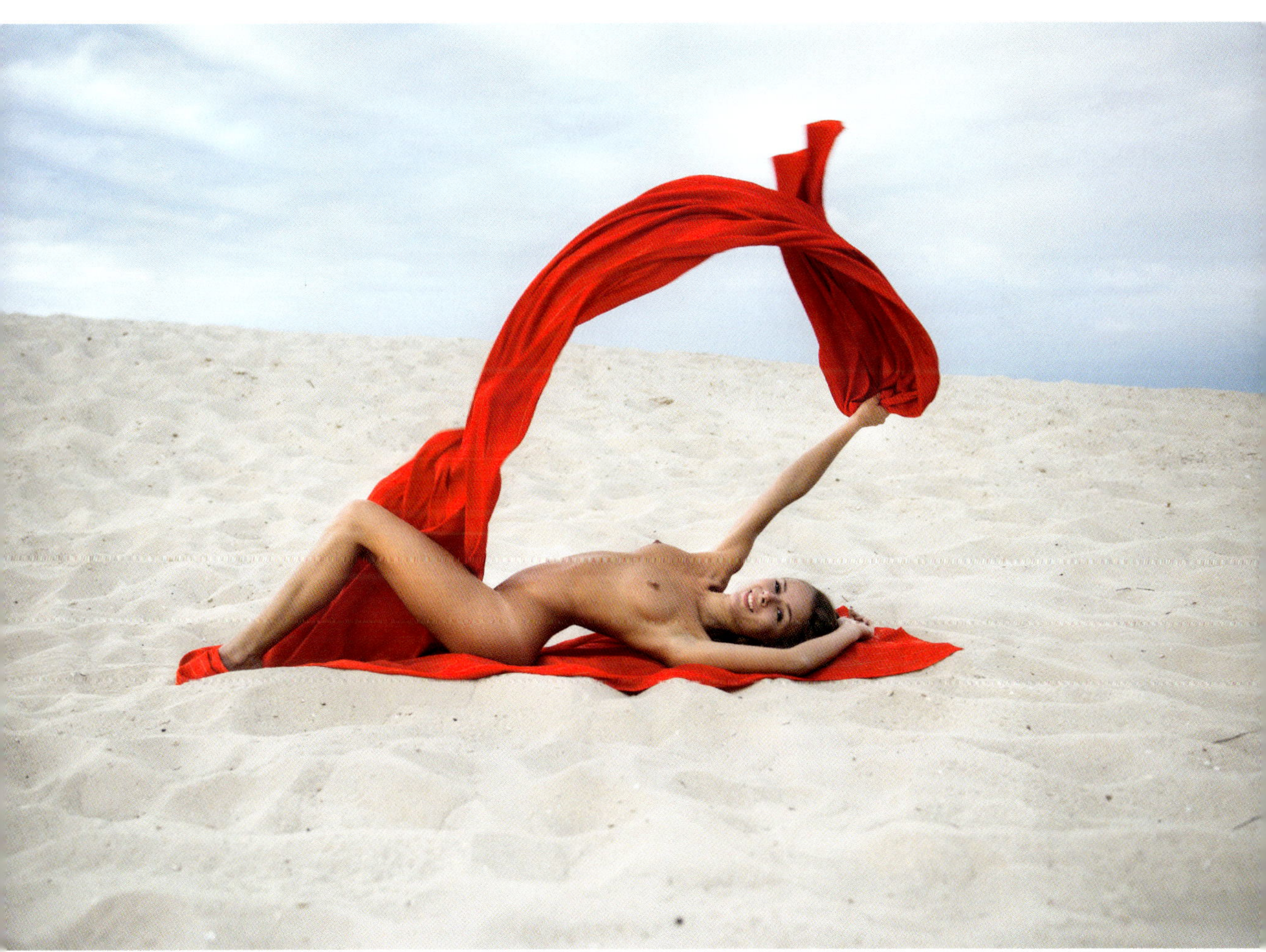

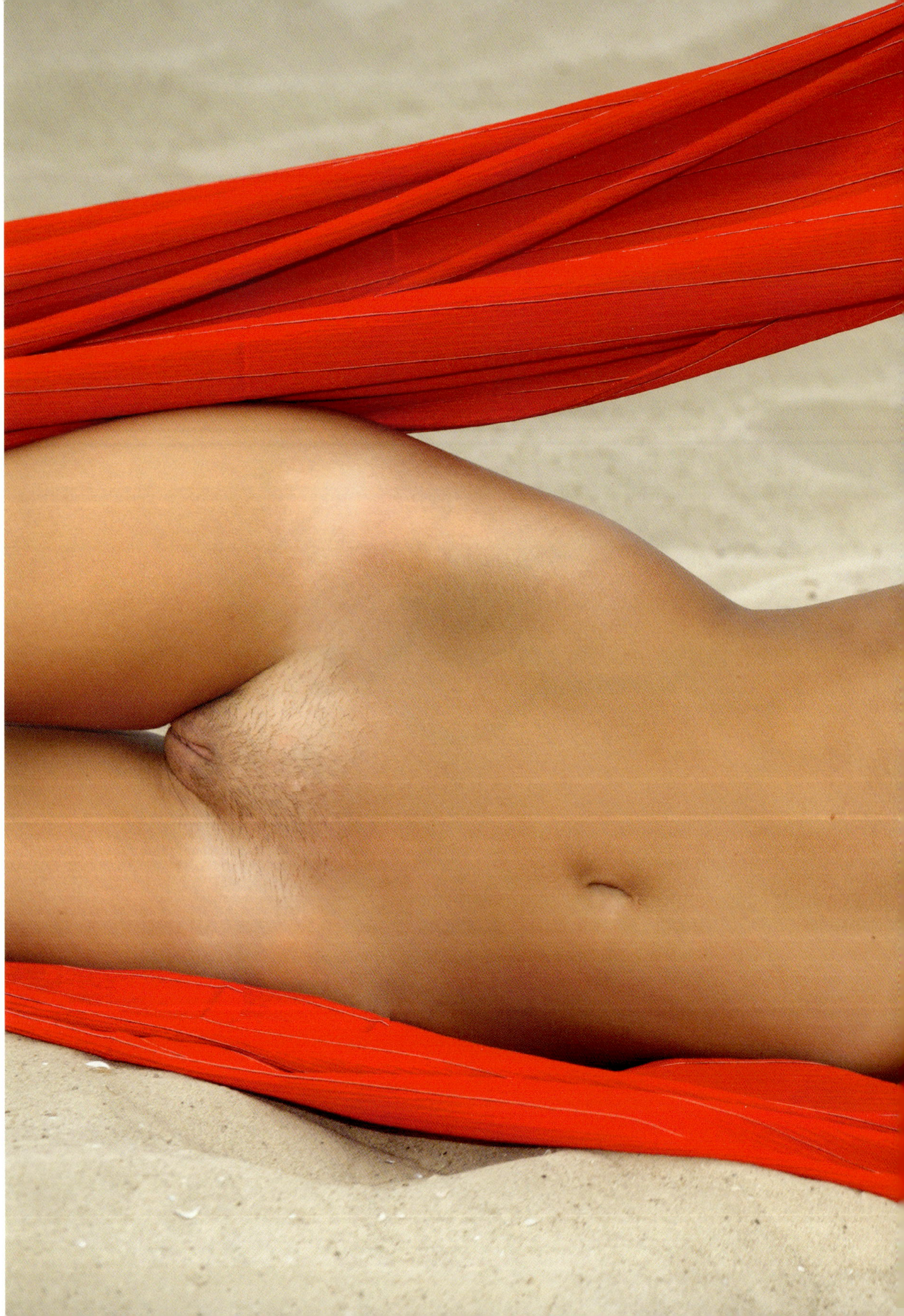

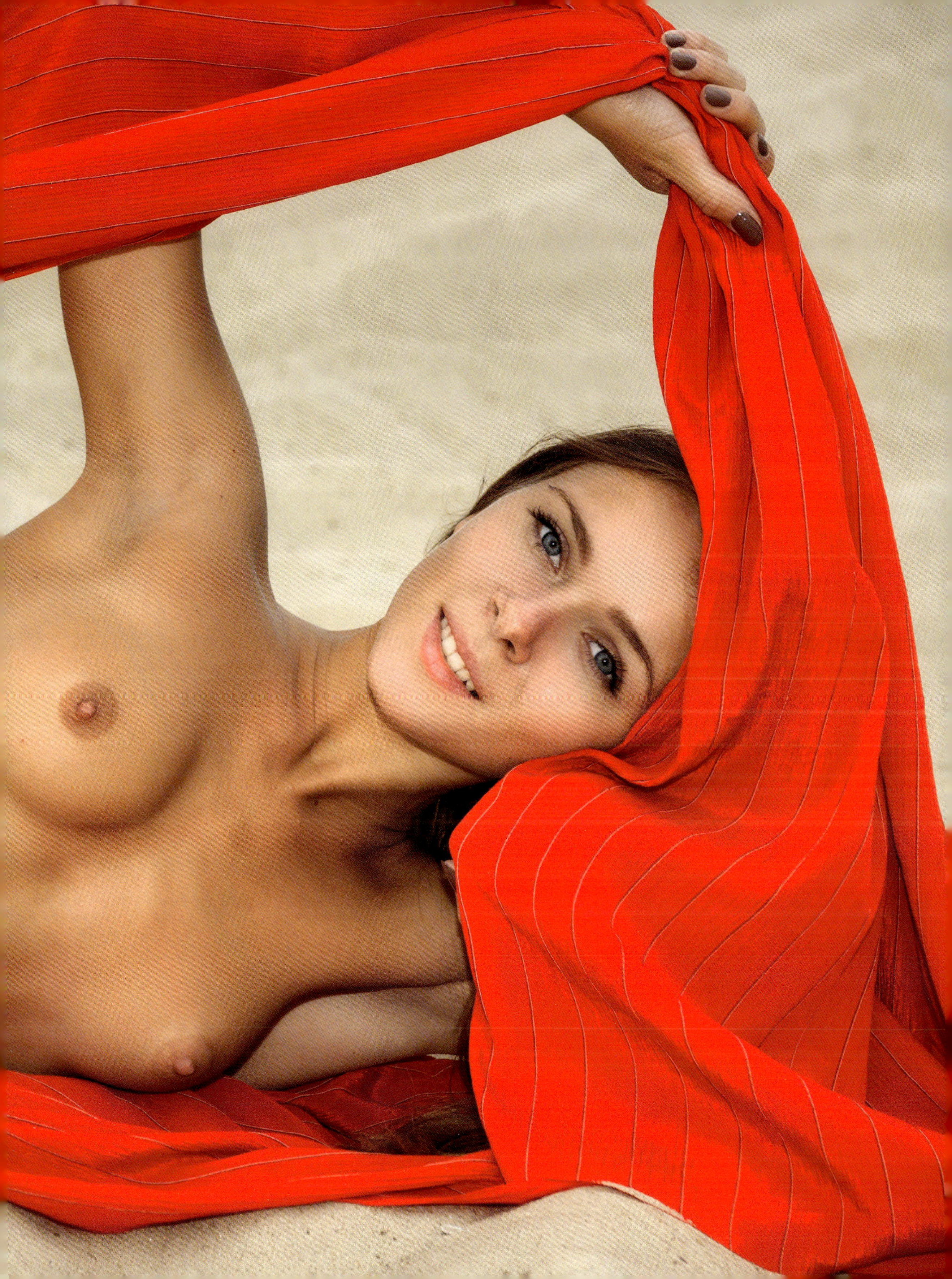

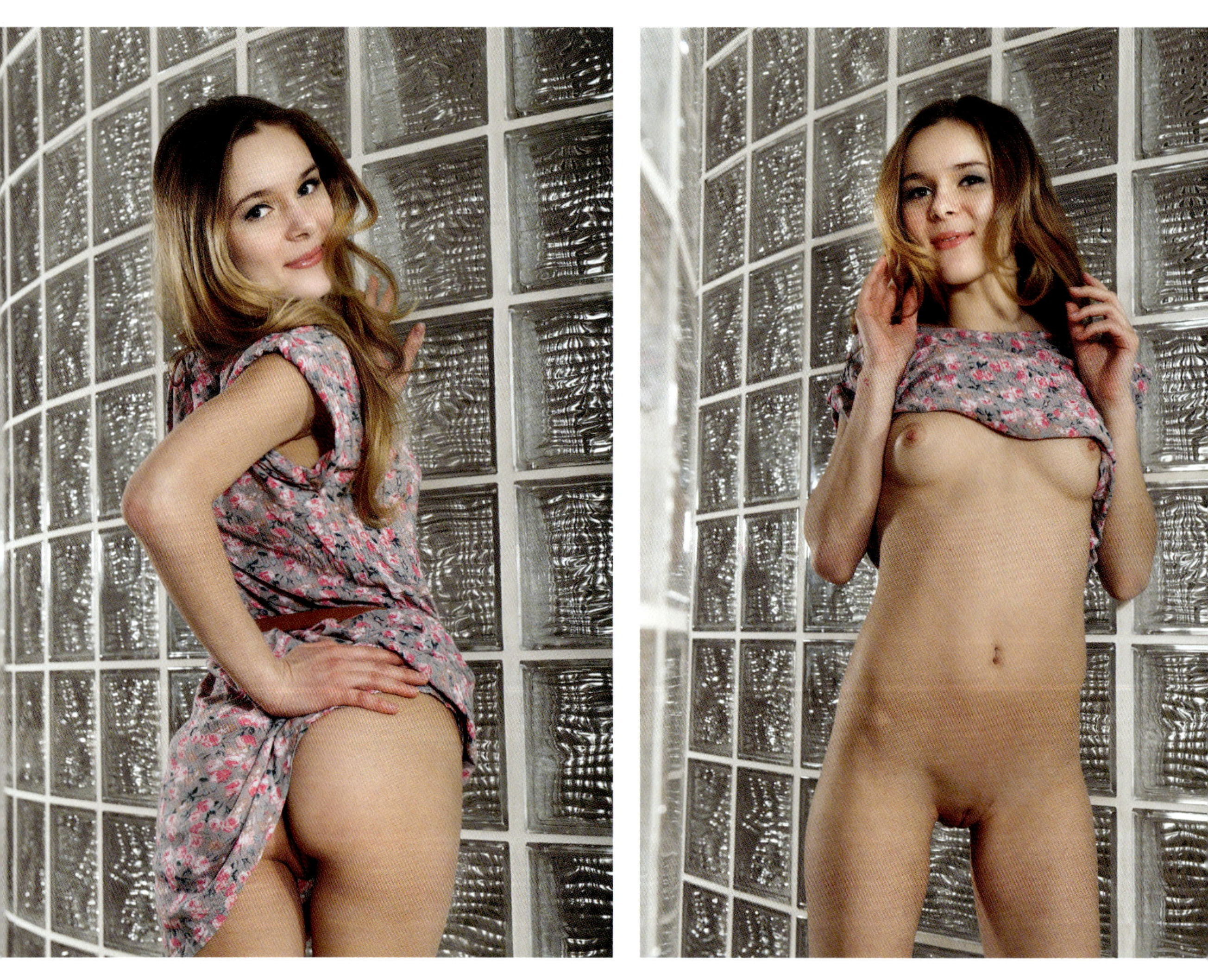

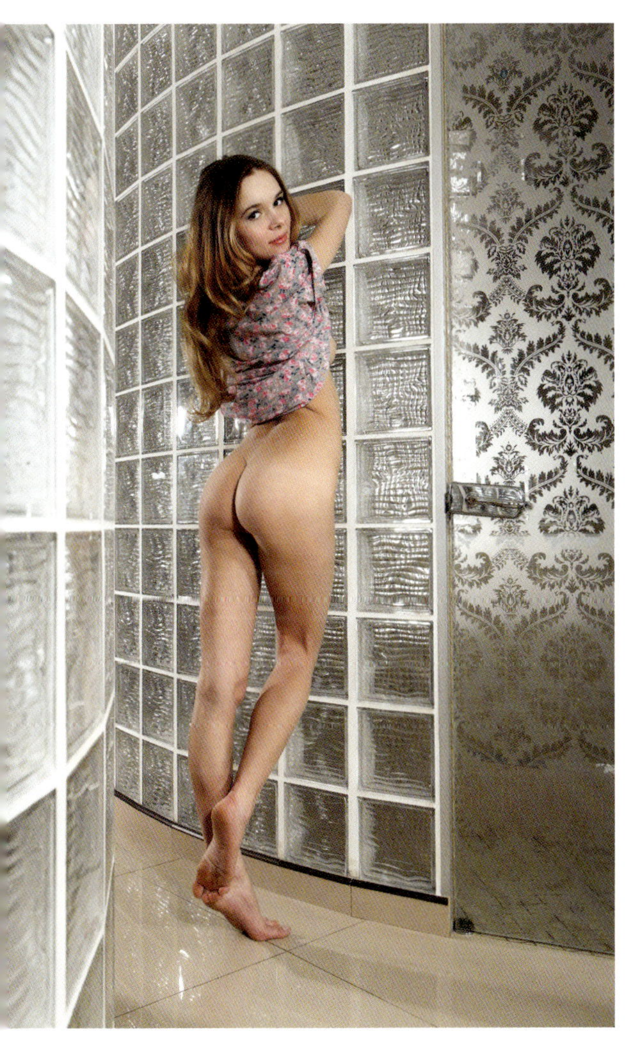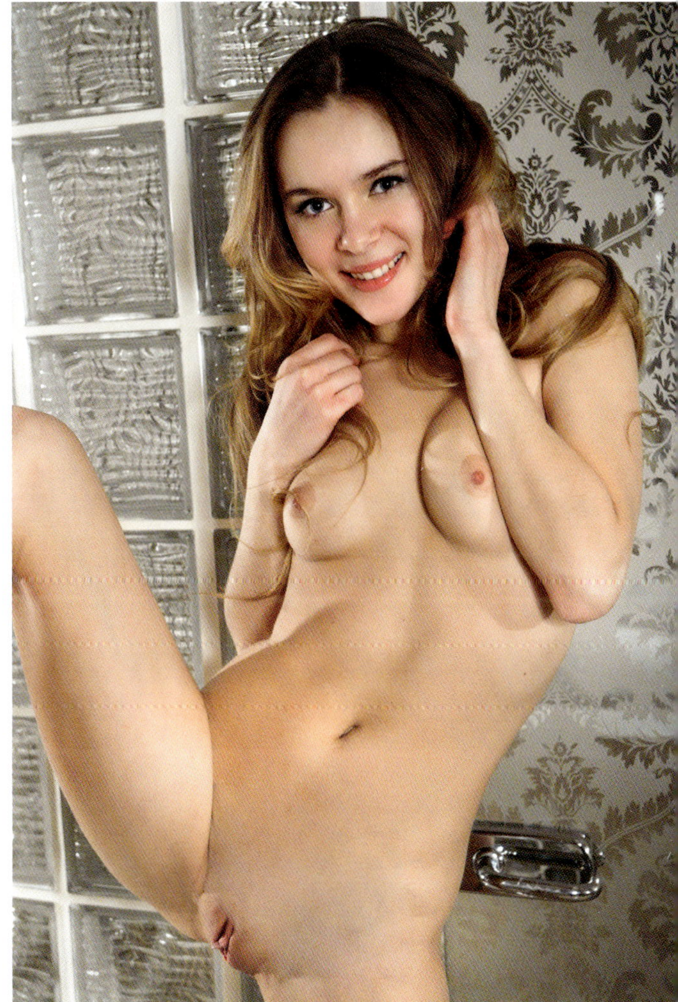

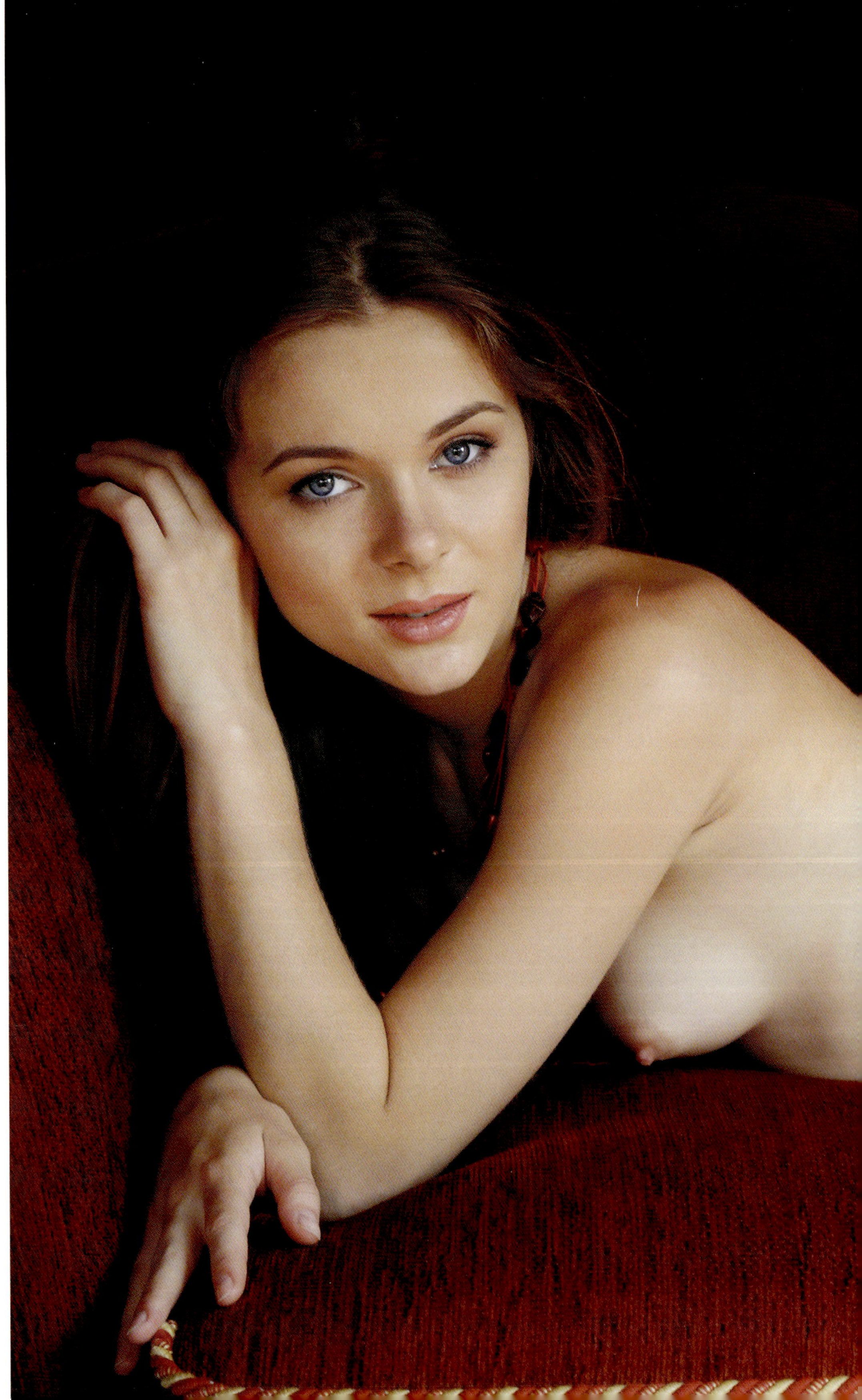

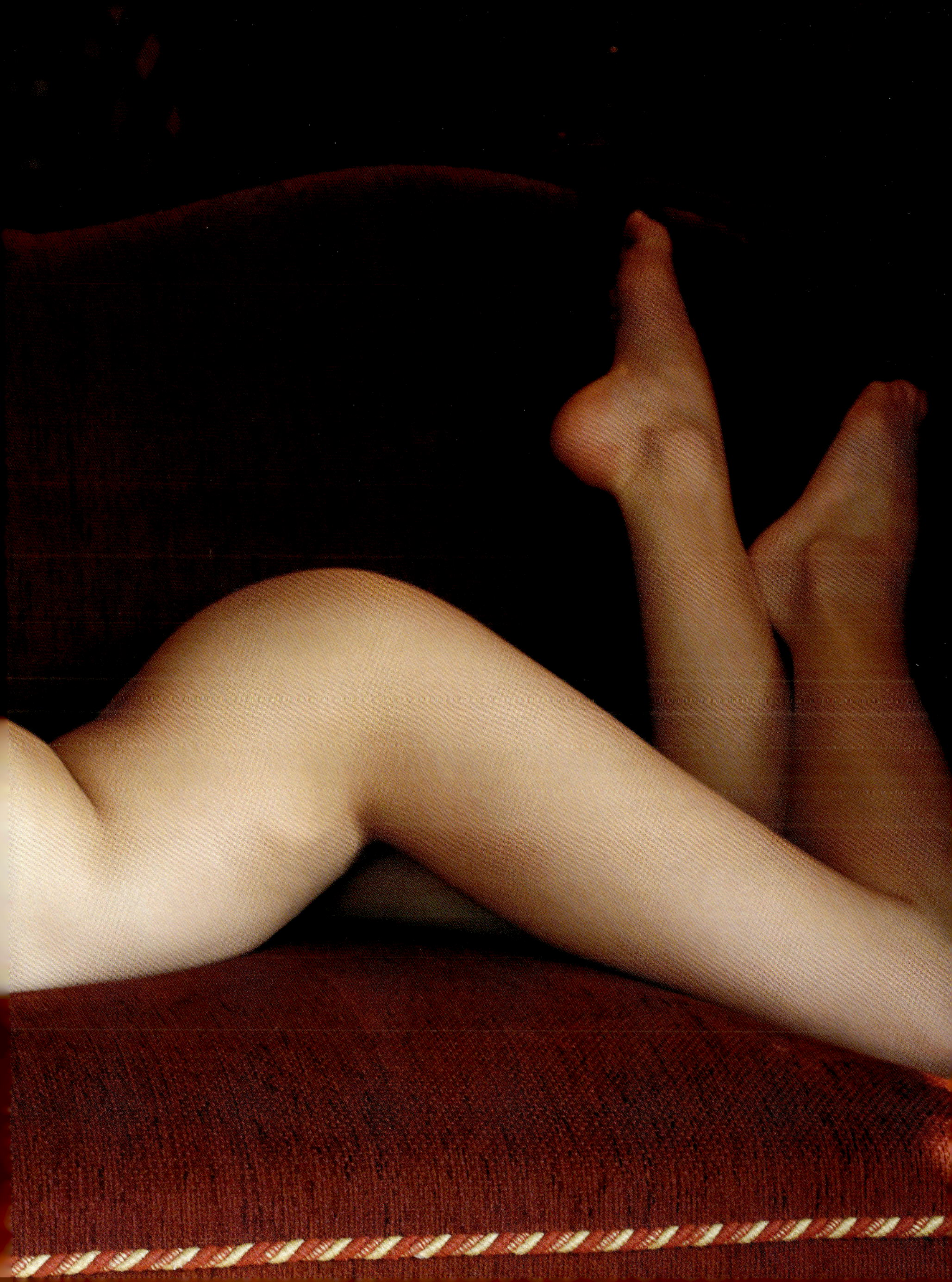

COLLECT THEM ALL: OUR MOST BEAUTIFUL

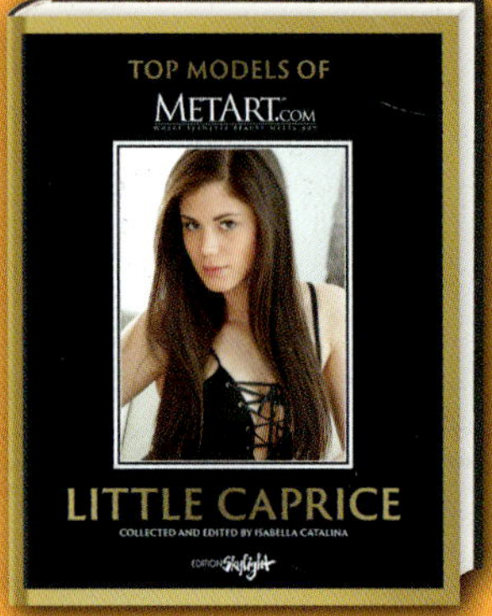

ISBN 978-3-03766-659-3

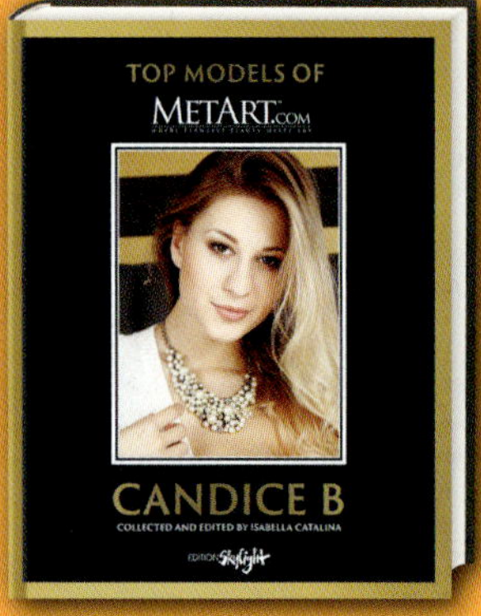

ISBN 978-3-03766-660-9

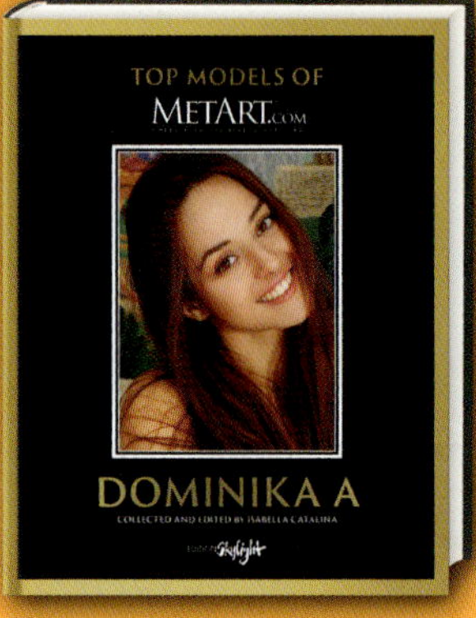

ISBN 978-3-03766-679-1

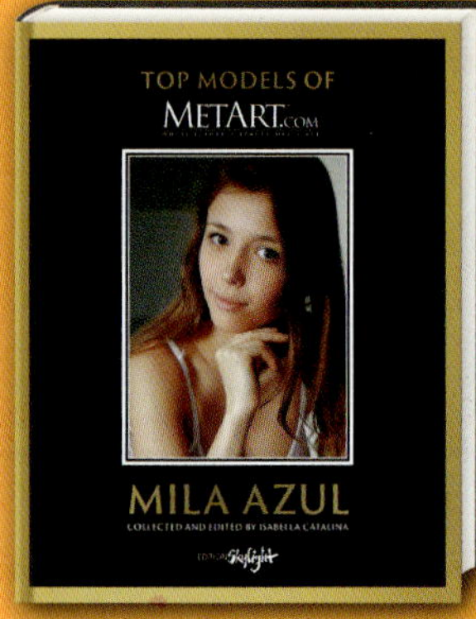

ISBN 978-3-03766-680-7

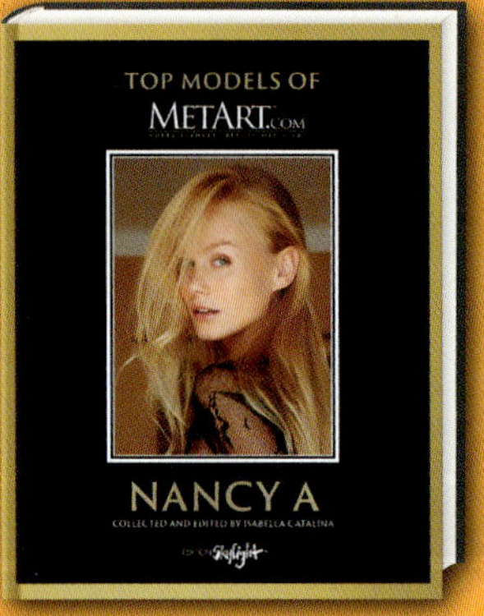

ISBN 978-3-03766-687-6

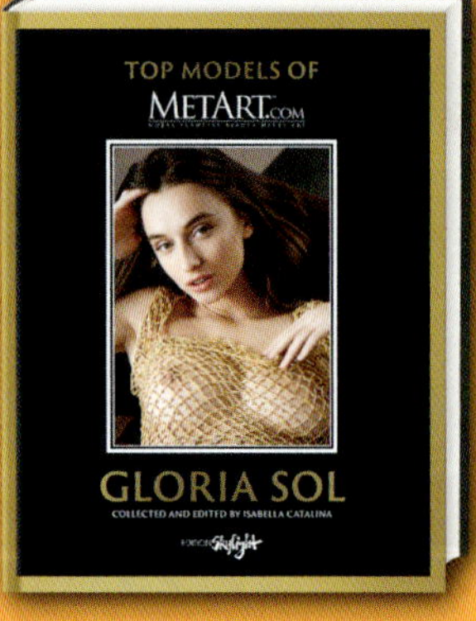

ISBN 978-3-03766-688-3

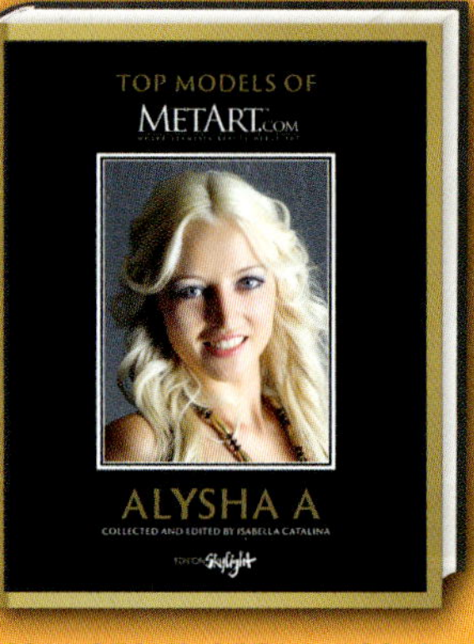

ISBN 978-3-03766-692-0

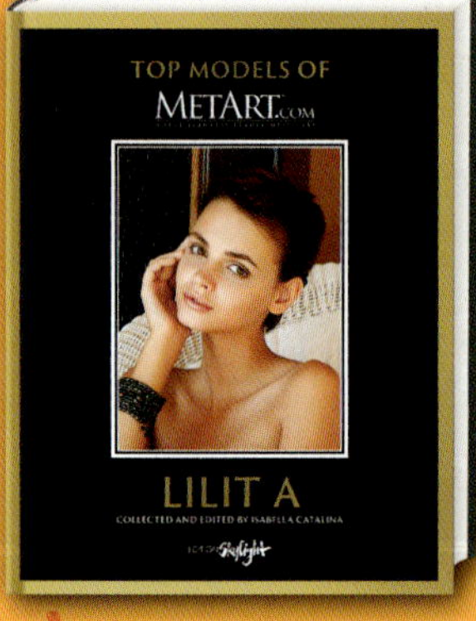

ISBN 978-3-03766-693-7

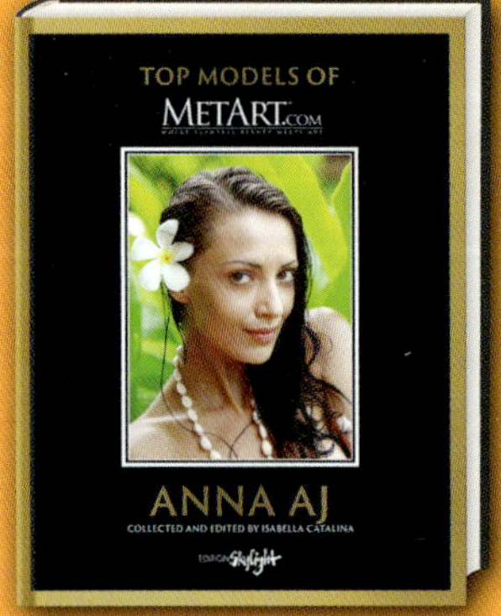

ISBN 978-3-03766-695-1

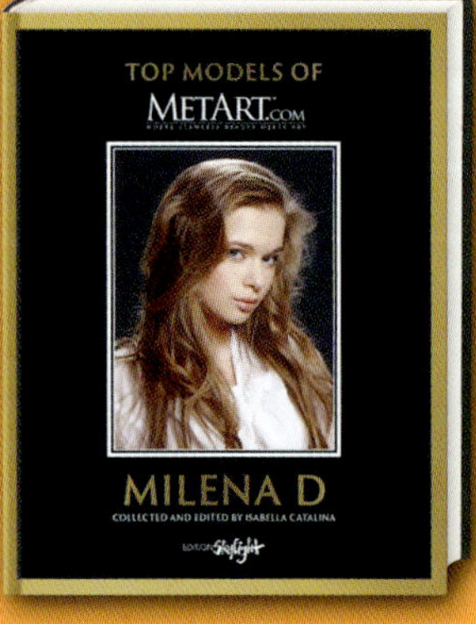

ISBN 978-3-03766-696-8

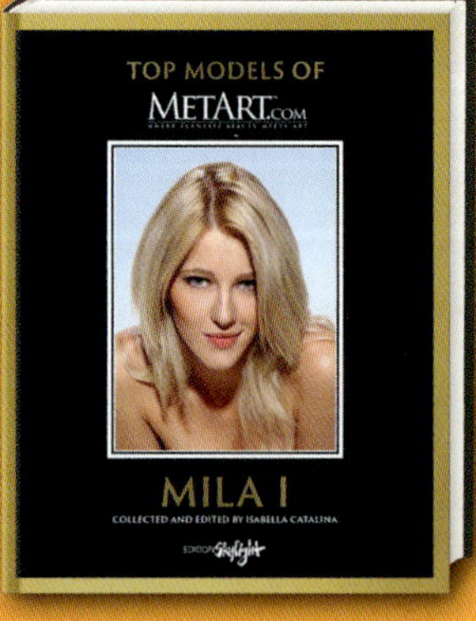

ISBN 978-3-03766-703-3

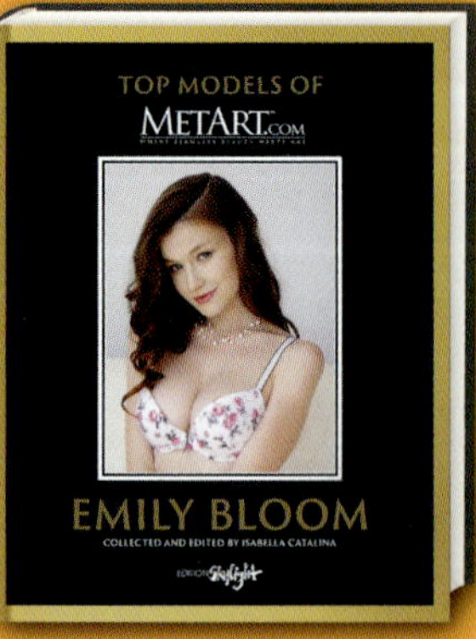

ISBN 978-3-03766-704-0

WWW.EDITION-SKYLIGHT.COM